THE REAL JESUS

GARNER TED ARMSTRONG

THE REAL JESUS

SHEED ANDREWS AND McMEEL, INC.
SUBSIDIARY OF UNIVERSAL PRESS SYNDICATE
KANSAS CITY

Library of Congress Cataloging in Publication Data

Armstrong, Garner Ted.
    The real Jesus.

    1.   Jesus Christ—Biography—Devotional litera-
ture.   2.   Christian biography—Palestine.   I.   Title.
TB306.5.A69   232.o'01   [B]   77-20002
ISBN 0-8362-0727-0

CONTENTS

Introduction:
Meet the Real Jesus

It's time you met the real Jesus.

It's time you knew Him as He was: sometimes brusque, abrupt and authoritative. Always thoughtful, philosophical and profound.

It's time you knew that Jesus could be the kindest and most gentle human being on earth, showing boundless love, mercy and forgiveness to those who genuinely asked for it and were in a repentant spirit. But it is time to recognize that Jesus could also radiate blazing anger and could hurl swift, incisive indictments at all posturing egotists, self-righteous religionists, simpering crowd followers, or even at His own beloved disciples when they got out of line.

It's time you knew that Jesus perspired just as you do; that He grew desperately hungry and tired; that He almost starved to death on one terrible occasion; that He suffered through the entire panorama of human temptations, passions and emotions which are common to us all; that He enjoyed good food and drink; that He appreciated feminine beauty.

It's time you knew that Christ could cry, shout, laugh and sing; that He could enjoy the rough camaraderie of men of His own age in an out-of-doors camp, or appreciate the glittering setting of fabulous feasts in the most palatial of estates.

It's time that you realized that Jesus was not a vagabond; that He was a professional builder in the construction business, combining the technology of "modern," first-century engineering with the art of the skilled craftsman.

It's time you knew the Jesus who was admired by officers high in the Roman army, who became a puzzle to Pilate, who was hated by the Pharisees, greatly beloved by His disciples, held in awe by the masses, detested by Judas, deeply admired by a proud

1

mother, intensely loved by John, rebuked by Peter, and who was just as intensely *human* as you are.

Few know that Jesus was a Jew; that He looked like any common, average Jew of His day; that He was so nondescript that He was frequently overlooked in crowds even among people who were seeking to put Him to death.

Few know that Jesus was not born on or anywhere near December 25;

—that, as a boy, Jesus learned a profession; that He became the senior member in a construction partnership; that He owned at least one and probably two homes of His own; that He paid taxes.

—that Jesus had a large family with at least six brothers and sisters.

—that Jesus slept indoors most of His life and frequently spent the night in the homes of very wealthy people, including Romans as well as religious opponents.

—that He was a personal friend of con artists, soldiers, fishermen, cheats, liars, thieves, crooked politicians, religious leaders and prostitutes.

—that Jesus did *not* come to save the world some two thousand years ago, that He has *not* been trying to save it since, and that He is *not* trying to save it today.

—that Jesus did not die of a broken heart; that He was not crucified on "Good Friday"; that He was not resurrected on "Easter Sunday"; that neither Jesus nor His disciples ever celebrated (or taught anyone to celebrate) Christmas or Easter.

—that Jesus had to prove to doubting disciples by incontrovertible evidence that He had truly been resurrected.

—that much of what He taught lies abandoned in the dust of history.

—that Jesus Christ is alive today, is planning to return to earth and has actually begun His "countdown" from heaven!

If your own values are those of the common person, the real Jesus may insult you, shock you, please you, challenge you, inspire you, surprise you, make you wonder. But He will never bore you.

CHAPTER 1

The Birth of Jesus:

The Greatest Story Never Told

Jesus was born sometime in the late summer or early autumn of 4 B.C.

The first time I ever made this statement to anyone I was viewed with a combination of doubt, incredulity, hostility and outright pity.

"How in the world could Jesus have been born *before Christ?*" I was asked.

It so happens that the present system in the Western Christian-professing world of counting years either prior to or subsequent to the event of our Savior's birth was not established until the work of Dionysius the Little, many, many centuries this side of the event.

In the events surrounding Jesus' birth, God managed to move a whole empire by causing the world leader of that time to establish an entirely new government bureau (the taxing and census bureau) which finally resulted in Joseph and Mary ending up in Bethlehem at the time of Jesus' birth! Part of the requirement of the vast worldwide census-taking was each family returning to the city of its origin ("And all went to be taxed everyone (into) *his own city*" (Luke 2:3-4), so since the Bible claimed Joseph was of the lineage of David (as both genealogical records in Matthew and Luke prove) he had to journey with his wife who was in an advanced state of pregnancy from Nazareth to Bethlehem, which is called the "city of David." The census in Palestine took place in our faulty chronological reckoning about the year 4 B.C.

From early on, Mary understood that she was pregnant. She

knew the meaning of the interruption of the normal menstrual cycle; after all, hadn't an angel actually told her this would happen?

Though it must have been nearly unbelievable, and there surely must have been moments of doubt, Mary's training and deep religious education, including the quality of her own character and the deadly seriousness of the impending persecutions and her knowledge of glances of those in her own community, must have all been weighing heavily upon her mind as she contemplated her gradually changing form, slightly swelling belly, and growing breasts.

Even though there probably had been many sessions between husband and wife, poring over those prophecies they knew referred to what was happening within the body of Mary herself, explaining why this shocking transformation in their own private lives had turned their little world upside down, they did not have perfect understanding of many vague references later revealed by the gospel writers, and by Jesus Himself.

Naturally, Joseph and Mary had been living with the pain of growing notoriety ever since friends and relatives learned of Mary's pregnancy. They were fully prepared to accept it, as Mary's humble statement, "Behold, the handmaiden of the Lord," clearly shows.

Still, it was tough, and they were as human as you and I.

Oh, there were close friends and relatives who knew the truth. After all, Elizabeth and Mary were cousins, and Elizabeth was carrying the baby who would grow up to become John the Baptist—both remembered the remarkable occasion when the two babies had reacted so obviously when the two expectant mothers met. Joseph and Mary could spend time with such people, away from the smirks and knowing stares of the hypocrites.

But they suffered when friends talked behind their backs; they hurt when former friends shunned them; they probably had second, or even third, thoughts about the tremendous burden they had assumed, as would any other normal human beings. But they had the courage to see it through.

It may have seemed a cruel twist of fate, to be required by the Romans to travel all that distance during the final, crucial month of pregnancy. It is clear that Joseph and Mary were not acting out any special predestined fulfillment of prophecy, or they would have seen the predictions that Christ was to be born in Bethlehem, and would have tried to travel earlier, at an easier time, and to have arranged accommodations more suitable than the hasty, last-ditch improvisation of a manger.

Neither could they have known that what had appeared to be a terribly difficult trip at best, would end up with their being exiles in a foreign country, waiting until Herod the Great had died.

Christ was not born on Christmas. Those who do not yet know this, or do not wish to know it, are either too firmly dedicated to tradition, no matter how pagan, or are too lazy to bother with simple research.

Abundant evidence exists which proves Christmas is utterly pagan in origin; as pagan as belief in Dagon, Vishnu, Baal, or Isis and Osiris.

Jesus was born in the autumn, though the exact date is kept carefully concealed. Look at the eyewitness accounts, written by those who were there. Even *Herod* didn't know exactly when Christ was born, or he could not have risked a massive uprising by his brutal edict to butcher helpless babies up to *two years of age!*

Most people have never heard the true facts surrounding Christ's birth; and lodged in their minds is only a purely mythological tale which exists only in fantasy and erroneous religious tradition.

The traditional view of Jesus' birth, with the loveliest manger imaginable on the face of the earth; sadly smiling shepherds leaning on their crooks; the Magi, gorgeously arrayed in obviously kingly robes with funny-looking crowns, opening up little gold boxes wherein are contained precious spices; a tiny baby nestled in the arms of a mother who stares sadly at him with a halo around her head and a sweet smile curving her mouth; maybe naked little babies flitting through the heavens, and a bright star seen in the distance outside—all this is repeated endlessly in millions of Christmas cards, religious books, journals and magazines, illustrated pages in Bibles, and on people's front yards, rooftops, in their driveways, along roadsides, and in displays in churches at Christmastime.

But the shepherds were not there at the birth. They came later. And there is no reason to suspect that the shepherds and the wise men ever crossed trails.

But let's ask a few questions concerning Jesus' birth. How did God manage to convince the lowly and humble classes that in fact a Savior was this day being born?

He did so by the most intricate collection of divine miracles, carefully interwoven into the fabric of history, extending so far back in time that it boggles the mind.

Few realize that Michael the archangel spoke to Daniel and delivered to him the longest single prophecy in the Bible (Daniel, the 11th chapter is personal testimony from the archangel Michael) informing him of a great struggle going on among arch-demons, and perhaps Satan himself. These were influencing the mind of the "Prince of Persia" in order to bring about some disruption in God's plan to cause Artaxerxes to allow the Jewish captives under Ezra to return to their homeland and reestablish the religious state.

Though it deserves a great deal of space, the miracles having to do with the precise moment of Jesus' birth, the decree of Augustus, the building of the temple, the beginning of His ministry, the decrees of Cyrus and Artaxerxes, and many other related events are tightly interwoven into a careful system of intricately fulfilled prophecies to form a network of incontrovertible evidence: the fact that Jesus Christ of Nazareth was in truth the Son of God.

All the religious leaders knew, and the common folk believed intensely in, Isaiah's prophecy, "Behold, a virgin shall conceive, and bear a son, and shall call his name Immanuel" (which means "God with us" in Isa. 7:14). They knew Isaiah had said, "The people that walked in darkness have seen a great light: they that dwell in the land of the shadow of death, upon them hath the light shined . . . for unto us a child is born, unto us a son is given: and the government shall be upon his shoulder: and his name shall be called Wonderful Counselor [Wonder of a Counselor], the Mighty God, the Everlasting Father, the Prince of Peace.

"Of the increase of His government and peace there shall be no end, upon the throne of David, and upon his kingdom, to order it, and to establish it with judgment and with justice from henceforth even for ever. The zeal of the Lord of Hosts will perform this" (Isa. 9:2-7).

But how would God manage to avoid the contemptuous slander of "impostor" heaped upon Jesus not only by His detractors, persecutors and religious antagonists, but even by His own closest disciples and personal friends? How would the common people, the meek, lowly shepherd and laboring class be convinced utterly that Jesus was in fact fulfilling the many prophecies of Isaiah, Daniel and others and was in fact the promised Messiah, that "Prophet" who should come to deliver Israel, and to qualify to inherit the throne of David?

First, God sent a humble group of shepherds from sufficiently far away that no one could claim collusion.

An angel appeared to them and said, "Unto *you* is born this day in the city of David a Saviour which is Christ the Lord" (Luke 2:11). They were not given any address, only a *"sign"* that they would find the baby wrapped in swaddling clothes, lying in a manger, meaning He would be so newly born that there would have been no opportunity for either the purchase or the making of clothes for Him, and He would still be wrapped in a soft blanket, not yet moved inside an inn or a private home, but lying in a bed of straw.

Obviously, then, the shepherds in journeying around the streets and the marketplaces of Bethlehem were asking from time to time where they could find a baby who had been born in a manger.

They were no doubt quite excited about the vision they had seen, and it is inconceivable that they were not elated with that combination of awe, fright, and yet subdued joy over having actually heard the voice of an angel, and seeing an overwhelmingly bright light seemingly coming very near to them out of the heavens. Thus they fully expected to find the Savior of mankind lying in swaddling clothes in a manger. They probably asked any number of people, and repeated time and again to the excited questions they were asked precisely what had happened.

Finally, with the question having been asked sufficiently about the town, perhaps one servant at a nearby inn recalled that Joseph or a friend had come, urgently begging the use of some basins and some heated water; that one of the females in the kitchen had rushed off to help during the birth; and that several of the women had been exclaiming about the fact that a poor woman had to be turned out in such an advanced state of pregnancy, when a lot of other people had been put up in more suitable accommodations, and were clicking their tongues about the unfortunate happenstance that the poor lady had given birth in a stable.

Actually, the Creator was succeeding in announcing the birth through three separate groups of individuals: the shepherds themselves; all the citizenry and the townfolk they asked and who subsequently became involved; and Joseph and his own family.

The events of the first few weeks after Jesus' birth caused widespread attention. It is evident that the Idumaean Herod (he was only partly Jewish) was terribly shaken by what he had heard.

The Bible says he was troubled *and all Jerusalem with him* (Matt. 2:3), and claims he gathered all the chief priests (who probably were Sadducees) and scribes of the people together and demanded of them where the Christ should be born (Matt. 2:4). All of the scholars were aware that this very likely was the time of the birth of Christ.

Pious frauds and sincere scholars—astronomers, astrologers, seers and soothsayers alike—were almost universally expectant that some great event would occur at *about this time,* and were looking for the Messiah.

When Herod called together the "chief priests and scribes of the people," this was tantamount to the President of the United States having a combined cabinet and Supreme Court meeting.

The "Supreme Court" of the Jewish nation was the Sanhedrin, and the greatest religious body of the nation declared in unanimity that Jesus the Savior *would be born* in Bethlehem, a city of David!

There is no evidence whatever of the length of time that elapsed from the moment the "star" (an angel, as shown by scriptures) appeared to the Magi in "the east" (most authorities believe Persia) until their arrival in Jerusalem; it could have been several weeks, or even months.

Following their interview with Herod, and his request that they "search out carefully concerning the young child," they went outside, saw the "star" again, and followed it until "it came and stood over where the young child was" (Matt. 2:9). This was in Bethlehem, a short distance over steeply plunging trails from Jerusalem. Contrary to the assumption of millions, Jesus and His parents had found more permanent accommodations following the hasty emergency quarters in the stable, and the Magi "came into the *house,* and saw the young child with Mary His mother, and they fell down and worshipped Him . . ." (Matt. 2:11).

That night, the wise men had a "bad dream," a warning from God, and sneaked out of the country without going back into Jerusalem. After they left, Joseph also had a dream. "Now when they were departed, behold an angel of the Lord appeared to Joseph in a dream, saying, Arise and take the young child and His mother, and flee into Egypt, and stay there until I tell you; for Herod will seek the young child to destroy him."

Joseph got up, hustled Mary and the baby, and any other servants or family members who might have been with them, into their clothes, packed and loaded the animals and took off *that same night,* hitting the caravan route to Egypt, probably swinging further into Arabia. They probably stopped at little-known camp-sites, avoiding the usual water holes and towns or villages along the way. Little did Joseph know that inadvertently he was fulfilling another prophecy which said, "Out of Egypt did I call my son" (Hosea 11:1).

Herod waited a few days, and then, in a fit of insane rage, "sent forth, and slew all the male children that were in Bethlehem, and in all the borders thereof, from *two years old and under,* according to the *time which he had carefully learned of the wise men"* (Matt. 2:16).

Since it was the major trade and commercial capital, Joseph probably had business interests in Jerusalem. His own building trade required that He deal from time to time with importers, distributors and craftsmen who were located there. So he and His family *may* have remained in Jerusalem up to about one year following Jesus' birth, though there is no actual proof. However, the murder of the children by Herod, risky even for a despotic king, offers some proof that Herod suspected the child would have been about one year of age, or even slightly older.

After Joseph and family had been somewhere in Egypt for a time, another dream occurred; an angel said to Joseph, "Get up and take the young child with his mother, and go into Israel: for they are dead that sought the young child's life" (Matt. 2:19-23).

The following verse indicates Joseph's first choice as a place to live probably would have been Jerusalem or its environs. "But when he heard that Archelaus was reigning over Judea in the room of his father Herod, he was afraid to go thither; and being warned of God in a dream, he withdrew into the parts of Galilee, and came and dwelt in a city called Nazareth; that it might be fulfilled which was spoken by the prophets, that He should be called a Nazarene."

Being a "Nazarene" merely meant He was a citizen of the city of *Nazareth.* He is called "Jesus Christ of Nazareth" several times in the Bible. Jesus was not an uncommon name (only the Greek form of Joshua); no doubt there were any number of individuals bearing the same name; it was quite common to name children after various attributes of God, or to include names of God (the prefix "El" and the suffix *"Yah"* were very commonly applied) in a person's name. The real Jesus was a Nazarene in the same sense a citizen of Chicago is a "Chicagoan," or someone living in Los Angeles is an "Angelino," or those in Paris are "Parisians." It was not a "religious" title of any sort, but a geographical and political term.

From the time of the young lad's return with His parents from Egypt to the city of Nazareth, there is no further mention of Jesus until the moment He is seen sitting in the temple, both listening to questions and asking His own questions of the most learned doctors of the law, and astonishing them with His understanding and His answers (Luke 2:46-52).

CHAPTER 2

Jesus The Creator—His Former Life

In later years, Jesus was always making some "outrageous" statement, the way the Pharisees looked at it. If something was true, He said it. If something was false, He called it so. For example, Jesus once said, "Your father Abraham rejoiced to see my day: and he saw it, and was glad." What Jesus *meant* by this was that He, Jesus, in His divine form was the very person who physically (through spiritual transformation) had *visited* Abraham (Genesis 18) and had related to him the reality of the coming of God's Kingdom; that Abraham, because he had proved obedient and faithful, would have a *part* in that Kingdom; that Abraham had known of the necessity of a Savior to come ("rejoiced to see my day") and had been glad.

The religious leaders didn't get it. Jesus was thinking in "another dimension"—the full knowledge and awareness of *who* He was, of *what* He was, of His spiritual background and timelessness, His great mission on earth, and His need to continually preach that great truth.

The religious leaders answered Him by a sarcastic, "You are not fifty years old, and have *you* seen Abraham?", implying He was crazy. Jesus then made another of those "outrageously" strange statements. "Verily, verily, I say unto you, Before Abraham was, I *am*"!

When Moses wanted to know what to say to the Israelites upon returning to Egypt on his mission of leading them in the Exodus, he asked God, "When I come unto the children of Israel, and shall say unto them, The God of your fathers hath sent me

11

unto you; and they say to me, What is his name: What shall I say unto them? And God said unto Moses, I AM THAT I AM: And he said, Thus shalt thou say unto the children of Israel, I AM hath sent me unto you" (Exodus 3:13-14).

"I am that I am" can also be taken to mean "I will be what I will be" or "I *continue to be* that which I *continue to be.*" I am the self-determined one, the life self-inherent, the One who is, and who always will be: the Eternal." (God is also called the "Amen," meaning, the "So be it," or "So it shall be.")

The Pharisees were familiar with Exodus 3:14, you can be sure. Thus, when Jesus plainly said He was that one who had said those words to Abraham, it just about snapped their minds. Forgetting all legality, propriety, or due process, they flew into a blind rage, and " . . . took up stones to cast at him: but Jesus hid himself, and went out of the temple, going through the midst of them, and so passed by" (John 8:56-59).

There are two other important scriptures relative to Christ's preexistence.

"In the beginning, God created the heavens and the earth." (Genesis 1:1)

"In the beginning was the Word and the Word was with God and the Word was God." (John 1:1)

In Genesis 1:1, the Hebrew word for God is *Elohim.* It is an interesting word with a *plural* form (the *im* ending.) A little research demonstrates that *Elohim* can indicate *more than one person*; and can be taken to mean a *family* of persons.

Through many portions of the Bible, Jesus reveals a *family relationship* in both the family of God and the family of man. While Jesus is called the Son of God, He is also called the Son of man, the Creator and Author of human life, the first-begotten from all humankind, the "firstborn among many brethren" (Rom. 8:29), the Captain and Author of our salvation, and the soon-coming King of Kings and Lord of Lords.

Notice that there is *duality* everywhere evidenced, not only in God's creation, but throughout the Bible when members of the Godhead are revealed.

Elohim means *more than one*, and, while not necessarily limiting the number, many other texts prove there was the Father (who no man has ever seen at any time) and the Son.

Therefore, in our modern English language, the beginning

text of the Bible would be more understandable if it were written thus: "In the beginning, the family of God, consisting of the Father and the Son, created the heaven and the earth."

John 1:1 is the second significant place in the Bible where the phrase "In the beginning . . . " is used.

"In the beginning was the word, and the *word was with God*, and the word *was God.* The same was in the beginning with God. All things were made by him; and without him was not anything made that was made" (John 1:1-3).

Here, the Greek word, *logos* (word) is used in reference to Christ. None of the other disciples who wrote of Jesus' life (Matthew, Mark and Luke) utilized "logos" in reference to Christ.

The Greek word seems to have a double meaning, referring to both "reason" and "speech." However, the idea John obviously had in mind is to convey the clearest meaning of those many long talks he and Jesus had privately, wherein Jesus conveyed to him the deepest secrets and mysteries of Jesus' own preexistent state.

You have the feeling, in reading the first chapter of John, that John is speaking from a great deal of experience, trying to recall words which Jesus Himself very likely used.

John's first chapter closely corroborates the fact that the Hebrew word *elohim* in Genesis 1:1 means that there was more than one member of the God family involved in the creating!

The "Word" was, then, the *executive member* of the Godhead, One of whom the Bible says "all things were made by him"!

Perhaps the clearest scripture absolutely proving that the Jesus Christ of the New Testament was the same Being who was the Eternal Creator of the Old Testament, the God of Abraham, Isaac and Israel, is Colossians 1:16: "For by him were all things created, that are in heaven, and that are in earth, visible and invisible, whether *they be* thrones, or dominions, or principalities, or powers: all things were created by him, and for him."

These verses very plainly show that this same Being who made all things, "was in the world and the *world was made by him*, and the world knew him not. He came unto his own, and his own received him not. But as many as received him, to them gave he power to become the sons of God, even to them that believe on his name: which were born [begotten] not of blood, nor of the will of the flesh, nor of the will of man, but of God." (John 1:10-13)

This unmistakable reference to Jesus Christ of Nazareth

clearly shows, without any interpretation or exegesis, that the creator being who is called "God" *(Elohim* or *YHWH)* in the Old Testament is the same individual who became the Jesus Christ of the New Testament!

Notice the next words, "And the Word *became flesh,* and dwelt among us (and we beheld his glory, glory as of the only begotten of the Father), full of grace and truth" (John 1:14).

The Word did the creating, and the Word "became flesh." What could be simpler than that? *abundant*

The New Testament is rife with scriptures concerning Jesus' attempts to convey the message which the Father gave Him. He said He spoke only as the Father inspired Him, spoke only *what* the Father gave Him. Jesus continually said He came to *reveal* the Father: He prayed to His Father, said He was returning to His Father, and showed, continually, a Father-Son relationship!

There is a great deal of further proof throughout the Bible on the prehuman origins of Jesus Christ! For example, He is called that "Rock" which followed the children of Israel in the wilderness ("And did all drink the same spiritual drink: for they drank of that spiritual Rock that followed them: and that Rock was Christ" I Cor. 10:4); and is referred to as that "Rock" in Deuteronomy: "He is the Rock, his work is perfect" (Deut. 32:4).

The personage who "emptied himself" and "became of no repute," and "was made flesh," born of the virgin Mary to become the baby Jesus in Bethlehem, was the *same individual* who created Adam, who saved Noah, who appeared to Abraham, who wrestled in the dust of the earth with Jacob, who called and spoke to Moses out of a fiery bush and a cloud, who parted the Red Sea and who spoke directly to His prophets, from the patriarchs prior to the flood on down to Elijah and others. Jesus Christ of Nazareth was the same personality of the Godhead or God family who wrote with His own finger the Ten Commandments and who ruled Israel.

The Bible absolutely *proves* the fact that Jesus Christ of the New Testament is the same person as the God of the Old Testament!

CHAPTER 3

Jesus' Childhood,
Education and Early Life

Despite the fact that the Bible gives us only the briefest view through a keyhole, as it were, into the events of Jesus' birth, and gives us only one sentence, that of Luke 2:40, about His boyhood, most theologians tend to portray Jesus in only two major moments of His life; that of His birth, as celebrated by the pagan adaptation of an Egyptian, Greek, Roman, Nordic and Druidic ceremony called "Christmas," or an equally pagan ceremony surrounding His death and Resurrection, which came out of ancient Babylon, Egypt, Rome and Greece, called "Ishtar" anciently, or "Easter" today.

However, God no doubt knew exactly what He was doing when He preserved only a few brief statements about Jesus' birth, and then spent more than 90 percent of the remainder of biblical texts concerning Christ's message—His life from age 30 onward, His ministry, His miracles, and His death, burial and resurrection!

So what was Jesus like when He was a small child? Did Mary ever have to spank Jesus? Was He a "normal" child in every way? Was there no necessity to train Him; to teach Him in the simplest ways as every parent should?

To find out, first let's consider His earthly parents.

They were, together with Mary's cousin Elizabeth (John the Baptist's mother), Zacharias, and a small minority of others, living a sincerely righteous life within the intent of God's laws. That meant they were physically healthy; following God's revealed laws about foods, exercise, diet, avoidance of the use of harmful substances, like drugs, and of overindulgence, or any excesses.

15

Mary was in perfect health. Remember, too, that the tiny fetus being shaped in her womb was guarded, each moment, not only by God's Holy Spirit, but by unseen angelic beings! Michael and Gabriel were both extremely busy at this time—and you can be sure that God the Father in heaven had commissioned His most powerful obedient spirit beings to keep close guardianship over that precious human life.

Mary would have had a "normal" pregnancy. There would have been no abuses heaped upon that tiny, growing baby within her by a thoughtless mother who deprived the baby of its needed nourishments. No smoking, no excessive use of stimulants or depressants, no careless accidents which could cause injury, no violent, emotional upsets, or a loud, screaming, unhealthy family environment.

That she was in excellent health is obvious from the fact that even in an advanced state of pregnancy, she made the trip from Nazareth to Bethlehem. Probably she could have ridden in a cart, or similar conveyance, pulled by donkey or horse, or even have ridden a donkey or a horse itself.

The presence of God's Spirit, and angels, together with the physical condition of Mary and her absolute obedience to health laws enables you to *know* that Jesus was a perfectly shaped and formed, healthy baby.

Now let's consider Jesus Himself. Did Jesus ever cry? *Why* do babies cry? Too many mothers don't know they sometimes cry because of a need for exercise; sometimes cry almost *automatically* from various stimuli on some occasions; as well as cry because they are hungry, or tired, or wet and uncomfortable.

Yes, Jesus cried. If He could weep at Lazarus's tomb because of the obstinate faithlessness of people, He could have cried as a baby because He was in need of a good workout, waving little arms and legs about, and filling His lungs.

But though He could cry when hungry, wet, or uncomfortable (there is no sin in crying and responding to the natural human emotions of infancy), Jesus was a completely different baby boy.

Every normal baby reaches that point in his infancy where his cries and wails of outrage take on a new tone of self-pity, anger, resentment or frustration.

The Bible reveals that the carnal mind (the natural human

mind with the spirit in man but without God's Holy Spirit) is *enmity* against God (Romans 8:7)! Millions do not know *why* they resent God's law, His way of life, and any directives from God in their private lives! Jeremiah 17:9 reveals that the human heart is *deceitful* and *desperately wicked* and asks "who can know it?"

As "normal children" we all grew up in our own environments to become gradually acquainted with all the feelings of racism, group instincts, competition, selfishness, pride, self-pity, vanity, and *self-consciousness* which made up the whole panorama of our earliest years, with all the "normal" frustrations, introversions, embarrassment, dashed hopes, successes, or despair.

How far back can you remember? Can you remember when you were three or four or five?

Chances are, you have only the dimmest or vaguest awareness of those early years of your life, but those recollections which *do* stand out are the ones that had to do with either major triumphs, such as successes in games, in some experience among children your own age or with your parents; or in deep disappointments or frustrations, such as playground altercations, being pushed and shoved by the neighborhood bully, or in having an intense "boy-girl relationship" with a neighborhood child, beginning sex experimentation; or in a host of other experiences which are common to human nature.

Though it's difficult for you to accept it or believe it, Jesus Christ experienced *none* of these!

From His beginning awareness of learning of words, that little baby, in whose little mind was the "Spirit of God without limit" could learn without the normal hostility and antagonism toward authority symbols, such as His parents or others around Him.

I can imagine how many times Mary must have told Jesus, "You are *different*, Jesus. You are the Son of God! You were not born in the same way all other little boys and girls are born—but by a divine *miracle*! You are a little Prince, born to become the King of Israel, and to be the Messiah sent to Israel and to all mankind."

I cannot imagine a human individual going through the fabulous series of remarkable miracles as did Mary who would not have continually sung that baby to sleep by rocking Him in her

arms, constantly thrilled and aware of His divine origins and the
great calling which awaited Him.

I can well imagine she must have made up songs of her own,
or even hummed some of the psalms about deliverance; that she
would have taught Him continually about every one of the
miracles, visions, dreams, miraculous appearances of angels,
and the events prior to and surrounding His birth and young
babyhood.

As Jesus grew older, His direct contact with the Father,
through the power of God's Holy Spirit, His deepening and
growing awareness of the "other dimension" of the always present
spirit world (angels were about Him from the time of His conception throughout His life) meant that His learning process was not
twisted by feelings that are common to the carnal mind.

If Mary could describe the reactions of her different children
(she had at least seven of them), she would no doubt have testified
that Jesus was her "best baby."

Ever hear of a "child prodigy"? Jesus was a child prodigy—
but *not* in the traditional sense. Jesus was a prodigy, if that is the
right word, in *wisdom* and *understanding*. He could perceive the
profound meaning and implication of God's Holy Scripture; He
could answer questions about the Bible that generations of scholars had argued over. He could expound and explain the Bible
with far greater perception and power than anyone else had ever
done. Jesus knew the Scriptures very well, but He probably didn't
have a perfect photographic memory. He had to *work* to learn the
Bible; He had to study hard with great diligence and dedication.
But when the time came to preach what He had learned, suddenly
Jesus burst forth with startling insight, brilliant analysis and
profound impact.

If He could astound the learned doctors of the law at age 12,
He could have already startled His fellow classmates in His classes
as well as His mother and father!

Jesus had God's Holy Spirit "without measure." A converted
person today, who has repented, been baptized, and received
God's Spirit is still *mostly carnal.* He is said to have received a
little "earnest" or "down payment" of God's Spirit, but, even as
Paul told the church members of Corinth, is "yet carnal." The
Holy Spirit is *there*, in the mind, but in a comparatively small
amount, and as Paul explained, helps us resist the carnal pulls,

but however sometimes *loses*. (Paul said, "The thing that I hate, I do, and that which I would do, I cannot seem to do.")

Not so with Christ, even as a tiny child. There was *no carnal reaction*. There was the *temptation* to react carnally, in exact measure to the level of understanding of His mind, depending on the age. But there was the help of the limitless power of God's Spirit, plus the protection of angels to help Him overcome such temptations.

Did Jesus suffer any of the "childhood diseases"? Unthinkable! Not only is there not the faintest whisper of evidence to indicate Jesus was ever "sick" a single day of His life, but there is every evidence to the contrary! In following the divinely revealed laws of God basic to good, physical health, Jesus' bodily resistance to any disease was especially high. There are laws involving human diet revealed in the Bible which have to do with the physical health and well-being of us humans which can only be known through *revelation*, and could perhaps never be known through the modern biochemical analyses of chemistry and nutrition. Consequently, Jesus' parents would have seen to it that He received the very finest diet available according to their means!

This meant that Jesus was eating whole grain foods, drinking raw milk from domestic cattle and goats (anyone can tell you that goat's milk, so long as the creature is fed a reasonably good diet, is much richer than cow's milk), and was eating lamb, mutton, beef, fish, fowl, and the common diet of a basically agrarian society where food was never "processed" in the sense that we know it today, where it was seasonal, natural, and healthful. Further, He had the protection of God's Holy Spirit throughout His life, and though there is no mention of it, if Jesus had ever ingested spoiled food, tainted meat, or anything of any nature that could have brought about physical debility or sickness, there is no doubt whatever that a divine miracle was instantly imposed, and that Christ was protected from any ill effects. (Jesus later predicted that His own disciples, in the conduct of their work in fulfilling the great commission He gave them, would not be affected by poisonous things, whether they picked them up accidentally as in the case of the Apostle Paul, who was bitten on the hand by a poisonous serpent while preparing a fire on an island, or whether they happened to ingest tainted, poisonous drink or other things dangerous to health!)

From His earliest babyhood, then, Jesus followed the laws of physical health. He ate right foods, got plenty of the right kind of strenuous exercise, a good full night's sleep every single night, and "grew and *waxed strong*" as a result!

What kind of games did He play? Did Jesus ever indulge in loud noises and fits of screaming, or throw tantrums as a tiny child? Was He ever given to outbursts of anger?

His play periods were different from those of most normal children of today, in that there were never any games of pretense, of sham, which required lying, "pretending" to be someone He was not, "hero worship" in the form of the "cops and robbers," "cowboys and Indians," played by so many millions of children today! (Or "Romans and Jews" or "Maccabees and Romans" back then.)

There were no feelings of self-importance, because there was no *vanity!*

If you took away vanity and a desire for attention, all the frustrations which bring about the psychoses, neuroses, mental handicaps and debilities which shape most of the rest of us, you would see a different picture indeed!

Whether it was a simple game of marbles or the other games Jesus might have played, you would never have seen a temper tantrum, a sudden burst of crying and fleeing home, the loud insistence at being number one, the playground altercations, the taunts at other children to make them feel inferior over a handicap, or any of what we call "normal behavior" in most children!

What kind of games *did* Jesus play? In the first place, perhaps the word "play" could never properly be applied to activities which occupied Jesus' time between His lessons, studies, learning Joseph's trade, and the other essentials of life such as eating, sleeping and working. If there was any "play," it was no doubt the *kind* of play that was totally *constructive!*

This means that Jesus, in applying the laws of God perfectly in His life and mind, would never have attempted to *take advantage* of someone else's weakness! If there were any games He played, they could not have been games constructed around petty vanities of human ego which make it all essential for the individual to *win*, no matter by what means! Jesus might have played "games" of the kind which could stimulate thought, help develop a vocabulary, develop physical skills, or perhaps even have contests to see who could finish some constructive project more quickly.

Jesus would have learned self-discipline and the development of physical skills by leaping, climbing, racing, swimming, possibly playing team games (such as our softball, basketball, soccer, water polo, etc.), which were inventions of the time. But as a boy He would never have gone beyond mere contests of physical strength which would not inflict either pain or injury on the other person.

Jesus most surely would have participated in all those rough-and-ready boyhood sporting endeavors which would build strong young bodies and give healthy outlet to youthful energies, but without the feelings of selfish competition.

That meant Jesus would surely have been involved in foot races, in tests of strength in regard to lifting, pulling, tugging, and other physical contests, including wrestling.

Wrestling has been a popular sport for millennia. It puts full focus on the character of the wrestlers as well as on their natural strength and technique. Wrestling, as a sport, without desire to injure or hurt the opponent, *builds* strength, develops perseverance, generates mental as well as physical endurance and instills personal confidence. We can be quite positive that Jesus wrestled as a boy. How? He had previously shown His interest! We can prove that Jesus, in His preexistent state, had wrestled with Jacob. This remarkable account in Genesis 32:24-30 shows how God developed the character of Jacob by wrestling with him for many hours.

There is no reason to assume the Bible requires that Jesus never once suffered minor nicks, cuts, bruises or abrasions. The Bible does explicitly point out that God had intended only that not one bone of His body should ever be broken, but there was no such restriction placed on the possibility of cuts or abrasions.

It would be doubtful, however, because of Jesus' careful attention to God's laws and also common sense about safety on the job and principles of fairness in all sports, that Jesus ever suffered any affliction or injury beyond a very minor nick to a knee or a finger.

Even in these cases, He could quickly look up to God His Father in heaven and ask that God heal the wound, and God could have answered instantly.

With His "other-dimensional consciousness" of God's Holy Spirit, Jesus totally rejected the group instincts. He never allowed Himself to become a member of a "gang." As a boy, He never limited His association to a certain clique—a select few who could find camaraderie in performing acts of vandalism, playing practical jokes on the elderly, beating up a member of a rival gang, stealing a farmer's crop, telling giggly tales of sex exploitation, or engaging in wild escapades during some political or religious holiday, as do children of our time.

Jesus knew that God was no respecter of persons, and followed that principle perfectly.

He thoroughly knew the proverb that said, "Don't let thine heart envy sinners, but be thou in the fear of the Lord all the day long" (Prov. 23:17). And, therefore, the excited tales of other neighborhood boys who would laugh privately about illegal or shameful exploits would not have been attractive to Him.

But Jesus *did live* through all of those 30 years prior to the beginning of His ministry. No doubt every single day and every single week of those years were jam-packed with living life in the most zestful, enthusiastic, and purposeful manner that has ever been known.

As the years went by, and Jesus' perceptions grew of exactly what He was to do, who He was and what His calling was, what lay ahead of Him only a few years hence, and the deadly seriousness of the great task before Him, there is no doubt He studied, thought, prayed, pondered and struggled with various thought processes in a way none of us can understand!

Concerning the matter of Jesus' education, this no doubt consisted of a manifold program, which was *superior* to the kind of education available to the average youth in our affluent societies of today.

Though the endless fables, oft repeated, were extant in Jesus' day—including many exploits of the "gods"; common polytheistic theological fantasies told and retold by the Greeks; fabled stories of Nimrod the hunter from Babylon and of the Pharaohs of old from Egypt; and even imaginative additions and trappings to the biblical accounts of Moses and the burning bush, the Noachian deluge, Samson and his strength, David and Goliath, and Saul and the witch of Endor—Jesus never believed them, and never wasted His time on them; nor did He grow up believing in fairies or childhood fairy tales. His education was *in the home,* in His father's trade and business, and was the most valuable kind available!

No other teaching methods can surpass private tutelage.

Families such as Joseph's would have been sufficiently prosperous to have hired a highly skilled private tutor, or even several, whose occupations consisted of teaching in homes in the region.

Remember, Jesus grew up in an area which was a virtual crossroads for trade and commerce, and where the worlds of Europe and Asia met. The area was at least bilingual, and many people grew up learning to speak three languages. There is every evidence Jesus spoke Greek as well as fluent Aramaic, and the Bible also indicates He spoke Hebrew.

How did He learn these languages? The community was mainly bilingual, and parents spoke two languages or more in their own homes. There were no doubt skilled linguists who came into Jesus' home and taught Him languages on a regular basis.

In addition to languages, the growing young boy would have been taught music, history, geography, the science of the time, and would have been especially learning the skills required in His father's building profession, which included physics, engineering, mathematics, trigonometry, and the many other disciplines required in the construction of either larger commercial buildings or private homes.

These skills would have included a sense of proportion, symmetry, beauty, harmonies of color, and adaptation to scale. Anyone who was so versatile so as to be involved not only in a choice of location, site preparation and the heavier process of laying of foundations and supporting structures, but even in the finishing of the interior, including the delicate mosaics and decorative features of such a home, would be considered far more flexible than are most people in similar trades today!

It is obvious Jesus would have known about art, literature, music, stoneworking and building skills, and history. Especially He knew about the Holy Scriptures from start to finish!

But this knowledge was not automatically inserted into His mind through divine fiat, but gradually *accumulated* as He developed and grew.

The Bible plainly says, "Though he were a Son, yet learned he obedience by the things which he suffered; and being made perfect, he became the author of eternal salvation unto all them that

obey him" (Heb. 5:8-9). Learning is a process. So is perfection.
Living perfectly for one day does not mean that an individual is
"perfect," for there is much to learn on the next day. Perfection is
not only a process of the guarding of perfect character and morality,
but also a process of acquisition of additional knowledge and
experience, which together can provide even greater understanding
and wisdom.

Because Jesus "experienced" human life in this flesh, He is
able to turn to God the Father as an experienced counselor and
adviser and explain on some occasions when a human's failings
have been particularly obnoxious and say to His Father, "Father, I
understand—please forgive that person!"

God's Word says Jesus learned "by the things which He
suffered," meaning that many object lessons were learned throughout His young and developing years through that continual awareness, however painful and disillusioning it may have been, of the
hypocrisies, the hates and jealousies, vanity, carnality and ego
which could afflict members even of His own family and close
friends.

Though the Bible calls Him a "man of sorrows and acquainted
with grief," this cannot possibly preclude the fact that Jesus was a
completely well-rounded personality who could lay His head back
and roar with laughter over something particularly funny; nor did it
preclude Jesus indulging in singing lilting songs on occasion; it is
likely that He was acquainted not only with the religious songs of
that time, but also knew of the folk music of several cultures. Could
the very personality of the God Family who invented within us
human beings that "universal language" of a deep appreciation for,
and a desire to participate in, music have not enjoyed singing? The
only insight that you can gain into Jesus' musical knowledge was the
fact of His deep desire to sing "one more song" with His disciples
following the "Lord's supper" on that final Passover.)

Joseph, while not well-to-do, would have comfortably and
adequately provided for his family. That included the ability to pay
for special Levitical teachers whose sole responsibilities were either
in the priestly or educational line, to come into his home as private
tutors on any number of days each week and to teach Jesus special
skills in musical instruments, and in the musical literature of the
day.

Thus it was that Jesus grew up not only being at least trilingual within the family, but also studying languages through those specially skilled in such, and learning at the feet of brilliant teachers who no doubt very quickly responded to the incredible aptitudes and insatiable thirst for knowledge the young lad possessed.

Did Jesus know the principles of nuclear fission? Was His mind so brilliant in that first century that He knew all there was to know about today's computers, satellites, business machines, jet aircraft, missiles, and all assorted space-age technology?

Of course not! Although through His awareness of material substances and the physical forces working upon them, Jesus' grasp of the basic underpinnings of historical and dynamic geology, paleontology, zoology, biology, history, and other related subjects, would have been far superior to those of His time, His growing awareness of His own origins and recollections of the fact that "before Abraham was, I *am*" would have given him a brilliant and incisive perception of geology and the actual formation and substance of the earth far beyond the most skillful of teachers of His time. But it was not necessary for Jesus' mind to acquire knowledge far beyond that which was not commonly available to the most learned and best-educated person.

Jesus was not a "space-age" person in a first-century environment; but He most assuredly *was* a visitor from outer space, and had knowledge surpassing those of His first-century environment by a great measure!

Here was a young lad who, from the time He was six or seven, was cheerfully going about His daily household chores, looking over His father's shoulder as He watched him work and listening wonderingly as He learned of all of the detailed things he was doing, going happily to His studies to learn to sing, perhaps to play on an instrument or two, to study the languages of His time, and to learn so many interesting and absorbing subjects that His mind was *constantly busy*. He had no time for the wasteful activities of most youth.

As soon as He was physically able, I am sure Joseph allowed Jesus tasks which would have developed His young body to make it "strong" as Luke reports. He could have been carrying stones, boards and lumber, mortar or plaster, and running errands, fetching tools, climbing up and down ladders, pushing, pulling, lifting, moving, sliding, and continually exercising until, at the end of a long day, He was ready for a good solid meal prepared by a wonderful cook and housekeeper, and to be tucked into bed following a session of prayer with the family, and no doubt some pretty serious private prayer of His own!

Luke shows how Jesus' parents went to Jerusalem every year at the Feast of the Passover. "And when he was *twelve years old*, they went up after the custom of the feast . . ." (Luke 2:42). As a boy of 12, He was very wise, and very well educated.

It is no accident that the Bible singles out Jesus' twelfth year as an important milestone in his life. Without my becoming overly laborious on the matter, suffice it to say that man is not the inventor of numbers, God is. The Bible is very clear on the fact that certain numbers bear certain significance. The number 12 represents "organized beginnings," or a perfect governmental number.

Further, 12 was the age when, according to Jewish custom, a young boy was expected to pass into the adult community. He began to assume more of the responsibilities of a young man of the household and the family's trade, and was looked upon as having crossed an important threshold at age 12.

Notice the account of Jesus' "debut" in the public eye from the time of His private boyhood until the time when He was about 12½ at the Passover in Jerusalem! "And when he was twelve years old, they went up to Jerusalem after the custom of the feast; and when they had fulfilled the days, as they were returning, the boy Jesus tarried behind in Jerusalem; and his parents *knew it not*; but supposing him to be *in the company*, they went a day's journey; and they sought for him *among their kinsfolk* and *acquaintance*: and when they found him not, they returned to Jerusalem, seeking for him" (Luke 2:42-45).

That statement tells you a great deal about the family structure. First of all, the very fact that Jesus' parents did not realize that Jesus had remained behind in Jerusalem for a *full day* indicates that Jesus was very mature for His age, well accustomed to handling responsibilities by Himself, and had the total confidence of His parents. Furthermore, by this time the other boys or perhaps both of the girls had been born. Twelve long years had gone by, and Jesus' brothers and sisters were no doubt along on this journey. Though Jesus was the only one, as the eldest, who had now (some six months earlier) grown into his more adult responsibilities, his other brothers, James, Joses, Simon and Jude, and either one or two girls or even more were probably along. That's why the Bible talks about "the company, and how they sought for him among their kinsfolk" and acquaintances.

Joseph and Mary probably searched through parts of the city where they fully expected to discover Jesus, probably among some of Joseph's associates and fellow tradesmen, suppliers or business acquaintances.

So it was with a great degree of surprise that they finally found him in the temple.

"And all that heard him were amazed at his understanding and his answers. And when they [Joseph and Mary and His family] saw him, they were *astonished;* and his mother said unto him, "Son, why have you treated us so? Behold, your father and I have been looking for you anxiously.' And he said to them, 'How is it that you sought me? Did you not know that I must be in my Father's house [temple courts]?' And they did not understand the saying which he spoke to them" (Luke 2:47-50, RSV).

Now that's interesting. Jesus' parents did *not* understand the meaning of what Jesus had done or said. This demonstrates that heretofore Jesus was *not* a totally out-of-the-ordinary child. He did not constantly tell everyone "who He was," not even His parents. Though they surely remembered the unusual nature of His birth, the passage of time and the normal ebb and flow of the mundane events of daily life dulled Joseph and Mary's realization of what Jesus was going to do. Jesus did *not* flaunt this preexistent life or the mission of this physical life, even as this realization must have come fully into His consciousness. No doubt by the time of this incident at age 12, Jesus knew who He was and what He had to do. Nonetheless, He maintained His "normal" life as a fine, bright, obedient, young Jewish boy growing up under His parents' care.

Jesus was a Jew.

As such, He knew a great deal of persecution throughout His life—for it wasn't easy growing up in an area of mixed races in His own homeland, including the dark and swarthy Canaanites, Syrophoenicians, Greeks, Romans, and various other races from the East, as well as a chance encounter with an Egyptian now and then.

The "Decapolis" or those ten towns of the plateau the other side of the Sea of Galilee—which spread from the southern shore of the Sea of Galilee considerably southward along both banks of the Jordan River and thence eastward for quite a number of miles into what is modern-day Jordan—were largely inhabited by Gentiles.

The land of Galilee, Samaria, Judea and Idumea were made up of various races or mixtures of races.

Jesus grew up in a multiracial, multilingual society, where a young Jewish lad, especially one in "business," would have encountered all the assorted forms of racism, prejudice, curses and epithets common even unto this day.

How did Jesus manage to stay totally free from racial bias?

The answer is that He had God's Holy Spirit without measure, and that the Spirit of God cannot tolerate the slightest inkling of racial prejudice or bias. (It is strongly implied that one of Jesus' own disciples was black—Simon the Canaanite—and thus even the underpinnings of the New Testament Church of God could have been multiracial.)

The very personage who became Jesus Christ of Nazareth had earlier created all the races of man!

I can well imagine that when the conversation turned to race, Jesus as a boy would never have taken great issue with someone who called Him "a dirty Jew."

Never could Jesus have laughed at ethnic tales which tended to belittle or ridicule the members of another race merely because of their color of skin, stature, language, general physical or cultural characteristics. He knew that He was come unto the world, as well as unto His own people, and that He would be the "light of all men" and finally "draw all men unto myself."

No doubt, through Jesus' young life, there were any number of smirking little ruffians who knew how different He was, and continually tried to trip Him up in His lifestyle and His ways. Also there were no doubt other groups who attempted to entice Him to join with them in plotting some thuggery or other.

But Jesus had been learning the deep wisdom of the Proverbs, and would have recalled what some of them had said, "My son, if sinners entice you, do not consent. If they say, 'Come with us, let us lie in wait for blood, let us wantonly ambush the innocent; . . . we shall find all precious goods, we shall fill our houses with spoil; throw in your lot among us, we will all have one purse.' "—Jesus would have remembered that Solomon said, "My son, do not walk in the way with them, hold back your foot from their paths; for their feet run to evil, and they make haste to shed blood" (Prov. 1:10-16, RSV).

"Chicken!" would not have dislodged Jesus from his stolid

refusal to engage in the vicious antics of youthful gangs, since He knew they were all a group of filthy, sniffing little cowards and very likely told them so.

Also, Jesus was not ashamed of His father or His mother, of their business, their home, their background, or their example. (Not that they were perfect, in the sense that there was never a cross word, or that they lived an absolutely flawless life.)

Jesus could grow up as a young boy remembering that He was the one who had inspired Solomon to write, "Rejoice, O young man, in your youth. Let your heart cheer you all the days of your youth, and walk in the ways of your own heart, and in your own sight: but you had better understand, that for every one of these things, even during your youthful days, God will bring you into judgment.

"Therefore, don't be sorrowful about it, but put away evil from your day-to-day physical life, because a great deal of childhood and youth is an empty pursuit for useless goals" (Eccl. 11:9-10, paraphrased).

CHAPTER 4

Jesus and His Family

In the beginning of Jesus' ministry, the narrative in the sixth chapter of Mark shows that He "went out from thence," that is, from the shores of the Sea of Galilee, and came into His *"own country"* meaning *Nazareth.*

The local officials in the synagogue were astounded when Jesus suddenly appeared in the synagogue of Nazareth preaching and teaching and, true to human nature, they used the ancient old dodge, "Just who does he think he is?"

The account says they were astonished and said, "From whence hath this man these things? And what wisdom is this which is given unto him, that even such mighty works are wrought by his hands? Is not this the carpenter, the son of Mary, the brother of *James,* and *Joses,* and of *Juda* and of *Simon?* And are not *his sisters* here with us? And they were offended at him" (Mk. 6:2-3).

Jesus was a member of a large *family.* The eldest of at least *seven children—at least* four brothers (all named) and two sisters *(plural!)* in addition to Himself. Notice that this account occurs in the very *beginning* of His public ministry; this was apparently His first official appearance in the synagogue in His hometown of Nazareth. By no stretch of the imagination could these rulers of the synagogue have been referring to men by the name of James, Joses, Juda and Simon, nor could they have been referring to "His sisters," in a *religious* sense. In no way could these religious leaders have meant that they understood that these individuals, whoever they were, were merely "acquaintances" of Jesus, and

30

therefore were "spiritual brothers and sisters" rather than flesh-and-blood kin. Remember, this was the very *beginning* of Jesus' ministry—the Pharisees knew of *no* disciples yet! These brothers and sisters would not have been "spiritual brothers and sisters" because there weren't any yet known!

These petty complaints of Mark 6:2-3 should tell us a lot. First, they knew He had great wisdom; they knew He was performing *miracles.* Second, their remarks indicate that Joseph, Jesus' legal father, was already dead, or they would have included him in their mention of the family members. Third, it proves Jesus lived most of His younger life in Nazareth; that He was a "carpenter" (contractor would be a better term today, as you will see), and that he had *four brothers* and *at least two sisters!*

For reasons of traditional doctrine, some religions refuse to admit this simple truth.

Some have argued, from Mark's account in Mark 3:31 of Jesus' mother and brother trying to communicate to Him through the crowd, that Jesus' subsequent statement is proof that there *were* no real flesh and blood brothers but only Jesus' brothers in the spiritual sense.

"And his mother and his brothers came; and standing outside they sent to him and called him. And a crowd was sitting about him; and they said to him, 'Your mother and your brothers are outside asking for you.'

"And he replied, 'Who are my mother and my brothers?'

"And looking around on those who sat about him, he said, 'Here are my mother and my brothers! Whoever does the will of God is my brother, and sister, and mother' " (Mk. 3:31-35, RSV).

Jesus *never failed* to turn a statement, a question, a situation into a vivid spiritual lesson concerning His calling, His gospel message of the coming kingdom, and man's brotherhood to fellow man.

In Jesus' mind was the fullest awareness of His heavenly origins; His direct relationship to the entirety of the human race by virtue of being the very Creating Agent of the first human beings; His kinship to His own people, to whom He was sent; and finally by virtue of His teachings to His own disciples and close circle of confidants, the "brotherhood" which existed between Him and this group. Remember, however, that the leaders of the synagogue in Nazareth actually knew the *names* of Jesus' flesh and blood brothers and listed each of them in their plaintive protest against Jesus' miracles and His teachings—unable to believe that a local man could possess such powers.

John 2:12 is very plain. "After this he went down to Capernaum, he, and his mother, and his BRETHREN, and *his disciples:* and they continued there not many days." Here, the biblical account written by John, that "disciple whom Jesus loved," very clearly shows that His disciples and His "brethren" were two different groups of people.

Now read the critical verse of Mark 6:3 *again.* As Jesus was teaching in the synagogue, some of His persecutors began to say, "Is not this the carpenter, the son of Mary, the brother of James, and Joses, and of Juda, and Simon? And are not his sisters here with us? And they were offended at him. But Jesus said unto them, A prophet is not without honour, but in his own country, and among his *own kin,* and in his own house."

Notice. Jesus plainly said, "Among his OWN KIN."

He plainly admitted, then, that He, the prophet who was being dishonored, was, at that time, in His own country, and *among his own kin.*

(The James who is mentioned here as one of Jesus' brothers is spoken of as "the Lord's brother" by the apostle Paul in Galatians 1:19. It was *this* James who later became the leading apostle of the headquarters church in Jerusalem (Acts 15:13) and who wrote the book of James. Also, one of Jesus' earliest disciples was James the son of Zebedee and the brother of John. Then, there was another man whose name was James, who was also one of Jesus' disciples, who was the son of Alphaeus, and who was sometimes called "James the Less.")

Jesus' brothers and sisters were no doubt *converted* following His crucifixion and resurrection (though there is no record that they all were).

The events of their entire lives; of living with and around this remarkable man, seeing the throngs following Him and the vast ministry, which reached such proportions that people flocked up to the Galilean hills from as far away as Jerusalem and all the environs of Judea, and from as far north as up into modern Lebanon of today, the "seacoasts of Tyre and Sidon," were a powerful witness to Jesus' own kin.

They had known of His growing preoccupation with His

ministry—His confrontation with Satan the Devil and His subsequent calling of His disciples—and had closely known of all the details of His ministry.

If there was any individual with the psychological hangup which would have represented a true *barrier* to accept the plain truth about Jesus' origins, it would have been His own flesh and blood brothers and sisters! (Incidentally, concerning these sisters, there is no reason really to limit the number of girls in the family to only two. There could have been three, or four, or even more.)

But the Resurrection PROVED it to them. They had grown up together; had eaten, played, worked, laughed and sung together; had taken lessons from their tutors together; and had been educated in the languages, history, geography, science and literature of the day together, most especially a thorough education in the sacred scriptures.

And what about Jesus' brothers? Did they all die celibates? Were none married? Did none of them survive that tumultuous first century following the establishment of the New Testament Church to live normal lives and raise families?

Peter was married (Mat. 8:14, Luke 4:38, I Cor. 9:5). There is no proof one way or the other there were any children; though it is safe to assume there most certainly were, since this was the expected custom of the time, and it makes a great deal more understandable how Peter and Andrew (who some authorities say was Peter's elder brother) were able to leave their family's business, and to follow Christ in His journeys. If there were strong young sons coming along, brought up in the trade of their father, as was Jewish custom and tradition, then the narrative of Peter's and Andrew's call makes more sense. Of course, there could have been other brothers not mentioned.

But do you realize what some of this implies?

It merely implies that the human physical family of Jesus Christ of Nazareth did not necessarily die in the first century; that some of those family members no doubt *did* survive and continue to build families and leave progeny after themselves. If this is true (and there seems every likelihood it is) then the descendants of those families directly related to Jesus Christ through Mary, that is, the progeny of Joseph and Mary and their ancestors, may still be walking this earth today!

Jesus, then, while *He* was not married, did grow up as a

young man with brothers and sisters, and was very definitely a "family man" in the sense that He, as the elder brother, became the leader of the family, and directly responsible for it.

Not one more word is heard of Joseph after the mention of the word "parents" in the second chapter of Luke. From that time on, whenever Mary and the other children are mentioned, they are *alone*. Obviously, though the Bible does not record the event, Joseph had died some time after Christ's twelfth birthday and prior to His thirtieth. Joseph is never mentioned, and is nowhere on the scene, during the entirety of Christ's ministry, or even at His death.

To some, it was even necessary for Mary to be "immaculately conceived," in order that Christ's birth could be as holy and "immaculate" as it properly should be. But, if Mary, why not *her* mother, grandmother etc.? For that matter, why not her father, and his father, and so on?

Interesting, isn't it—how some of the major doctrines of professing Christianity cannot be found in the Bible? There is no mention whatever of Mary being "immaculately conceived" and the words aren't even used in the Bible.

Because of Augustinian guilt complexes, religious folk have taken the completely erroneous notion that sex is dirty, filthy, evil, and, even if necessary for the propagation of the human race, it is surely something of which to be ashamed.

For some to entertain in their minds that Mary was conceived in the same way they were—by the ghastly, evil, "dirty" method of (blush!) sexual intercourse—is unthinkable.

If Mary were "immaculately conceived" by a divine miracle, then *she*, and not Jesus, was the "first begotten" of God. This tends to place Mary *above* the Son of God, at least in form if not in substance. This seems to be the religion of millions. But the Bible teaches no such doctrine.

While Mary is deeply respected and honored in memory of her sacrifice (for that's what it was!) in humbly accepting the calling of God to be chosen as the human mother by whom the very God of life would become human, there is no teaching whatever from Genesis to Revelation that she is to be *worshiped*. Respected, loved, yes; but worshiped, no. The Bible instructs that God (the Family of God including the Father and the Son) *only* is to be "worshiped"!

(The doctrine of the worship of Mary is as nonbiblical as is the fable of the Trinity. Mary was said to have been found "with child of the Holy Spirit." [As an aside, if the Holy Spirit were a person, then Jesus prayed to the wrong Father! Trinitarians admit that the Father is a distinct person of the Godhead. If He is the Father God, and the Father of Jesus, then it was He, by and through the limitless power of His Spirit, called the "Holy Spirit" that performed the miracle of Christ's begetting as a human being.])

Mary was not "dirtied" or "defiled" or in some way unworthy of being named the mother of the son of God because she was conceived in the same way you and I were conceived.

God "invented" marriage, and *commanded* that a man and his wife "become one flesh" in the normal, wholesome embrace of human love, in sexual intercourse. God says, "Marriage is honourable in all, and the bed undefiled . . ." (Heb. 13:4).

Neither was it a shame for Mary to have *other* children, after Jesus was born; and yes, these were conceived through sexual union with her husband. Even the plain language of Matthew 1:24 ought to tell any thinking person that. The Bible says, "Then Joseph being raised from sleep did as the angel of the Lord had bidden him, and *took unto him his wife:* And *knew* her not until she had brought forth her firstborn son: and he called his name JESUS."

Even the translators of 1611 could not bring themselves to give the proper rendition of the Greek word by admitting it should have read, "And did not know her carnally until after . . ." or some similar rendering which would have made the verse more obvious.

The fact that Joseph "took unto him *his wife*" is rather plain. The fact that Jesus was the "firstborn" implies a "secondborn," and so on. The fact that Joseph "knew her [carnally] not *until*" after Jesus was born is plainly indicative of the fact that Joseph *did* "know her" in full sexual intercourse *after* Jesus was born.

At the time of the annunciation and their journey to Bethlehem for the birth of their first child, Joseph was unable to afford anything more than a pair of turtledoves as a dedication sacrifice (Lev. 12:8; Luke 2:24). Apparently, he could not afford the price of a lamb.

This has been taken by some to imply that Joseph and Mary

were in a state of near poverty. While obviously not "wealthy" by any standards, Joseph, however, was an industrious worker and a more than adequate provider. Remember, they had been forced to make an arduous journey at a critical time in Mary's pregnancy. No doubt, it required extra expense for proper animals and conveyances to insure Mary a comfortable trip. Further, there was the problem of taxation, of enforced payoffs to various petty officials, Roman soldiers or others along the route.

The family God selected to be the human guardian and physical mother of the very Son of God would have measured up to the strictest standards of God's own laws of industry, labor, honesty and thrift.

God's laws established principles of hard work, and Joseph would have followed those principles diligently. There was no spiritual or biblical requirement that Joseph and his family be wealthy; but there is every reason to believe there was a strong requirement that he measure up to the biblical "work ethic" of the Old Testament.

The biblical principles demanded that a man be energetic and hard-working enough to lay up for "his children's children" indicating that each tradesman was fully expected according to God's Word to be successful enough that he would, at the end of his life, have provided a sufficient estate that even his grandchildren would be given a little head start in their own careers.

So, accepting the biblical account at face value, then, it is simply inconceivable that Joseph was anything less than moderately successful; not necessarily wealthy but certainly not poor. He would not have had a single child more than he could have afforded or provided for; and each of the children would have been partners with him as soon as his physical stature and grasp of the trade allowed.

The word "carpenter" relating to Joseph is very misleading in modern terminology, and is far better rendered "stone mason" or "artisan." The Greek word is *tekton* and most biblical authorities agree it had a far wider application than merely the term "carpenter" as it might be applied today. In our specialized societies, carpenters are thought of as those who work with sawn and hewn lumber, and primarily work only at pounding nails into boards.

Ask a modern carpenter if this is "all he does," and he will very likely give you a lengthy lecture about the *many* skills required to become a good carpenter.

However, during the day of Jesus Christ, "carpentry" included much more than just the fabrication of wooden dwellings. Most of the homes were a combination of stone, mud and clay, hewn beams and "lumber."

The city where Jesus spent much of His early ministry around the Galilean area was Capernaum. I have been to Capernaum several times, and have seen the remnants of the porches, the arches, the mosaics, and the walls of the buildings which were there during the time of Christ.

Capernaum, at that time, was a beaming, modern, beautifully sculptured Grecian-type city. It was filled with beautiful multi-leveled homes which had large central gardens, mosaic walks, fountains and even, believe it or not, indoor bathrooms and steam baths!

The homes of the wealthier class at that time were marvels of architecture, and a far cry from the stone and adobe hovels imagined by many as being the general domicile of the time.

A "carpenter" would have to have a certain familiarity with mathematics, engineering principles (working with block and tackle, levers, and knowing how to construct arches and cantilever overhanging balconies, etc.) and especially would have to be skillful in finishing work, such as interior surfaces, mosaic hallways and walkways, and would even have to know a certain amount about plumbing.

For, during that period and in the first two or three centuries thereafter, home plumbing included indoor water, which was delivered via a system of pipes and could be cut off by valves just as in a modern home today.

From their earliest age Jesus and His brothers learned the skills of the trade, and Jesus, as the older brother, could well have been the one primarily concerned with keeping of family records, payment of bills, ordering of materials, the writing and signing of contracts, and the required barter, both in the marketplace and with passing caravans, for tools and building supplies.

From earliest moments of boyhood, Jesus, James, Joseph, and later little Simon would perhaps run down to the public market when they had heard the tinkling of the bells of a long heavily laden caravan coming through the area from the trade routes from the north and the east, realizing that it might be a timely opportunity to purchase some finely made tapestries, rugs, yardage of fine fabrics for Mary and the girls to make into clothing, or perhaps even some of the famous metal tools, adzes, drawknives, chisels and heavier quarrying tools produced by the nations to the east.

Probably by the time Jesus was in His late teens or early twenties, His legal guardian Joseph was dead. The family business passed into the hands of Jesus, his eldest son, together with the other brothers.

Jesus grew up in a *family* environment, with an intelligent and well-educated group of young men and women maturing under the careful guardianship of Joseph until his death, and later under the love, warmth and sympathetic concern of Mary.

A greater grasp of the New Testament would lead any thinking person to ponder whether the great God—who shows us that the family represents the most basic building block of society, the underpinning of civilization, and the unit which is held up in the Bible as a divinely ordained unit and used as a direct analogy of the relationship between Christ and His Church—would have been an only child, and never would have known the sharing, giving, close relationship of a family.

The family's concerns were Jesus' concerns for the bulk of His life on this earth. While His intensive studies and private tutelage sessions, plus His countless hours spent in fervent prayer and even fasting from time to time, were diligently preparing Him for the tumultuous and challenging ministry He was later to fulfill, from His boyhood and on up through His early teenage and beyond, Jesus learned that close-knit experience of living among the members of His own family and the conduct of a family trade.

The family took yearly trips to Jerusalem on the occasion of annual holy days, and perhaps went twice a year or even more. Other shorter trips might have included a visit to the Mediterranean Sea in the Syrophoenician coastland (a place to which Jesus resorted for a much-needed rest during a particular stressful part of His ministry later on), to the snow-covered mountains of Hermon, or down into the beautiful Sharon valley and to the Mediterranean.

Was Jesus ever cheated?

Surely, Jesus' reputation as a tradesman was one of total honesty and generosity, and there were no doubt a great number of individuals who felt He was "an easy mark" for shyster deals.

Jesus would have never entered into a loud argument with other tradesmen, suppliers, or homeowners about alleged mishandling of money or goods. His entire message later showed that gentle and meek spirit of a willingness to accept abuse, of turning the other cheek, of gladly handing a man an inner garment and also giving, if required, an outer one, and if, being pressed by a Roman soldier riding the mail circuit to carry the heavy mail sacks, not only to walk the required mile in the cool mountain elevations of Nazareth's beautiful conifers, but to go an extra mile or so down the trail with the Roman before turning back home.

It is a great mistake to erase from your minds the entire life story, personality, boyhood, family environment and building trade of Jesus the carpenter, and try only to imagine Him in some superreligious postures, as a mature man during His ministry, gleaned from a few accounts in the gospels.

Though God did not intend to give us a lengthy biography of Jesus' boyhood, neither did He want the terrible perversion of the plain truth concerning Christ's early life, which portrays Him as an only child, a sorrowful-eyed vagabond who seemingly appears out of nowhere at about age 30 and begins challenging the religious leaders with His strange doctrines.

CHAPTER 5

Jesus in Palestine—
the Historical Facts

The importance of Jesus Christ's life and death is recorded in the New Testament. Yet for those who do not accept the New Testament as accurate history, other records have been preserved which clearly show that the human life of Jesus Christ was fact— not fiction.

In times past and present, some atheists and agnostics have gone so far as to claim that no real evidence exists outside the New Testament to prove that Jesus of Nazareth actually lived and died. And the New Testament, of course, is dismissed as a pious fraud.

It is true that no record of the crucifixion of Jesus has come down to us from Pilate himself. But other records *have* been preserved which do mention Jesus of Nazareth. These records are *non*-Christian in origin and, hence, can be regarded as neutral, disinterested, historical proof of Jesus' life and subsequent crucifixion by the Romans.

Writing around the end of the first century A.D., the Roman historian Suetonius tells us that in A.D. 49 the Emperor Claudius banished all Jews from the city of Rome (an incident also mentioned in Acts 18:2): "He expelled the Jews from Rome, on account of the riots in which they were constantly indulging, at the instigation of Chrestus" (*Claudius*, 25,4).

"Chrestus" was a common misspelling of the name of Christ. These riots were probably a result of the recent arrival in Rome of Christianity, which would have caused considerable dissension in the Jewish community there, as it did elsewhere (see, for example, Acts 21:31). Writing many years later, Suetonius doubtless misunderstood the police records of the rioting and took the name of "Chrestus" to refer to some individual of that name.

A more detailed account of Christ comes from the Roman historian Tacitus. Writing between A.D. 115 and 117, Tacitus tells us that in A.D. 64 the Emperor Nero tried to blame the disastrous fire in Rome on the Christians. Tacitus then goes on to describe these Christians: "They got their name from Christ, who was executed by sentence of the Procurator Pontius Pilate in the reign of Tiberius. That checked the pernicious superstition for a short time, but it broke out afresh—not only in Judea, where the plague first arose, but in Rome itself, where all the horrible and shameful things in the world collect and find a home" (*Annals*, XV,44).

From Tacitus's comments it is clear he had no sympathy for Christianity. Yet for him there was no question that its founder actually lived and was executed by Pontius Pilate while he was procurator over Judea several decades earlier. Tacitus was not writing from hearsay. He was a Roman historian of note; he had access to official court records, diplomatic correspondence and Roman archives. Aside from his pagan, anti-Christian bias, his account is a reliable confirmation of the New Testament account of Christ's death and its aftermath.

Roman historians are not the only ones who tell us of Jesus of Nazareth. Ancient Jewish traditions preserved in the Talmud also mention Him. Jewish scholars generally agree that some traditions of Jesus' death by crucifixion were maintained among the Jews for several centuries after the event and were finally put in written form in the Babylonian Talmud about A.D. 500. One such passage—which some think refers to Jesus, though a number feel it refers to someone else—reads as follows: "On the eve of Passover they hanged Yeshu and the herald went before him for forty days saying, He is going forth to be stoned in that he hath practiced sorcery and beguiled and led astray Israel. Let everyone knowing aught in his defense come and plead for him. But they found naught in his defense and hanged him on the eve of Passover" (*Sanhedrin*, 43A).

Another account of Jesus is found in the writings of the famous Jewish historian Flavius Josephus of the first century A.D. However, historians feel that the passage was later altered by a Christian scribe to make Josephus say that Jesus was possibly the Messiah—something Josephus himself probably did not write.

However, one Jewish scholar has rendered the passage as follows: "Now, there was about this time Jesus, a wise man; for he was a doer of wonderful works, a teacher of such men as receive the truth with pleasure. He drew over to him both many of the Jews and many of the Gentiles. And when Pilate, at the suggestion of the principal men among us, had condemned him to the cross, those that loved him at the first ceased not so to do; and the race of Christians, so named from him are not extinct even now" (Klausner, *Jesus of Nazareth*, pp. 55-56).

Josephus also mentions Jesus briefly in another passage which scholars feel is quite genuine: "He [Annas] convened a judicial session of the Sanhedrin and brought before it the brother of Jesus the so-called Christ—James by name—and some others, whom he charged with breaking the law and handed over to be stoned to death" (Josephus, *Antiquities*, XX,200).

Many other accounts, mostly fragmentary, have come down to us besides the ones that are quoted here. Many of these give further details which corroborate the New Testament accounts of Jesus. These documents so vindicate the New Testament record that Professor Klausner stated: "If we possessed them alone, we should know nothing except that in Judaea there had existed a Jew named Jesus who was called the Christ, the "Anointed"; that he performed miracles and taught the people; that he was killed by Pontius Pilate at the instigation of the Jews; that he had a brother named James, who was put to death by the High Priest Annas, the son of Annas; that owing to Jesus there arose a special sect known as Christians; that a community belonging to this sect existed in Rome fifty years after the birth of Jesus, and that from the time of Nero, the sect greatly increased; regarded Jesus as virtually divine, and underwent severe persecution" (*Jesus of Nazareth*, p. 62).

False concepts of a false Jesus would be at least partially removed by understanding more of the environment that was Palestine during Jesus' day. Few understand the true picture of Jesus as framed in the social customs, the type of architecture, the flow of commerce and business, and the whole panorama of Jewish life during that Herodian period.

It is incredible that so many books of theological research, Bible dictionaries, histories of the Holy Land, and other works on the life and time of Jesus use the illustrations of a

Palestine of the turn of the century—the old woodcuts, travelogue photos, and oft-reprinted scenes of the bleak ruins of ancient cities, Bedouin tents, camel caravans, filthy streets and rocky, barren hillsides—which tend to leave the impression that this *is* the Palestine of the time of Christ.

Nothing could be further from the truth.

The land that is now drastically depleted, mostly deforested, heavily eroded and reduced to dust, was, almost nineteen hundred years ago, a verdant, beautiful, rich part of the world, virtually unrivaled in industry, wealth and strength.

If you could have walked the streets of the cities of Capernaum, Nazareth, through any of the confederation of the "Decapolis"—the ten towns in the Galilean region—you would have been startled by the quality and wealth. And Jerusalem itself? You would have been even more amazed than were Jesus' own disciples over the beauty, magnificence and size of Jerusalem, especially of those buildings associated with the temple.

In ancient times, God had promised the Israelites a land "flowing with milk and honey." One remembers the account of the spies sent to search out the land who came back with tales not only of giant men, but of fruits and produce so abundant and so large that they are virtually unknown among modern agricultural products today.

The implication of the account of one cluster of grapes being carried on a pole by two men is clear; each grape must have been about the size of a plum or a lemon!

"And they came to the Valley of Eshcol, and cut down from there a branch with a single cluster of grapes, and they carried it on a pole between two of them; they brought also some pomegranates and figs.

"And they came to Moses . . . and they told him, 'We came to the land to which you sent us; it flows with milk and honey, and this is its fruit' " (Num. 13:23-27, RSV).

The early Israelites weren't only impressed by the gigantic size of the fruits and produce of the land—they were frightened to death at the size of the people living there! They said, ". . . all the people that we saw in it are men of great stature . . . and we seemed to ourselves like grasshoppers . . ." (Num. 13:32-33). It is logical to have expected that the largest, and therefore strongest, peoples would populate the richest areas.)

The land of Israel combines every variety of climate, from the perennial snows on beautiful Mount Hermon and the cooler higher elevations of Lebanon, to the more pleasant warmth of the valleys of Galilee, and the tropical and humid climate of the Jordan River facing the Mediterranean Sea. According to the most ancient records, every fish imaginable teemed the waters of that country (fishing was a major industry as evidenced by some of Jesus' own disciples' occupations) and birds and wild fowl were abundant.

In your mind's eye, you need to imagine a country more like some of the western mountain states of the United States— perhaps portions of northern or central California, but in a much smaller area, encompassing a deep depression (such as Death Valley) wherein lies the Salt Sea and the terminus of the Jordan River, together with lofty snow-clad mountains, higher elevations festooned with conifers of every sort, especially the world-famed "Cedars of Lebanon," seemingly endless corn and pasture lands, terraced hills covered with olives and vines, glades and pleasant valleys bubbling with springs and streams. Naturally, by the time of Christ, a great deal of the land had been abused and no small amount of depletion of natural resources and subsequent erosion and loss of arable soil had already occurred. Still, it was immensely richer than it is today.

Therefore, although many glowing accounts of the beauty of that land exist in the books of Exodus, Leviticus, and some of the major prophets, descriptions of pastures which seemed to be "clothed with flocks" and of "the land of milk and honey" may not have been quite so accurate by Jesus' day. Nevertheless, abundant literature exists, and archaeological finds substantiate, that the Palestine of Jesus' day was luxuriously wealthy in natural resources; dotted with towns and cities that were resplendent examples of the finest engineering and architectural principles of that day and represented one of the most important possessions of the Roman Empire. Palestine was prized for its exports of fruit, grains, olives, wine, oils, spices, and the by no means meager returns to Roman treasuries from the heavy system of taxation imposed upon the people.

Herod was a great builder. Not only was the temple during

Jesus' day an absolute marvel of glittering stone and beautiful architecture, but there were so many fortresses, palaces, temples, amphitheaters and public monuments that it was said even in far-away Rome that some structures of the area of Palestine were among the very finest in the empire, looked upon as a jewel in the crown of Caesar himself.

Try to imagine the city of Capernaum, which in fact was a most important city, and frequently mentioned by the writers of the Bible in connection with the life and ministry of Jesus.

Millions of Bible illiterates think of Christ's ministry as having taken place in the streets of Jerusalem. Many suppose His "Sermon on the Mount" was probably delivered on the "Mount of Olives" adjacent to Jerusalem—few seem to understand *most* of this ministry was conducted in northern Israel, around Capernaum and the dozens of towns in Galilee.

Galilee was a motley collection of many races and religions, distinctly tainted with foreign and distasteful elements, in the opinion of the religious bigots of Jerusalem.

Galileans were generally regarded as a crude, half-breed lot, looked upon with varying degrees of pity and contempt. The present-day attitudes of some New Englanders toward those from Dixie with a "Southern drawl" might be an appropriate analogy. That's why the intellectual and spiritual leaders of Jerusalem called Christ and His disciples a crude and "unlearned" lot, without academic or spiritual credentials.

Even though Jesus grew up in Nazareth after His family returned from their exile in Egypt, Joseph's business took him and his sons into the other cities and towns in the Galilean area. Remember that a young Jewish boy was expected to join the adult community at about age 12; that it was a sober time of Roman occupation, heavy taxation and poverty, ferment and potential for rebellion (there had been a spate of abortive attempts at Maccabean revivals), and the fear of the life-and-death power of the religious leaders, as well as the oppressive rule of the previous Herod.

It was hardly a cheerful time for carefree young children to grow up with time on their hands for endless play and daydreams. Jesus had been taught His father's trade from His earliest youth, and no doubt labored, first at His father's side (Joseph), and, following Joseph's death, as the head of the family and its business.

His building trade was well known throughout the area; and, just as it is quite common for a contractor or a carpenter to live in a home built with his own hands, by his own design, or by his own firm, so Jesus and His brothers, Joses, Simon, Jude and James, together with their helpers, must have constructed a large home for their family in Capernaum.

That home in Capernaum and the city itself are prominent in the early ministry of Jesus. When Jesus would return to Capernaum He was said to have been "at home" (Mark 2:1, RSV). His disciple Matthew (also called Levi), writer of the first of the gospels, was a resident of that city as well (Matt. 9:9).

According to archaeological discoveries, the city of Capernaum, like many other port cities, seemed to be divided into two distinct sections. The one part was almost wholly devoted to the fishery industry, the other to the business and residential sections of what was one of the finest cities of that part of the world.

Peter and Andrew both lived in nearby Bethsaida, along the shore of the lake a few miles further south (Mark 1:29), and Peter owned a home there (Matt. 8:14; Mark 1:30; Luke 4:38).

Try to imagine that you are standing in one of the main streets in Capernaum. You would no doubt see houses of all types, differing in size and scope depending entirely upon the substance and wealth of the owners; the houses would range from small cottages only 30 or 40 feet square, on up to large homes of the fairly wealthy of two or even three stories or more. While not common, it would not have been rare to see any number of homes of two stories or more which would have featured rich architectural embellishments of pillars and decorative friezes, built in the style of the Roman villas of the same period.

On entering such a home, you would have noticed the beautiful stone work, or marble or more expensive stone, the walls painted with delicate colors such as vermilion (or whitewashed), and a large interior courtyard, where you would have seen a pool and possibly a fountain. Opening to either side would be living quarters, and to the rear and upstairs would be large public rooms for dining and family meetings. A wide stairway of beautiful quarried stone would lead directly from the street up the side of the home to the rooftop. Building codes of the time required that the large rooftops be provided with decorative handrails to protect people from falling. The roof would probably have been paved with brick or stone, or possibly one of the cements used at the time. The roofs always sloped slightly toward the front, so that the cisterns (sometimes contained even within the homes themselves) were filled with rainwater by ducts which caught the rains of the wet season.

It would be quite common to see families of the cities of Palestine—including Jerusalem and those of the Galilean area—gather in the cool of an evening on their rooftops for discussion or to call to the neighbors across the way. Actually, the way the homes were built it was possible to go from roof to roof. Rabbinic literature spoke of the "road of the roofs." Read Jesus' statement in Matthew 24 of one who might be caught on the housetop during the time of severe national crisis. (He was speaking both of the destruction of Jerusalem in A.D. 70 and of a time called in the Bible "the Great Tribulation" yet ahead.) Jesus told them not to come down to take anything which might be in their house, indicating that they could use the "road of the roofs," passing from roof to roof until, perhaps at the final home in the block, they might make good their escape by descending to the ground.

Once, Jesus was gathered together with His disciples and a large crowd of people *inside His own home* in the city of Capernaum. A group of people, desperate to have their sick friend healed, took up the stones of the roof and let the sick man down into the large upper room where Jesus was. "And again he entered again into Capernaum after some days; and it was noised that he was *in the house.* And straightway many were gathered, insomuch that there was no room to receive them, no, not so much as about the door: and he preached the word unto them. And they came unto him, bringing one sick of the palsy, which was borne of four. And when they could not come nigh unto him for the press, they uncovered the roof where he was: And when they had broken it up, they let down the bed wherein the sick of the palsy lay. When Jesus saw their faith, he said unto the sick of the palsy, Son, thy sins be forgiven thee" (Mark 2:1-5).

This reveals that Jesus was in a home which was obviously *His own.* It was noised abroad that He was "in the house" which is rendered by other translations "at home." This also illustrates the fact that those who were so anxious to have their friend healed were easily able to climb to the rooftop via the outer stairway.

Jesus was in His own home, either in a large upper room capable of accommodating more than one hundred persons, or, possibly, in a large central courtyard that was a feature of Jewish homes of that size and scale. Servants' quarters and the vestibule for guests were located near the front, sleeping quarters around both sides, and larger upper rooms toward the rear with a large family kitchen. It was not unusual for such homes to have interior fountains with plantings, and many of them would have been open to the outside air, not unlike those Spanish villas designed at a much later time.

Jesus' ministry centered around the area of Capernaum, and later, the city where He grew up and was so well known, Nazareth. The synagogue into which He entered and healed the man with a withered hand on the Sabbath (Mark's third chapter) was no doubt the synagogue of the city of Capernaum.

He was teaching "by the seaside" (Mark 4:1) of the Sea of Galilee. Capernaum occupied its northwestern shore. When the fifth chapter speaks of Jesus going "to the other side of the sea, to the country of the Gadarenes," it refers to the Golan Heights of today.

CHAPTER 6

What Jesus Looked Like

What did Jesus look like?

Scripture indicates Jesus was neither outstandingly tall, nor outstandingly short; He was therefore of the average height of the average Jewish young man of His day. Research suggests that men were somewhat larger then than they subsequently became during the Middle Ages; consequently Jesus could have been between 5' 7" and 5' 10".

His physical stature would have been similar to any other average laboring person who had spent his growing years lifting, tugging, pushing, pulling, carrying, and enjoying hard work out of doors.

The Bible states that the body is the "temple of the Holy Spirit," indicating that Jesus must have had a strong, healthy body. Furthermore, the Bible reveals that Jesus was made in the exact similitude of the Father.

Since Jesus in His prehuman life and God the Father did the planning and designing of the human body, it is logical to conclude that Jesus had a flawless or perfect human form.

This, by itself, is not necessarily unique. There are many millions who are so blessed with that right combination of muscular development and symmetry so as to appear perfectly and equally proportioned, yet without the bulging muscles of a professional weight lifter or the opposite extreme of gawky thinness.

Jesus looked like what He was: a commonplace Jew of first-century Palestine. And as such, Jesus could have been either blond, redheaded, or dark-headed. There is no way to really tell, since members of the family of Judah can regularly exhibit any of this range of complexions and/or colors of eye or hair.

If we may speculate, it may be reasonable to postulate that Jesus could have looked somewhat like his physical ancestor, David.

There is evidence that David was "ruddy" in complexion, meaning he was fair skinned, and probably red haired. David also wore a beard. He was shorter in stature than his other brothers, yet was well muscled and quite physically strong.

The picture of David as the young dark-haired lad with a sling in his hand that is popular in some family Bibles may be erroneous according to the biblical descriptions of the man, but then an exact picture would be impossible to draw, since there is no physical description in sufficient enough detail.

If following the reasoning that Jesus was from David's own lineage, and that David was in fact a type of Jesus Christ, if there is any such "type and anti-type," perhaps Jesus could also have been fair-skinned and red-haired (freckle-faced also?).

Of course in one sense, it is *not important* what Jesus looked like or what He wore! It frankly *doesn't matter* what His skin color, skin texture, color of eyes and hair were! It doesn't matter what His clothes were made of. What *does* matter is what Jesus *said,* what He *taught,* what He *promised!*

God does not honor one skin color, one facial "look," one style of clothing. God created *all* human beings to have an equally enormous ultimate potential regardless of external appearances.

So the only thing about Jesus' appearance that is somewhat important is that you understand that the cherished concepts of the "Jesus" of the pictures and movies are false.

As we grow older, we come to realize there are "types" of facial and bodily builds, and we tend to categorize people we have met and known into those "types"!

Some individuals are noticeably outstanding because of either physical attractiveness or ugliness—and we tend to remember them because of their most distinguishing characteristics: beautiful eyes, large ears, protruding chin, high cheekbones, perfect teeth, a unique smile, an unusual nose. Some people project the picture of absolute beauty in perfect proportions, others must live with the knowledge that they are physically ugly.

Jesus was somewhere in between. He was that type of person who, though reasonably attractive in the sense of having a pleasant enough face, did not call attention to Himself because of any outstanding characteristics. Jesus was neither "beautiful" nor ugly. He was commonplace, quite ordinary. He had the kind of face which could easily become lost in a crowd. He looked average, normal, regular—an everyday kind of person.

Doubtlessly, Jesus' eyes could become as fiercely intense as any other human being in a moment of anger. (Yes, Jesus became angry on occasion, though never from the normal human stimuli, never for the normal reasons and never with the normal consequences.) Jesus' eyes could radiate and express the full range of human emotions from amusement and good humor, to pain and sorrow, to deep thoughtfulness and profound compassion.

Jesus' face and countenance would change with His changing moods as much as ours do, but there is no reason to assume that His face was any more "expressive" than that of any other average person.

The face and particularly the eyes have been called "the mirror of the soul." It is, after all, fairly simple to deduce what a person is feeling if you simply look at the expressions on his face. It of course helps to know all the inputs and to be aware of the flow of the conversation. But, all by itself, the human face paints a masterful picture.

There are certain facial expressions which convey to other human beings ranges of emotions which I thoroughly believe never crossed Jesus' face.

Did Jesus ever reveal on His face a sly, devious or mischievous look?

I doubt it. He could never "fake" a look, masquerading behind a false deceptive expression. The look coming out of Jesus' eyes and across His countenance was always precisely the look which portrayed honestly and forthrightly what was going on inside His mind.

He had God's Holy Spirit without measure and without admixture. You have met any number of people you would say have an "open, honest look" and others who tend, perhaps because of deep-set eyes, a shifty glance, dark brows or low hairlines, to have a sly or devious look.

I would rather assume Jesus' look was the former, and that there was a frankness, earnestness and openness about His countenance which men would find attractive, yet not especially outstanding. Jesus was serious, but certainly never threatening.

That same directness of appearance would no doubt change, like a beautiful landscape during a thunderstorm, to blazing anger, when circumstances warranted it.

The look of profound agony on Jesus' face when He "groaned within himself" over the people's lack of faith as He was about to raise Lazarus from the dead could be contrasted with the look of piercing outrage which He would have displayed as He spoke the words recorded in Matthew's twenty-third chapter, "Woe unto you, scribes and Pharisees, hypocrites!"

Then there would have been the look of mature yet kind indulgence when He gently chided his own mother at the marriage feast at Cana in Galilee when He said, "Woman, what in the world am I going to do with you?" The faint quirk of indulgent humor, showing mild but understanding displeasure, expressed at the corner of His mouth and with a slight furrowing of the brows could be contrasted with the look of real emotional and physical pain over the hopelessness and the utter faithlessness of some of His closest personal friends at Lazarus's tomb.

Jesus was in fact the kind of a guy you would have loved, but only if you too were filled with God's Holy Spirit, or could be utterly and totally honest with yourself about who and what you were.

To the higher social classes, especially the religionists of his day, He was the kind of guy you could easily hate.

But to the little folk, the maimed, the sick, the blind and the tormented, He was in fact the kind of a guy you could love.

Jesus had average facial texturing and coloring, with average length hair. We might call His hair length "mod" today, since that was the cultural norm at the time—somewhat longer than the hair styles of the 1940s and 1950s and somewhat shorter than the long-haired hippie look of the 1960s.

There is no doubt that Jesus wore a full, yet neatly trimmed and well-groomed beard. (It would be almost impossible to argue around the fact that Isaiah's prophecy said He "gave his cheek to those who pluck the hair" by alleging it was only a day and a half's growth to which they applied pinchers or tweezers.) Beards were the custom of the time, and there is no reason to assume that Jesus appeared smooth shaven.

He followed conscientious practices of personal hygiene.

Even at the account of the last supper, when Peter began to argue that Jesus would "never wash his feet," Jesus said, "He that is bathed doesn't need to wash anything except his feet" thus proving that all the disciples and Jesus had had opportunity for a bath prior to coming to the dinner.

Most believe false conceptions about the "dusty roads of Galilee" where they envision a perpetual drought, one muddy creek winding down the middle of the desertlike, rocky wasteland called the "Jordan River," and the "Holy Land" as a bleak, hostile and barren landscape where dust, dirt, fleas, flies, bedraggled camels, braying jackasses, and dusty people in dusty robes made up the whole scene.

Not so. As has been shown earlier, the land was a verdant beautiful area of greenery, conifers, orchards, fields of vegetables and grain, with rippling brooks and streams, wells, and indoor bathing facilities in some of the homes.

There were both hot and cold springs in the areas where Jesus lived and worked, and you can be absolutely sure that the great God who so insisted upon cleanliness in the camp of Israel, who gave and made a matter of *law* the most rigorous attention to personal and communal hygiene, would have followed the practice of daily bathing, meticulous grooming of His person, trimming of the hair and beard, and deliberate choice of His clothing. All with care and concern, but totally devoid of fetish and obsession.

It is important to note that even Jesus' outer garments were of such quality that the Roman soldiers were industriously gambling for even His undergarments at the foot of His crucifixion stake.

His outer garments consisted of a coat or cloak which was seamless and, one is tempted to assume, was not unlike Joseph's coat of "many colors."

Perhaps it was plain, perhaps it had tribal colors or decorations, but at any event, it was in commonplace good taste and of fine quality, just like any number of dark suits worn by businessmen at dinners today.

A lack of showiness in this dress would have been one of the reasons that Jesus managed on several occasions—prior to God's own appointed and intended time—to elude His pursuers in the riotous melee of a swirling mob of people. How could Jesus have so escaped His attackers if He looked distinctly different from the other people of His day? Surely a pasty-white face, exceedingly long hair and a glowing, golden halo could have been easily spotted!

No, Jesus was *plain*. And it was only His similarity in physical appearance (a beard certainly helps when there are hundreds of them about) as well as the similarity of the garments He wore that enabled Him to lose Himself in a crowd "passing by in their midst" and thereby succeed in escaping.

The quality of the clothing was extremely fine in first-century Palestine.

Housewives still speak of "sheets and linens" today, though mostly they are really speaking about cheaper cottons and synthetics. But the purchase of fine handmade linens can be a costly acquisition indeed.

Linen was handmade and was durable enough to last for many years during Jesus' day.

Many other kinds of fabrics were woven by the people of that country, and the Bible speaks of velvets, purples, fine linens, and many kinds of personal clothing, as well as draperies and tapestries.

Jesus' inner garments would have been of lightweight cotton, linen and/or wool. The outer coat was almost surely wool.

Check the price tags on a 100 percent wool suit today and compare it with other kinds of fabrics; it may change your mind about thinking that all of the fabrics of Jesus' day were crude by comparison to ours.

Even as architecture during His day and further back in history was superb—who could ever hope to duplicate the pyramids of Egypt, the fabulous hanging gardens of Babylon, the Colossus of Rhodes, the temple of Solomon's day, Herod's amphitheaters, deep water ports and palaces?—so it is that the finely made hides, skins, fabrics and the like during Jesus' day would be fabulous possessions for any family even in our time.

The *real* Jesus epitomized what God would look like as a man—well groomed but not affected, well dressed but not clothes-conscious, clean but not antiseptic, dignified but not "distinguished."

CHAPTER 7

Jesus and John the Baptist:

Incongruous?

John the Baptist's condition was desperate. He had just been thrown into prison, following his insistence that Herod would be breaking God's law to live in adultery. Then he heard, through several of his disciples, the rumors about Jesus' growing ministry.

From the beginning, John had shunned material substance and consequently had become known as a frugal, austere person who "neither ate nor drank" (never banqueted or drank any alcoholic beverages). Furthermore, John "had his raiment of camel's hair, and a leathern girdle about his loins; and his meat [food] was locusts and wild honey" (Matt. 3:4). This was seen as in complete contrast to Jesus, who attended any number of sumptuous dinners, and who did, notwithstanding opinions to the contrary, take a glass of wine with a meal now and then.

Because of the camel's hair, leather, and seemingly strange diet (grasshoppers, ugh!), John is usually type-cast by Hollywood as a wild-haired, crazed-eyed, ferociously gesticulating freak with streaks of dirt down his face, a rat-eaten, torn, ancient old camel skin, complete with traces of hoof and udder, on his back, and a shepherd's crook in his hand. He is imagined to be constantly spewing out inane condemnations, punctuated by spittleflecked stentorian thunder. John is seen to be leaping wildly about in various Jesus films like an inmate from a mental asylum playing the part of an African witch doctor.

Ever purchase a camel's hair coat? They happen to be among the most expensive. The Bible says nothing about a whole camel *skin*, loosely draped over a scrawny, filthy freak. But it does say John wore a coat of fine, durable, camel's *hair*.

Even today the finest leathers are handfinished, handsewn, handmade. John had a "leathern" girdle; a wide, all-purpose belt which contained pockets for personal items—not strange at all, since it was a common item of apparel of the day. (And, after all, millions of men still avoid having their trousers cascading over their ankles by a band of cow's hide around their middle; today it's called a belt.)

John's diet has been argued for decades. The Bible says that his main staple was food found in the wilds; locusts and "wild" honey. Today, "wild" honey is coveted by those who insist the healthful benefits of using natural sweeteners are infinitely more salubrious than either sugar or saccharine. Perhaps "locusts" seems strange to most; but, then, many a gourmet restaurant features shrimp, lobsters, oysters, escargot, squid, eel, and, you guessed it, grasshoppers. (Strangely enough, only the last was designed by God as fit for human consumption! See Leviticus 11:22 for a surprise.)

Like many other parts of the Bible, Matthew's encapsulated view of John's life-style is only a quick, partial sketch, intended to convey the general concept of a person who had eschewed a sumptuous pattern of living.

John was conducting a very great ministry: thousands had been baptized by him in the waters of the Jordan River and elsewhere. But now it seemed he was doomed to die because he had refused to sanction Herod's lustful marriage plans. Though most miss the subtleties in the account, could it have been that John was genuinely hurt that Jesus had not dropped everything, rushed to his side, and, if not at the very least comforted him, perhaps even have performed a miracle to free him?

Consequently, perhaps it was John himself who had sent his disciples with a petulant message to Jesus.

Jesus was at a town called Nain, where a great miracle occurred; that of raising the son of a widow from death right while he was being transported on a bier to his grave.

The disciples of John heard the rumors of the great event, now rapidly spreading, and told John, in prison, all about it. When John in turn sent the disciples back to the town to talk with

Jesus they said rather chidingly, "Are you he who is to come [meaning the Messiah] or shall we look for another?"

Luke's account could imply that John had rehearsed his disciples on exactly how to phrase the question; and sure enough, when they met Jesus they did exactly as John had requested (Luke 7:18-20).

During their visit with Jesus a crowd surrounded Christ. Many were virtually waiting in line to bring children, husbands and wives, friends and relatives to be cured of many diseases, including leprosy, and to have demons cast out of those possessed. Blind individuals in the area were being healed by Jesus; all this as a direct result of the rumors following the raising of the widow's son.

In the midst of this setting, Jesus told John's disciple, "Go and tell John what you have seen and heard: the blind receive their sight, the lame walk, lepers are cleansed, and the deaf hear, the dead are raised up, the poor have good news [the gospel] preached to them" (v. 22, RSV).

This statement seems to fulfill several portions of the book of Isaiah, and is in fact, a partial summary of the human ministry of Jesus Christ.

All of the great miracles He performed were done either spontaneously, out of deep compassion for human grief (as in the case of the son of the widow at Nain) or as a direct result of distraught people pressing themselves *upon Him.*

However, following this powerful statement, in which Jesus, true to His own continuous teachings, essentially urged John and his disciples to "judge by the fruits," Jesus told John's disciples to take to John the *eyewitness* account of exactly what they had seen *accomplished,* rather than a clever story from the lips of an individual who had a good argument. As His last statement, Jesus turned to the disciples of John and said, ". . . and blessed is he whosoever shall not be offended in me"!

A fascinating though easily overlooked comment! What does it mean? Obviously Jesus was gently *rebuking* John's disciples and through them perhaps even John himself. Jesus was reminding John that each of them was fulfilling a specific calling and purpose in life. John had been ordained of God to conduct a great ministry to "prepare the way" for Christ's first coming as a human being; John was the "voice in the wilderness" typifying a voice of truth in spiritual darkness. Jesus, on the other hand, was fulfilling the calling of His Messiahship in a much larger dimension, being continually sought out by hundreds who had heard of His miraculous healing powers and who pressed upon Him so insistently that on some occasions He had to escape the crowds and get away into a private place to rest.

After John's disciples left, Jesus felt it necessary to explain the seemingly harsh remarks He had made to them, and so turned to the multitude and said words to this effect, "Well, what in the world did you go out into the wilderness to see? Did you expect to find a man quavering like a reed shaken in wind or a man strong enough to stand up for his principles and demand an explanation? What did you go out to see? Someone clothed in fine and soft raiment? Behold they that wear soft raiment are in king's houses.

"But what did you go out to see? A prophet? Yes, I'll tell you that and much more than a prophet because this is he of whom it is written: Behold, I send my messenger before thy face, who shall prepare thy way before you" (Malachi 3:1).

And Jesus went on to say, "I am telling you the truth: among those who are born of woman there has never arisen a greater man than John the Baptist—still, he that is but little in the Kingdom of God is greater than John!"

John the Baptist was Jesus' second cousin, since their mothers (Elizabeth and Mary) were first cousins. John's ministry was fulfilling the prophecy that an "Elias" would come to "prepare the way" in the wilderness (spiritual wilderness) for the Messiah that would come.

John had a powerful effect on the people. He was very widely known and highly controversial. Yet John knew his own limitations. He continuously stressed that "There is coming after me a Person much more powerful than I, and I'm not fit to stoop down and untie His shoes! I am immersing you in water, but He will immerse you in the Holy Spirit" (Mark 1:7-8, paraphrased).

John had warned the hypocritical Pharisees of their attitudes—He told them that they were represented by the analogy of a "tree that doesn't bear good fruit," and predicted that, ". . . even now is the axe laid unto the root of the trees: every tree that brings not forth good fruit is hewn down, and cast into the fire. . . ." Jesus was to repeat this same saying to His disciples later.

Gathering to listen to John, in addition to the common

masses of people, were a heterogeneous collection of Roman soldiers, Pharisees, Sadducees and publicans (publicans were tax collectors). Different groups clamored for answers following John's inspired preaching about repentance. He surely attracted attention and generated controversy since he had begun by a direct attack upon the religious leaders. He had said, "You generation of snakes; who warned you to flee from the wrath to come? Bring forth fruit [evidence] fitting to prove you are really repentant; and don't kid yourselves by saying in your hearts, 'We are the descendants of Abraham'; because I'm telling you God is able to create out of these rocks children to fulfill God's promise concerning Abraham's seed. Even now is the axe laid unto the root of the tree . . ." (Matt. 3:7-10 and Luke 3:7-9, paraphrased).

Some of the crowd asked what they should do, and John said, "He that has two coats, let him share with him that has no coat at all; and he that has plenty of food; let him learn to share with those who are hungry . . ." (see Luke 3:10-11).

The tax collectors wanted a special answer, too. John said, "exact no more than that which is required by law." Inevitably, the young men serving in the Legion asked their own questions: "How about us; what should *we* do?" John said "Don't treat people brutally, with violence; don't extort from anyone, or accuse anyone wrongfully; and learn how to be content with your own wages!" (v. 14, paraphrased).

Groups of people were discussing this remarkable phenomenon—for example, they were intrigued by a ceremony in which a person walked out into the water, professed he was sorry for his sins, and was "baptized" by being lowered into the water in solemn symbolism of repentance for his past life. It was a poignant experience.

Some began to wonder whether John was the Messiah. After all, didn't almost everyone hear rumors that the Messiah had finally come; that He was forming a secret army; that He was already marching on Jerusalem; that He was collecting ships in secret harbors for an attack on Rome itself?

The Jewish people were an occupied, oppressed nation. They were also impoverished, especially in Samaria and some parts of Galilee. They desperately hoped for a champion, a deliverer, a Messiah to come and free them and to begin building a kingdom with some of the lost grandeur of David and Solomon.

John knew about the rumors. He tried to dispel them, and at the same time both prepare the common man to accept Christ as the Messiah and warn hypocrites that Jesus would step squarely on their painfully sensitive consciences.

"I am, for a fact, baptizing some of you with water; but there is coming after me One that is much greater than I am, whose shoes I am not fit to unloose. He will baptize you both with the Holy Spirit [in the former case] and with *fire* [in the latter]: His fan is in His hand, and He is ready to use it to thoroughly clean up the threshing floor. He will gather the useful wheat into His garner: but the chaff He will *burn up* with unquenchable fire . . ." (see Luke 3:16-17).

From this ominous warning of Gehenna fire for rebellious hypocrites came the incredible misunderstanding in the minds of some that a "baptism with fire" is some strange charismatic experience accompanied by glossolalia (speaking in strange "tongues"), though it is obscure how anyone could misunderstand the two-part message of John. (I long ago took the word "almost" out of my statement, "People will believe *almost* anything . . .")

The biblical truth is that John was baptizing by *immersion,* meaning plunging completely *into* the water. For the Greek word *baptizo means* immersion. There is no linguistic justification whatever for the corruption of the term in an attempt to give biblical approval to various traditions of religious organizations whether dipping, pouring, sprinkling, dabbing, spraying, or hosing down a group of cavorting believers with a fire hose attached to a street hydrant.

Then follows the account of Christ's own baptism.

John was stunned. He had extolled Christ's calling, His character and sinless nature; he knew Jesus didn't need baptism, and said as much. Then Jesus from Galilee came to John, where he was baptizing in the Jordan, to be baptized.

John would have stopped him. "I have need for you to baptize *me*," said John, "and you are coming to me?"

"Don't worry about it, John," Jesus answered, "Let me go ahead with it; because I must fulfill an example of total righteousness."

Jesus walked out into the water, and John baptized Him.

Some saw a beautiful dove seemingly materialize out of the sky, and light on Jesus. Some thought they heard a distant roll of thunder, and those nearby heard a voice as if out of the sky say, "This is my beloved son, in whom I am well pleased." (Matt. 3:13-17, paraphrased).

The gossip was carried immediately as far south as Jerusalem; for when the Pharisees, the Sadducees, the publicans and Romans who were in the vicinity saw and heard these events, especially John's strongest affirmation that Jesus was the true Messiah, it was a startling announcement.

Remember, John the Baptist conducted a wide-ranging, well-known, public ministry. He attracted huge crowds and continually preached a powerful message of repentance. He knew that "the law and the prophets were until John," and that after that Jesus Christ would bring grace (unmerited forgiveness for past sins and crimes) and mercy.

As if in a concerted effort to perpetuate the myth of the false Jesus, a major television film called "Jesus of Nazareth" presented the same traditional views, albeit with a remarkable amount of actual Scripture utilized in the story.

This latest Hollywood venture into the "Jesus business" pretty much followed the pattern of those that have gone before, with one important exception: they showed both the agony of Christ's death on the stake, *and* His total surprise at the knowledge God had forsaken Him just prior to the moment of death.

But for the most part, it was the usual stuff. The "Jesus" in the picture had the standard stare. Since Hollywood has followed Broadway's lead in the single-word titles (*Hair* and *Jaws*), perhaps they could have entitled this picture "Eyes." From start to finish that's what you were aware of.

In the enactment of Jesus' baptism, there is enough level-eyed, baleful staring going on to mesmerize a whole den of cobras in a mongoose pit. Apparently, the movie directors think Christ always tried to get across tons of meaningful thoughts by a hyp-notic-like, level-eyed, unblinking, glazed stare. By the time John and Jesus were through staring at each other, with little knots of people standing around like so many totems staring at both of them, you found yourself cherishing the uncontrollable wish that at least one of them would blink. But no, they never did.

In the film, the baptism of Jesus is portrayed with the "John" who does the baptizing appearing as a bedraggled, unwashed, scraggly, bearded, wild-haired character who looks more like an escapee from a prison farm or a harried mental patient than he does a prophet of God.

But then, how would Hollywood directors, typecasters, producers and their special advisers from the clergy be expected to know just what a "prophet of God" looks like, let alone John the Baptist, who walked the earth almost two thousand years ago?

The Bible accounts indicate that John was baptizing *in the River Jordan*, where there was *"much water"*! The television show indicates John standing in what appears to be a still, stagnant mud hole, in water about up to the knees.

Striding out of the crowd comes the traditional "Jesus" in a somewhat soiled white robe, with long, flowing and uncombed black hair, a black, wispy beard and mustache, and a level, staring, flat, baleful, noncommittal, yet somehow strangely intense stare. His eyes seem to probe ahead of him like two blinding headlights on full bright, never deviating from left to right, and with never a blink to clear the dust of the land from his eyeballs

John the Baptist picks up from his present duties and takes a few steps forward as a hush falls over the entire crowd in the scene. The alleged "Jesus" continues striding forward toward John with this intense gaze fixed almost half crazed upon him, until he stops a suitable distance away. John then utters the words which are fairly close to Scripture, although in their attempt to stick too close to the King James version of the Bible, the directors asked their actors to use an almost verbatim wording which is neither necessary nor required. Instead of paraphrasing the intended meaning into the colloquial language of our time which would have been far more understandable, John mutters a subdued and stilted version of Matthew 3:14 saying, "I have need to be baptized of thee, and comest thou to me?"

The "Jesus" of the show then answers, true to form, "suffer it now: for thus it becometh us to fulfill all righteousness." Then He walks on forward out into the muddy slough, and for some unknown reason, drops to his knees so that He is covered in water up to about His waist. Jesus bows his head forward, and the "John" in the picture advances toward him, cupping his hands together, and summarily pours (some might wish to believe they saw the water "trickle, or even drip a little!") a double handful of water over "Jesus' " head.

There is no dove (Hollywood's special effects may be able to create a King Kong, but to reproduce the dove might have offended some people, though I cannot imagine who) and no booming or rolling sound of thunder or voice which says "this is my beloved son in whom I am well pleased!"

Instead, the "Jesus" in the play lifts that level, staring gaze to John once again, wades out of the water, and slowly disappears all by himself up a dry creek bed in a lonely, rocky, brown, totally treeless and barren landscape.

In the film Jesus appears to be followed by no one, though in the actual biblical account, He was with any number of other individuals, including Philip, who took another of John's disciples and spent that same evening with Jesus in a nearby home where he was staying. The following day they went all the way to Bethsaida, found Peter, and brought him back to the area where Jesus was staying near John's baptismal site.

The errors in this film are many. In the first place, there is no indication whatever in the Bible that it is required of Jesus Christ that He always act weirdly, strangely, rudely, or even frighteningly.

How would you feel if some total stranger walked straight up to you, and without ever saying a word, merely stared with fierce-eyed intensity into your eyes for uncounted moments as if waiting for you to receive some "spiritual" message?

You would probably wonder whether, (1) the man was insane, (2) he was trying to mesmerize or hypnotize you, (3) he was demon possessed, (4) he was deaf and dumb and couldn't speak, (5) he was trying out for a part in a new Jesus movie. Movies of this kind are of necessity filled with dozens of errors merely through the apparent need to produce a "Jesus" who satisfies everybody.

Therefore, those who believe in a form of baptism called "sprinkling," or another form called "pouring," could be at least partially pacified and go away exclaiming to each other that it at least *appeared* that there was some water sprinkling rather than pouring (or vice versa) from John's hands.

Those who believe in immersion could at least be partially pacified, though not totally, since they saw Jesus with their own eyes wading down at least to about knee deep water and then kneeling in the water so that he was at least 50 percent immersed.

Jesus' baptism was the formal announcement of the beginning of His ministry. It was only the next day that John proclaimed to those standing around, "Behold the Lamb of God, which taketh away the sin of the world. This is he of whom I said, After me cometh a man which is preferred before me: for he was before me. And I knew him not: but that he should be made manifest to Israel, therefore am I come baptizing with water" (John 1:29-31).

CHAPTER 8

Choosing His Disciples

Jesus had no doubt spent many months in Capernaum during each year over a span of at least 18 years. He *knew* many of the people; and He actually knew the families from which He would eventually choose His disciples.

Millions assume that Jesus recognized His disciples through some mysterious, mystical perception and convinced them to follow Him through an equally mysterious, hypnotic power. The popular image is that Jesus was dreamily strolling along the seashore one day and beckoned to a man named Peter, and said, "Come, and follow me, and I will make you a fisher of men." Peter, it is supposed, took one look at this beautiful man in white, with long brown locks, pointed beard, a multicolored halo around His head, and was so mesmerized he instantly dropped the net he was mending and, zombie-like, trudged off after Jesus.

Ridiculously false.

Joseph had known Jona closely. Jona's two sons, Peter and Andrew, had grown up in their father's trade, fishing, just as Jesus and His brothers' education had included stonework and building. Jona believed the Scriptures—believed a Messiah would soon come. That belief was equally strong in his two young sons as they developed. Peter married (it is not clear whether Andrew was married by the time of Christ's ministry), and had taken over the family fishing business by the time John the Baptist's ministry had grown so large.

Bethsaida, Peter's home town, was a distance to the south from Capernaum, along the western side of the Sea of Galilee.

There is no doubt Peter and Andrew had heard of Jesus and His brothers. Who knows, maybe "Joseph and Sons, Contractors" had built Peter's home in Bethsaida? Perhaps Jesus' family had likewise purchased fish from Peter's family?

It was Andrew who was following John the Baptist, as one of his disciples. When John saw Jesus, he made it clear to his disciples, including Andrew, that this was the Messiah.

The following day after the baptism of Jesus, John and two of his disciples were standing together and saw Jesus pass near.

One of them was Andrew, Peter's brother. After this brief discussion, they followed Jesus, arriving where He was staying about two hours before dark (John 1:37-40), and stayed for the remainder of the day.

John (Jesus' closely loved disciple, not the Baptist) says in his account that, ". . . they came and saw where he was staying, and they stayed with him that day . . ." (John 1:39).

The next day Jesus went to Galilee and ran across Philip who was also from Bethsaida, Peter and Andrew's home town. He told Philip to follow him, and Philip immediately found Nathanael (who could have been a well-known prophet), and told him they had found that Jesus of Nazareth, the son of Joseph, was in fact the prophet of whom Moses and the prophets did write. Nathanael wondered aloud whether anything good could come out of Nazareth, and so Philip invited him to come and see for himself.

When Jesus saw Nathanael coming to see if he could identify Him, Jesus said, "Look, there is an Israelite for a fact, who is without guile!"

Nathanael wondered aloud, "Where could you have known me from?" Jesus answered, "Before Philip called you and you were sitting under that fig tree, I saw you." Nathanael said, "Master (Teacher), you must be the Son of God; You must be the One who is King of Israel!" He was a student of the Scriptures, and knew the time was near. That he should meet a person with such superhuman powers of observation convinced him. Jesus used Nathanael's quick judgment as an opportunity for an invitation to wait for more fruits; to see the works he would perform in the future, and referred to the ultimate setting up of God's kingdom on earth.

No doubt, they asked Him many questions and were tremendously impressed by His knowledge, His wisdom, and the calm intensity with which He spoke. Andrew and the other man (not identified) asked, "Rabbi (which is to say, being interpreted, Master), where dwellest thou?"

"He saith unto them, Come and see. They came and saw where he dwelt, and abode with him that day: for it was about the tenth hour." Remember, Jewish days began with sunset, so these men spent at least the next two hours with Jesus, and, possibly, remained the night and part of the next morning.

Andrew then went to get his brother Peter. He wanted to tell him that Jesus was definitely the Messiah; and when Andrew introduced him to Jesus, during the ensuing conversation, Jesus said: "Thou art Simon, the son of Jona: thou shalt be called Cephas, which is by interpretation, a stone" (John 1:41-42).

The *Greek* word for "stone" is *petros.* Jesus had a definite purpose in mind for calling Simon "Peter"—made clear by reading Matthew 16:18 and Ephesians 2:20, where Peter is plainly a part of the *foundation* (as a "stone") of the New Testament Church. Jesus Himself is the *Rock* (petra) of Matthew 16:18 (see also Deut. 32; I Cor. 10:4), and the chief cornerstone of the Church, while Peter, together with the other 11 (except for Judas, replaced by Matthias later) made up the *foundation.* (The number 12 always signifies "organized beginnings" in the Bible and is found in connection with perfect government structures—ancient Israel, the Church, and the Kingdom of God.)

Now that you know about the first *formal* encounter between Jesus and Peter, you can read the account in Matthew 4:18-19, and it makes much more sense.

Jesus was now beginning His ministry. He had *finished* His careful selection of a big group, numbering 120 in all, who were to be His disciples (students). "From that time Jesus began to preach, and to say, Repent, for the kingdom of heaven is at hand.

"And Jesus, walking by the Sea of Galilee, saw two brethren, Simon called Peter [it was Jesus who had so named him "Peter" on an earlier meeting!], and Andrew his brother, casting a net into the sea: for they were fishers.

"And he saith unto them, Follow me, and I will make you fishers of men. And they straightway left their nets, and followed him" (Matt. 4:17-20).

Jesus showed He knew who Peter was: knew his father and family background, *prior* to this event. Remember, Jesus *prayed for hours* about these appointments. There was no "magic" to it, no strange "pied piper" calling, no siren song. Jesus knew the character of these men and selected them quite deliberately.

The same is true with the calling of Philip. Philip lived in the same town as Peter and Andrew, Bethsaida. Jesus *knew* these people—He had lived and worked in these towns for those 18 years from about 12 to age 30, the beginning of His formal ministry.

CHAPTER 9

Water into Wine

Following the choosing of the disciples in John 1, the scene immediately shifts in John 2 to a marriage celebration in Cana of Galilee, during which Jesus performed His first, and perhaps most famous and controversial miracle.

Let us first read the biblical account in the book of John.

Jesus' mother was there and Jesus and His disciples were called to the marriage. "And when they [Jesus and the disciples? Or all the guests?] wanted wine, the mother of Jesus saith unto him, They have no wine.

"Jesus saith unto her, Woman, what have I to do with thee? mine hour is not yet come. His mother saith unto the servants, Whatsoever he saith unto you, do it. And there were set there six waterpots of stone, after the manner of the purifying of the Jews, containing two or three firkins apiece. Jesus saith unto them, Fill the waterpots with water. And they filled them up to the brim. And he saith unto them, Draw out now, and bear unto the governor of the feast. And they bare it. When the ruler of the feast had tasted the water that was made wine, and knew not whence it was: (but the servants which drew the water knew;) the governor of the feast called the bridegroom, And saith unto him, Every man at the beginning doth set forth good wine; and when men have well drunk, then that which is worse: but thou has kept the good wine until now. This beginning of miracles did Jesus in Cana of Galilee, and manifested forth his glory; and his disciples believed on him" (John 2:3-11).

First of all, whose marriage was it? Mary seems to have a

significant role in the feast since she feels responsible enough to ask Jesus to perform a miracle. Was the marriage that of a close friend, business associate or family member, or maybe one of Jesus' own brothers or sisters? It also seems as if Jesus Himself could have had some responsibility with regard to the food and the drink, because of the way in which His mother appealed to Him. It makes one wonder, too, whether they were establishing a home at Cana for a member of their own family.

The marriage feast took place "the third day" after Jesus' baptism. Much can be learned from an examination of Jesus' miracle of turning the water into wine—about the personal habits of Jesus, about the knowledge of Mary, as well as about the prohibition policies of some of the teetotalers who claim to derive their teachings from the Bible.

Quite a number of people from Nazareth and/or Bethsaida and Capernaum, as well as the town of Cana, must have attended.

A wedding feast in those days was not unlike a Jewish wedding feast today. It probably featured many hundreds of invited guests, and there would have been feasting, a fair amount of drinking, and no doubt live musical entertainment with ample toasting, joyful camaraderie and good wishes on the part of family and friends for the bride and groom.

John focuses on one particular occasion near the end of the festivities when the large number of guests had finally exhausted the supplies of wine. It is necessary to mention here a few points about the English word "wine" and its Greek derivation.

The Greek word used in the inspired text is *oinos,* and it is used on at least two other occasions in the New Testament where the obvious meaning indicated the intoxicating effect of alcohol: "And be not drunk with wine, wherein is excess; but be filled with the Spirit," (Eph. 5:18), and "with whom the kings of the earth have committed fornication, and with the wine of whose fornication the dwellers on earth have become drunk" (Rev. 17:2, RSV).

In both of these accounts it is obvious the Greek word *oinos* is referring to a beverage which, when taken to excess, can make one drunk. Perhaps it is useless to point out that there was no refrigeration; that "grape juice"—as some would have the drink that Jesus created be—was kept either in stone jars and/or goat-skin bags and would ferment quite rapidly in any event. But "grapejuice" was not involved, nevertheless; it was *wine.*

Think about the implications of the biblical account. As was stated, Jesus' mother was apparently such a close friend or relative that she was helping serve in some fashion, for she came to Jesus when she discovered the wine had been exhausted and said, "They have no wine."

There happened to be six water pots of stone in the home which were used for purification rites or foot washing.

Judging by the number of stone jars (six) and the number of firkins in each (two to three)—which were either nine and one-half or twelve and one-half gallons apiece—the most conservative estimate is that there had to be at least 120 gallons. Allowing approximately eight normal glasses of wine to a quart, four quarts to a gallon, that means that about 3,840 glasses of wine were available. So unless that marriage feast was the most drunken orgy in history (which it wasn't), there had to be a minimum of 500 people there to drink all that wine. And to have already exhausted a normally provided supply and still to claim that they were out, there were probably more than that. On the other hand, since the wine cellar of the individual giving the wedding was possibly depleted, this may have been replenishment without implying any specific quantity that was drunk before the wedding was over. Also, it was common for weddings to last for several days, even a full week.

Jesus did not know everyone there, but there were guests and servants who would carry the memory of what He did for the rest of their lives and would talk of it to others. By the time they were elderly people, even if they never became converted and members of the church, they certainly must have told everybody else in their hearing about "the water becoming wine." They all probably told their grandchildren about that great miracle.

Jesus must have known the master of the feast and the young couple, one of whom may have been a member of His family. He could well have been chatting with them and congratulating them, talking with the other people around them—about marriage, about mutual friends, about the political situation.

When Mary came to Him, at least some of His disciples heard it—we know John did, since he wrote it down.

Mary said, "They are out of wine." Why did Mary say that? What did she expect?

Jesus retorted, "Woman, what in the world am I going to do with you? Don't you know it is not time for me to reveal who I am in public yet?" Jesus spoke rather chidingly, though with respect (the King James English makes it harsher than the reality).

Mary was, nevertheless, quite assured that Jesus would respect and fulfill her request since she turned to the servants and immediately stated, "Whatsoever he says for you to do, do it."

These surprising remarks show that Mary knew that Jesus *could* do something about the wine situation if He wanted to. But how could she know with such certainty? Wasn't this Jesus' first miracle?

Mary's request to the servants, "Whatsoever he tells you to do—do it!" is as strong a statement of faith as any found in the New Testament; whether a Gentile officer asking for the healing of the servant, or the father of the lunatic begging for Christ's mercy.

Mary's statement is similar to the statement of the man that had the demon-possessed son who said to Jesus, "I know you can heal him; all you have to do is just tell me that it is your will." It is also similar to the statement of the Roman officer who said, "You don't have to bother coming home to heal my servant but if you just tell me I will believe it. I understand an order because when I tell a man to go, he goes, and when I tell him to come, he comes."

Mary's statement to Jesus, "Jesus, they are out of wine," conveys such absolute assurance of Jesus' ability to perform a miracle that it had to come from knowledge of Jesus' past experience.

The miracle of turning the water into wine was indeed the first miracle of Jesus *recorded* in the Bible. But the strong inference is that it was *not* the first miracle of His life!

Mary's certainty of success couldn't have come from guesswork. It couldn't have come from supposition. It couldn't have come only from what she thought He *might* have been able to do.

Obviously Mary was confident. She had to have known that Jesus had miracle-working powers. No doubt during the course of the 30 years of Jesus' life, Mary had had at least a few occasions to witness such powers.

From her earliest moments of training the young child, Mary was urgently intent upon explaining to Jesus again and again all the events that had occurred from the time of the appearance of the angel and his pronouncement to her; to her meeting with Elizabeth and the sudden leaping of the two babies in the wombs;

to the muteness of John's father Zacharias, and the birth of John.

During His young boyhood, how many possibilities for accident or injury were there? After all, His father was a contractor of some note; his profession demanded the kind of labor which may have involved everything from obtaining raw materials to site preparation, laying of foundations, hewing out cisterns, waterways and drainage ducts, to the actual erection of small cottages and larger homes and buildings.

In such a trade, there is ample opportunity for accidents which could cause crippling injury or death.

Had there been times when, just as a large stone might have toppled from a parapet upon one of Joseph's laborers, one of Jesus' own brothers or upon Jesus Himself, the young boy simply pointing at the stone said in a quiet but firm voice, "Stay still"?

Had there been occasions when Joseph, Jude, Simon or perhaps one of the girls had come running to Mary, with a broken bone, dislocated arm, a smashed finger, or a deep cut? To presuppose that a family of at least seven children could survive all of those many years until the eldest son was age 30 without the usual run of household accidents, potential for accident and injury on the job, and the attack of disease, would be ridiculous.

I don't think any family of seven kids in the building industry in that kind of environment could grow up without incurring some injuries.

Seven kids?

You could very easily imagine the scene if Jesus' brother Joses came running in one day when Jesus was 11 and Joses was only 6, holding his little arm with a strange bow in it and crying at the top of his lungs. Realizing that he had broken his arm, Jesus may have walked up to him and said, "Don't cry, Joses," and just reached out and healed it. This would have had to have been very private, just within the family. But His mother surely knew about it.

One can imagine that there might have been times when a disfiguring scar might have marred one of the girls' faces or when one of the boys might have had a crushed instep, and Jesus healed them. Or Joseph could have been bent over a load of mortar that Jesus had just delivered to him as they were working on a wall. When Jesus was about to go up and take some to His brother James, He may have seen a bunch of bricks on the top of the parapet about to fall. Perhaps, as the bricks began to topple, Jesus commanded them to stop.

Probably, in a quiet family environment, Jesus had prayed to His heavenly Father that close personal family members could be healed and they had followed His urgent admonitions that they tell no one else about it; keeping it very quiet, limited only to the immediate family.

It is doubtful that any of Jesus' brothers would have taken His supernatural powers for granted; Jesus certainly would have warned them against "tempting God," taking unnecessary risks, exposing themselves to either danger or disease merely for the novelty of running to Jesus for a quick healing when necessary.

Therefore, it may be safely assumed such miracles were few and far between, for even His own brothers refused to believe He was the Messiah later. But there had been sufficient experience for Mary to have such profound faith that even following Jesus' gentle rejoinder, she knew His love for her and respect for her request would override His reticence, and so she turned to the servants and told them, "Whatever He tells you to do, do it!"

The turning of water into wine at Cana may have been His first "public miracle," but there is every reason to conclude that it was far from His first miracle!

Much additional insight into Jesus' personality can be gleaned from the account of the miracle in Galilee.

For one thing, stories were frequently spread about Jesus that He was a "glutton and a winebibber," which resulted in His chiding the Pharisees on one occasion that they were never satisfied, no matter what He did.

He explained that they were like little kids who called the tune, but if you didn't dance to the precise tune they called, you seemed to be a misfit, and they were disappointed in you.

He told them that John the Baptist had come neither eating nor drinking, and the religious leaders claimed that He was demon-possessed; but that He, Jesus, had come both eating and drinking (as He did frequently in expensive homes with leading officials, Roman officers, religious leaders, or at marriage feasts such as this one) yet was criticized for being both a glutton and a "winebibber" (meaning a "wino").

The Bible, of course, clearly condemns drunkenness. It clearly condemns excesses in *anything*, which would include drinking too much water! There are sins of commission and sins of omission, and there are sins of excess.

However, there is not one word in either the Old or the New Testament which forbids a human being to drink either strong drink (*tirosh* in the Hebrew, meaning liquor), or wine or beer, so long as it is taken in appropriate moderation on appropriate occasions, and is never abused.

Jesus *did* enjoy a glass of wine from time to time.

Do you?

If you do, then you probably know that wine tends to aid not only in digestion, but in conversation and humor as well.

There is no doubt whatever that Jesus, entering into animated and laughing conversation with other guests at that feast, also enjoyed the wine with them too.

Judging from Hollywood's attempts to picture the creepy, long-haired effeminate they think is Jesus, one would imagine they would have Him sitting off in some dark corner staring rather balefully at an opposite wall with a sorrowful look on His face, saying absolutely nothing except the required biblical pronouncement according to the Gospel of John.

What an insult it would have been for Jesus, who was head of the family business, whose younger brothers and mother were there together with His students, to sit mournfully in a corner with nothing but a level, steady, vacant gaze in His unblinking eyes! The leader of the feast, together with the bridegroom and the bride would all think the man was a little odd, and it would have cast a dark cloud over the festive occasion.

But the real Jesus was simply not like Hollywood of today and theologians of yesteryear have pictured Him.

He was an animated, healthy, robust, outgoing and effervescent personality.

He could throw His head back and laugh to the very depth of His being at some humorous incident. He was totally well rounded in personality with that combination of sincere interest in others, deep empathy for their frailties and misunderstandings, combined with lively interest in their lives. Jesus was the kind of scintillating conversationalist who would have been an absolute joy to have at any party.

CHAPTER 10

Encounter with Satan

Jesus spoke at great length, in private, to His disciples about His encounter with Satan. The accounts of both Matthew and Luke, together with Mark's one paragraph establishing the chronological place of the event (just before the beginning of His ministry and just after His baptism), prove that Christ discussed the event in detail with His disciples. Obviously, there were important lessons to be learned.

Mark said that the "Spirit immediately drove Him out into the wilderness"—showing that the very strongest spiritual compulsion was within Christ; that He *knew* the confrontation with Satan was necessary; that He had to overcome and conquer the world-ruling spirit (Eph. 2:2), Satan the Devil. Jesus was qualifying to take over rulership of all of the governments of the world—and He had to defeat the present ruler at his own game, according to his own rules, on his own battlefield. It was to be the supreme battle, and the enemy had all the weapons.

Previously named Lucifer ("shining star of the dawn," or "light-bringer") this great being had formerly been one of the three named archangels, and a personality extremely close to the God family, an individual known from the beginning. Jesus said "I saw Satan as lightning fall from heaven." Jesus was *there*, and *took part* in an *earlier* battle with Lucifer (Isa. 14; Ezek. 28) which had literally convulsed the heavens, rent the earth, exploded stars and planets, and filled space with the junk of a gargantuan, titanic battle.

Anyone who wants to take the Bible *literally* as an actual

communication to man *from outer space,* from *God,* would see the results of Satan's rebellion and battle against God in the panorama of universal destruction that is evident in the bleak, crater-pocked face of the moon; the desolate, lifeless waste of Mars; the impenetrable Venusian atmosphere; the billions of asteroids, meteors, and comets; all the space dust and gas. All the universe gives testimony to the primal war in space that defies human imagination.

Satan had been confined to the earth—been "chained" by God's decree (in a state called "hell" in one place, but translated from a Greek word, *tartaroo,* which is used in only one place), but was allowed to hold sway *over* the earth. Satan was a prince reigning over total destruction, when that Person who was later to become God in the flesh came upon the scene as outlined in the first chapter of Genesis.

Once, the earth had teemed with billions of creatures. The atmosphere was completely different from today; almost universally tropical, with no polar ice caps, and with abundant, thick, luxuriant foliage providing both food and shelter for billions of creatures. Lucifer was originally given the earth as his responsibility. But the Bible says he tried to use earth as a base for his attempt to overthrow God from His throne. He failed, and, as John wrote in Revelation, his "tail" (comet-like?) drew a third part (of course! there are only three archangels mentioned in all the Bible) of the "stars of heaven" (a common Bible symbol for angels) and "cast them down to earth" (read Rev. 12:3-9).

The total destruction of the earth was the result; and the massive burial of whole continents teeming with plant and animal life, multiple billions of creatures, resulted in the storage of fossil energy for the use of man in the countless thousands of years yet in the future.

If scientists believe the earth to be 4½ billion years old, there is no quarrel with Scripture—neither does 10 billion years make any difference.

There was, according to the Bible, an earlier, *perfect* creation. Also included were the spirit beings, among them Lucifer. But the resultant cosmic battle literally wrecked a good portion of the universe. Frustratingly to Lucifer, even in the destruction on earth he was to provide future fuel and energy sources to God's greatest creation of all—mankind—destined to rise ultimately to a position even greater than that originally given to Lucifer and his angels.

John's twelfth chapter of the apocalypse (meaning "to reveal," not "to destroy") is a quick summary of the whole time period from the conception of God's plan for His church, Satan's rebellion and earth's destruction, Satan's attempt to destroy Christ through Herod's decree to kill all the children, *and* the encounter in the wilderness with Jesus *personally*.

"And another portent appeared in heaven; behold a great red dragon, with seven heads and ten horns, and seven diadems upon his heads. His tail swept down a third of the stars of heaven, and cast them to the earth. And the dragon stood before the woman who was about to bear a child, that he might devour her child when she brought it forth; she brought forth a male child, one who is to rule all the nations with a rod of iron, but her child was caught up to God and to his throne," (Rev. 12:3-5).

Jesus knew what Satan looked like; both in an earlier, beautiful state, and in a later, more grotesque and ugly condition. He is called a "serpent" and a "dragon," as well as "the cherub that covereth" in the Bible.

When Ezekiel saw the strange creatures covering God's throne he "knew that they were cherubs." Most people believe cherubs appear as naked babes with cupid's bows and arrows—and few realize that cherubs appeared to men in ancient times; that some of them were tremendously famous from the time of Adam until Noah as the guardians to the garden of Eden.

Cherubim were able to manifest themselves as lions, oxen, men, and eagles; or as an aggregate of all four. Ancient mythology preserves these huge spirit creatures in stone as the "winged bulls of Bashan" on ancient Assyrian king's palaces, and even as recently as 1975, with new discoveries of even greater civilizations in ancient Syria, a wooden bull with a man's head overlayed in gold was recovered from ruins believed to be contemporaneous with ancient Sumeria. Search the great museums of Britain, France, Germany, and Egypt, and you will see hundreds of examples of the worship of "the host of the heavens" in the form of men with eagle's heads (common in the inscriptions of ancient Egypt, and in Egyptian tombs) as "gods"; winged bulls featuring the heads of men and lion's claws and other assorted mixtures of these four.

When God placed two cherubim with "flaming swords" to guard the way to the tree of life, they *remained* there from that day until the destruction of Eden in the flood. Remember, that means about one-sixth of all recorded history—a considerable time! The tales repeated down through time from the children of Noah, all of whom had *seen* those cherubim, gave rise to the mythologies about winged dragons, flying serpents whose mouths breathed fire, who guarded mysterious castles at the top of craggy hills, filled with fabulously valuable treasures.

Giants and their mythical treasures, St. George and the Dragon, the winged flying serpent which was worshiped by the Incas and Aztecs (Quetzalcoatl, meaning "flying serpent")—these are all mythological tales, endlessly repeated and embellished, stemming from human encounters with cherubim.

When God told Moses to decorate the interior trappings of the tabernacle in the wilderness with "cherubim," Moses didn't ask God, "Yes, but what do they look like?" He *knew,* especially since he had come from a background of the royal courts of Egypt.

Jesus knew exactly what to expect when he encountered Satan. He knew Satan didn't appear as a funny, mischievous man in a weird red body-stocking complete with pointed ears, a tail with spears' tip, and a trident in hand. He knew Satan could appear as a *man,* or as a *cherub,* or as a *winged flying serpent.*

What *is* a "dragon," after all, but a "winged flying serpent"? When the devil appeared to Adam and Eve they weren't at all startled to hear a strange-looking creature having serpentine, dragon-like form (but probably standing upright, like a *tyrannosaurus*) speak to them in audible voice; for they had no standard of comparison. The fact that God, using serpents as a *type* of Satan, cursed the serpent and *from that time* decreed he was to "crawl on his belly" in the dust of the earth strongly indicated there were serpentine creatures that stood upright prior to that time.

Jesus knew that He was meeting one of the most powerful spirit beings in the universe; He knew that He would have to stand the test of the most appealing, magnetic, powerful personality on earth; that He was going to match wits with the vilest, most subtle, cleverest, most cunning, and superbly (if perverted) intelligent creatures in the universe! He knew that *humanly, of Himself,* He didn't have the strength and will to overcome a spirit being of such power. He would need *super-*

human strength, *spiritual* strength from a *righteous* source, and the very help of the Father Himself, as well as the power of friendly angels.

Jesus *intended* to overthrow Satan. He was to combat the "prince of the power of the air" and conquer him! He was to meet the "lord of the dead" and displace him! He was to allow Himself to be subjected to the greatest test of His human life to date, and had to depend utterly on God the Father for His help to overcome!

That's why He had fasted for so long! The Bible says Christ "learned by the things which He *suffered,*" and Christ intended to come to *know* that weaknesses *can be overcome* with enough help from God!

Read the account of Jesus' confrontation with Satan just prior to the beginning of His ministry. The story is revealed in the fourth chapter of the book of Matthew. "Then was Jesus led up of the Spirit into the wilderness to be tempted of the devil" (Matt. 4:1).

When Jesus was "led up of the spirit" it is obvious that He had been, by this "sixth sense" of the awareness of the spirit world, in such close communication with His heavenly Father through prayer that He *knew* that it was time for this great confrontation—the supreme battle of *will* between the fallen archangel, Lucifer, and the One who was coming to unseat this Satan and qualify to be the World Ruler. (Perhaps He had received either a very vivid dream, a vision, or even heard an audible voice from an angel. Or He might have just "sensed" it was time.)

Jesus, with His brilliant mind and the outpouring of God's Holy Spirit "without measure" no doubt knew the Scriptures as no man before or since!

He was, after all, the "Word personified," as it were, and so was very thoroughly aware of the examples of *fasting* just prior to a great crisis or a great event in the Bible. He knew that Moses had fasted 40 days and 40 nights, prior to receiving the Ten Commandments on Mount Sinai.

He knew about Elijah's 40 days and 40 nights of fasting, and knew this would also be required of Him in order to utterly divest Himself of any reliance whatsoever on any material crutch, upon any remote temptation to depend upon a false feeling of "self-reliance," but, in this weakened state, after having spent countless hours in deep and soul-searching *prayer,* would be equipped to withstand the worst temptations Satan the Devil could throw at Him.

It says, "And when he had fasted forty days and forty nights, he was afterward an hungered."

The word "hungered" in context implies much more than just "hungry" the way it may appear to us. No living human being today could have the willpower and self-control, together with the physical stamina and strength to endure a full 40 days and 40 nights fast.

Jesus was nearly at the point of death; he had almost starved by the time Satan the Devil came to Him and hurled every conceivable temptation His way. After the initial temptation of trying to get Jesus to obey his whims by converting stones into bread, Jesus made one of His most important pronouncements. (And a statement that is almost universally misunderstood by millions of professing Christians today, who would rather live by "some", and *not* "every," word of God.)

Jesus said to Satan, "... It is written, *Man shall not live by bread alone, but by every word that proceedeth out of the mouth of God!"*

Then Satan began to probe to find if there was any *ego* there, any vanity, selfishness, or desire for power or self-importance. Finally Jesus *gave a command,* and the Devil was forced to obey! "Then saith Jesus unto him, Get thee hence, Satan: for it is written, Thou shalt worship the Lord thy God, and him only shalt thou serve" (verse 10).

Now read the next verse! "Then the devil leaveth him, and, behold, *angels* came and ministered unto him." What does "ministering" mean? What would you do if a person who was very dearly beloved to you were discovered in an emaciated, starving state, a condition of almost complete physical and mental exhaustion?

Remember, these "angels" did not appear like little pink-cheeked bare babies with bows and arrows—but as mature, kindly, competent, and swiftly efficient men!

From the time the One who became Jesus Christ of Nazareth—who was the God of the Old Testament—appeared unto human beings Himself (He wrestled in the dust of the earth with Jacob, sat in the shade of Abraham's tent on the plains of Mamre, talked to Moses from a cloud on Mount Sinai), to the other accounts in the Old Testament of angelic appearances, you can learn that angels always appeared to human beings *as men!* The two men who were the objects of the perverse lusts of the citizens of Sodom, and who had to drag Lot and his family out of the city just prior to its destruction, were *angels,* manifesting themselves as strong, human *men.*

Jesus had no doubt slumped to the ground or was seated with His head in His hands, following this exhausting encounter when a strong arm encircled His shoulder and a deep resonant voice said, "Here, take a sip of this."

When you "minister" unto a person in this state of exhaustion, you will no doubt provide warmth in the form of blankets and a place to lie down, and give sparing amounts of something appropriate like beef broth or some other richly nutritious and easily digestible food.

This encounter also serves to illustrate the fact that, when it was needed, angels, who were always around Jesus in unseen, spirit form, would manifest themselves as human beings, and give Jesus even the physical sustenance and protection that He needed, and that He was constantly attuned to that "other dimension" of the heavenly presence of His Father and His righteous angels.

So, in the greatest spiritual battle ever fought, a battle that was absolutely necessary in the plan of God for Jesus Christ to overcome Satan, the Captain of our Salvation qualified to take over rulership of Earth from Satan.

CHAPTER 11

Jesus' Faith

Jesus could only look forward to an early death. He would be beaten into an unrecognizable hulk, tortured, ridiculed, abandoned by friends, mocked by enemies and finally crucified. Before His 34th birthday, He would be hanging on a stake, naked and dead. All this He knew, and knew fully, throughout His adult life.

Under these circumstances, most of us would be so self-pitying, and would harbor such feelings of martyrdom, that we would only find it possible to moan and groan, doing the very most effective job of eliciting sympathy from others over our terrible plight.

But Jesus had perfect faith.

Faith is conviction. It is the full assurance that, according to God's specific promises, certain events such as miracles, healings and the exorcism of evil spirits—which were given as signs and testimonies to unbelievers, and as aids in the conduct of Jesus' work and ministry—would absolutely occur whenever Jesus desired it.

Jesus *knew* who He was; knew from whence He had come, and knew precisely what the future held.

Perhaps the analogy of an individual who, as a result of a blow on the head, loses his recent memory and then gradually regains it, could be applied to Jesus. Through a process of visiting familiar scenes and meeting with familiar faces during Jesus' young life, and continually as He absorbed more and more of the written word of God, plus direct personal communication with

His Father through deep sessions of prayer, coupled with fasting, His awareness grew and grew until He came to "re-remember" the tremendous amount of spiritual knowledge He once had had.

When Jesus told some of His persecutors, "Before Abraham was I AM," He revealed an unusual amount of insight into this concept. Not only did Jesus *believe* He was the Son of God through His mother's teaching, but He also knew this through His own personal contact with God, and encounters with spirit beings, both obedient angels and evil spirits!

Therefore, Jesus *knew.*

To millions of professing Christians, "faith" is an elusive "something" everyone wishes to have. All seek it through diverse sorts of physical and psychological phenomena; traveling to one place and another; trying to fix or set their minds in a particular channel; attempting to follow routines or ceremonial procedures; going to a famous "faith healer" and trying diligently to bolster up one's nagging doubts by any number of psychological and spiritual exercises or tricks.

Jesus' faith was so superb that, when it served an effective purpose, He quite literally had power over the elements. Yet this was not always the case, for on one occasion when He came among some of the religious teachers of the town where He had grown up, Nazareth, He was "unable to do any mighty work there, save that he laid hands on a few sick folk." In this case, Jesus was said to have "marveled at their unbelief," thus illustrating the fact that, as the Bible reveals, especially in cases of healing, it seems to require both "faith mixed with faith" to produce the miracle.

On a number of other occasions strange miracles occurred which were supportive of Christ's Messiahship and which dumbfounded and amazed His disciples as well as others, including detractors and persecutors.

When Jesus walked on water, He knew He would be buoyed up and simply stepped out on the water as if it were concrete or solid ground. Here He was, strolling about on the surface of the glassy waters of the Sea of Galilee when Peter looked out in dumbfounded amazement and recognized Jesus. To Peter, this was another novel "trick" of some sort, and He assayed to leave the boat and walk right out to where Jesus was, feeling that whatever applied to Jesus most certainly would have applied to Peter as well.

Peter *thought* he might be able to walk on water, but Jesus *knew*. Immediately, Peter began to sink into the water, and Jesus had to reach out and pick him back up by another miraculous act, and give him a gentle chiding about his lack of faith.

In order to provide a further miraculous testimony to His credentials, on one occasion Jesus told His disciples to go to a nearby body of water, catch a fish, and they would find a coin in the fish's mouth!

Wonderingly, they did precisely as He said, and sure enough, there was the coin.

Again, anyone who decides to take it upon himself to be a one-man critic of the Bible could simply decide he has discovered that one "loose brick" somewhere in the foundation walls of Holy Writ which renders him skeptical of the entirety of the remainder. For the purposes of this book, whether the reader believes it is mere theory or practical fact, the Bible is accepted as being the divinely revealed will and purpose of a great infallible God who cannot lie. Therefore, though most skeptics would immediately claim they disbelieve the miraculous, for miracles cannot be explained by physical or scientific means, for the purposes of explaining the personality and character of Jesus Christ these miracles are accepted as bona fide fact, as much a fact as is any physical law.

Jesus' faith was built on certain *knowledge*. He knew His Father heard His prayers; and though He did not have "X-ray vision" like the fabled Superman from Krypton, He did have both the insight and the ability to read the thoughts and hearts of human beings by a combination of body language, the looks in their eyes, as well as a very great amount of spiritual perception which some might call mental telepathy.

Therefore, on some occasions when an individual seemed to have a great deal of faith, Jesus would immediately answer the request for healing or for the expulsion of a demon.

On other accounts, even though one sincere believer might have asked for a miracle, Jesus asked that the unbelievers be put out of the environment prior to the healing taking place. On another occasion a Roman soldier, a captain over one hundred men, begged Jesus to come to his home to heal his sick servant.

Jesus turned and pointed out to His own people that He had not found such faith in all of Israel using the analogy of the Roman soldier.

The military man had said, "You don't need to come all that distance if you don't want to, Lord; I know all you need to do is give the word and it will be done! After all I'm a military man; I am a captain over a hundred men. If I give orders for a man to come, he comes; if I say go, he goes. Therefore, all you have got to do is give the orders and I know my servant will be healed!"

Following the Roman's analogy, Jesus gave the object lesson to His own disciples that He had not found such an example of straightforward, simple faith, "No, not in all Israel." He told the Roman, "Go your way, and as you have believed it will occur to you" (Matt. 8:8-10, paraphrased).

On the occasion at Lazarus's tomb, Jesus also reveals that He was in an attitude of prayer a great deal of the time. Upon nearing the tomb, He was met by Lazarus's relatives who came out weeping and wailing and wringing their hands in absolute anguish, telling Him, "Oh Lord, if you had only made it a few days earlier—but it's too late now, for poor Lazarus has been dead for four days already!"

Then follows another of the misunderstood texts in the Bible. Almost everyone remembers hearing the shortest verse in the Bible, "Jesus wept."

Few seem to know *why* He wept. Most would assume it was because of His feeling for poor Lazarus, or the terrible loss of His loved ones.

But wait. Read the inspired account and you will see that Jesus lifted His eyes to the heavens, and said loudly enough for a few of His own disciples to hear it, "Father I thank you that you have heard me, and I know that you hear me always."

And finishing this brief prayer as if an addendum or postscript to lengthy prayers said in private previously, Jesus said in a loud voice, "Lazarus, come out!"

Miraculously, and throwing stunned disbelief and shock into the detractors as well as disbelieving joy into the hearts of his loved ones, Lazarus stood up and came out of the tomb still wearing the grave clothes, whereupon Jesus said, "Loose him and let him go" (John 11:31-44). The account proves Jesus *knew* what He would find and knew of the surety that God was going to answer His prayer to miraculously resurrect Lazarus from death itself.

Therefore, it is utterly impossible that the brief two-word verse, "Jesus wept," could imply either sorrow for Lazarus, or for His loved ones.

But study Jesus' life carefully and recall the example of His "being grieved at the hardness of their hearts" on another occasion when a miraculous healing was to take place, or His expressions of grief at His disciples' lack of faith in the case of the healing of the boy who was possessed with a demon that was trying to destroy his life!

On this occasion, the distraught father came to Jesus and told him that the disciples had *tried* to cast out the demon but were unable; the father was despairing because apparently the spirit was literally trying to destroy the boy, by throwing him into any water nearby, or even into a fire; and the young lad was "torn" by fits and seizures which caused a great deal of trauma and pain.

Jesus commanded the spirit to come out, and even then in the last frenzy of hate, the demon was said to have cried with a loud voice and brought about another violent fit prior to his departure.

Later, the disciples had asked why they were unable to cast the demon out and Jesus said, "Oh ye of little faith," and told them that this kind "will not come out except by a great deal of prayer and fasting."

He knew that His disciples were spending nowhere near as much time in prayer as they should; and He also knew very obviously that they were not fasting anywhere near as often.

Obviously, then, because of Jesus' grief over examples of lack of faith, and the hopelessness of human anguish, His emotion at the tomb of Lazarus was more one of anguish and deep personal grief because of *their lack of faith*, than for any other cause.

It was, perhaps, similar to the anguish of a loving parent, who, though trying time and time again to teach an important object lesson to a child, sees the child slip up repeatedly, only to hurt himself severely. The parent cries out in anguish over the seeming inability of the child to learn the lesson.

Jesus wept at Lazarus's tomb not because of any frustrated feelings of hopelessness, sense of loss, or even necessarily deep compassion toward a loved one; for He knew Lazarus was going to walk out of that tomb in only moments! He wept simply because He was in deep personal anguish over the continual lack of faith of these people!

A custom of the day required the continuous wailing of members of the family over a protracted period of time, and could also even feature the actual hiring of professional "wailers" to do so on the occasion of a funeral.

Remember, this wailing and weeping was still going on after *four solid days.*

Jesus had faith, then, to work whatever miracles were absolutely necessary for the proof of His authority; for the presentation of His true credentials as the Messiah of mankind; for demonstration of the "power of the kingdom of God," for the casting out of demons, for the healing of the sick, and also for a testimony to His own disciples that they might have the courage backed by faith at a later date to perform miracles which Jesus said would be "even greater than these."

The "faith" experienced by most humans today is more of a frantic hoping, a quest, a desire, a deep and sincere thirst for something wanted than it is the calm, full-bodied, confident *assurance*, the *foreknowledge* that certain events are *going* to take place prior to their occurrence!

The greatest detriments to faith are fear, pain, doubt, or vanity. Perhaps the first three are obvious, but what about vanity?

Of assurity, though many would-be faith healers would desperately like to utilize some supernatural power for the propulsion of themselves into a theological limelight to create a vast following, God is never going to honor a request either in private or in public for miraculous events or for the healing of the sick merely to satiate ego and vanity.

On the other hand, how does one explain seemingly incontrovertible cases where individuals claim they had been healed miraculously on such occasions?

Notwithstanding the allegations of circus freaks, appearing and disappearing goiters, people who are not really crippled after all, what of those cases which would seem to defy scientific investigation? Perhaps there is another answer.

Jesus revealed another principle concerning faith: He said on more than one occasion that an answer to prayer would be "according to faith"!

When Jesus said, "It will be done, or it will occur according to your faith," He is throwing the burden of proof and the direct weight of responsibility squarely back on the shoulders of the supplicant.

It is not impossible to imagine occasions where individuals who were looking *beyond* the alleged human healer, looking directly toward Jesus Christ's own personal sacrifice (the Bible reveals, "by his stripes were ye healed") *could be*, under those circumstances, miraculously delivered from physical illness or deformity.

Careful study, however, of the examples of the healings found throughout the four gospels, cannot turn up one single healing done in a carnival-like atmosphere for the purpose of gaining attention.

Rather, there are any number of examples where even though a miraculous healing *did occur*, Jesus privately warned the individual who had been so blessed, "Tell no man, but go your way and show the gift to the priest as the law of Moses commands."

Thus, after performing the ceremonial ritual of cleansing in the case of blindness or a disease such as leprosy, Jesus strongly urged most individuals who were greatly blessed by being healed that they "tell no one about it," in order that Jesus would not bring too much persecution upon Himself too soon.

What a far cry is this quiet, once-in-a-while blessing, extended toward sincere supplicants, from the blatant circus-like attempts of individuals who proclaim themselves to be evangelistic healers and who advertise widely that they are going to provide a "double portion night" every Tuesday at 10 o'clock!

Perhaps the greatest example of the tremendous assurance which Jesus possessed and which resulted in a miracle is the occasion when He and several of the disciples were aboard a fair-sized boat in the Sea of Galilee, and an unusually strong desert wind arose which caused huge whitecaps to nearly swamp the boat. Jesus was in the bottom of the boat asleep and finally was roused by all of the frightened chatter by the disciples who thought the boat was surely going to sink.

Coming on deck, Jesus merely looked at the intensity of the storm, and gesturing to the waves and wind, said, "Peace, be still."

The waves began to die down, and within only a matter of

minutes, as can occur after the passage of a violent windstorm when a lake which had been tempestuous only minutes before can become almost glassy-still, the lake took on a great calm.

The disciples were absolutely dumbfounded and said, "What manner of man is this that even the winds and the waves obey him?"

On this occasion, while many might be tempted to see Jesus in the role of showman, merely gesturing or posturing in an attempt to gain popularity or notoriety, He was actually saving several lives, including His own!

While the account is cursory at best, there is every reason to believe it was a serious enough storm that if Christ had not intervened, it quite literally would have meant the sinking of the ship.

Skeptics would be tempted to say, "Well, so what, He could have walked on the water anyway, couldn't He?" But again, this book is not intended to "bring you to the Lord" or to convince anyone who wishes to disbelieve, but to set forth the simple truth about the personality, nature and character of the real Jesus Christ of Nazareth as closely as the personal eyewitness accounts will allow.

Perfect godly character would have absolutely demanded that Jesus never utilize any special supernatural powers for the mere purpose of show.

Furthermore, any attempt to utilize supernatural powers for such a purpose would have meant the automatic cancellation of miraculous powers in the first place! Nothing is more detrimental to faith than vanity and ego!

Entirely too many people feel miracles are "credentials" of *personal* righteousness, holiness and power, instead of aids to evangelism. "Signs" were utilized by God's prophets to dumbfound and convince skeptics and unbelievers; special blessings from time to time have come from God in especially outstanding cases to display God's mercy. But most assuredly, God will never permit real godly miracles to be prostituted in a form of spiritualistic gimmickry for the purpose of inflating the ego of would-be spiritual leaders.

Even as the teaching of the real Jesus is virtually intolerable to so many today, it was also intolerable to the religious leaders of His day. Jesus actually attempted to begin the formal segment of

His ministry by honoring His own country, sadly but fully expecting to be rejected by His own people.

Some interesting doctrinal truths are discovered in Jesus' first rejection at Nazareth.

Read Luke's account, chapter four, verses 16 through 30, and you will find that He was appearing in His own hometown synagogue. Jesus had already been in Judaea and had understood that the Pharisees were rumoring that He was becoming more of an important figure than John, allegedly baptizing even more people than John, and therefore looming as a larger competitive threat in the religious marketplace (at least in their minds). So Jesus left Judaea and went again into Galilee. However, it required Him to pass through Samaria (John 4:1-4).

It was during this journey that Jesus met the woman at Jacob's well and gave the Samaritan woman the lesson about "living water."

Following Jesus' miraculous ability to tell the woman many details of her past, plus His plain teaching about a "well of water springing up unto eternal life," many of the Samaritans began to believe that He must be the prophesied Messiah or Savior. It was only two days later (John 4:43) that Jesus went into Galilee. He had said earlier (Luke 4:24; Mark 6:4; Matt. 13:57) that no prophet has any acceptance in his own country.

In Luke 4:16, Jesus was in Nazareth, where He was brought up, and *"as His custom was, he went into the synagogue on the Sabbath day."* On this occasion, according to the custom of the synagogue, He was asked to read. He found the place in Isaiah where it was written, "The Spirit of the Lord is upon me, because he has anointed me to preach the good news to the poor. He has sent me to proclaim release to the captives and recovering of sight to the blind, to set at liberty those who are oppressed, to proclaim the acceptable year of the Lord" (Luke 4:16-19, RSV). After reading this segment from Isaiah 58:6 and 61:1-2, He rolled up the scroll and gave it back to the attendant and sat down. There was a protracted silence, with all eyes still upon Him, when He confidently proclaimed, "This day is this scripture fulfilled in your ears."

He went on to proclaim Himself as the Messiah who was actually fulfilling those centuries-old pronouncements from the scroll of Isaiah. Everyone listened intently, and began to wonder at both the eloquence and the vast biblical knowledge, as well as at the sincerity that gave His words a ring of truth.

But true to His predictions, their hometown prejudices began to get in their way.

Some began to reason, "Isn't this Joseph's boy?" Many of them had perhaps not paid much attention to Him in the last several years, though some few must have recognized Him as the young man who had grown up right in the city as a laborer at His father's side and who had been conducting His father's business together with His several brothers since Joseph's death.

Recognizing their beginning doubts He said, "Probably you are going to repeat to me the tired old parable 'Physician, heal yourself!' Since we have heard all those marvelous rumors about what you did in Capernaum why don't you do the same things right here in your own hometown and show us?" He went on to say that "no prophet is acceptable in his own country."

Then followed a very concise statement which is impossible for most people to believe, even today.

Jesus said, "I am telling you the truth—there were many widows in Israel during the days of Elijah when the heaven was shut up three years and six months; and great famine came over the whole country. In spite of all the terrible duress, Elijah was not sent to any of them but only to Zarephath in the land of *Sidon* unto a woman that was a widow." (Obviously, the implication was that even though a major prophet of Israel, Elijah was sent to a Sidonian and therefore to a Gentile.)

He continued, "Also, there were many lepers in Israel during the time of Elisha's prophecies, and *none* of them was cleansed but only Naaman the Syrian" (II Kings 5:14).

They were all so enraged at His obvious inference that great prophets and men of God who were champions and heroes of Israel had actually turned away from their own people because of their paganism, and had been sent to isolated Gentiles for special purposes, that they "were all filled with wrath."

As the men in the synagogue heard these things they "rose up, and cast him out of the city, and led him unto the brow of the hill whereupon their city was built, that they might throw him down headlong. But he passing through the midst of them went his way" (see Luke 4:22-30).

Much can be gleaned from this account—not the least of which is additional confirmation about the obvious plainness of Jesus' appearance, necessary for Him to be able to lose Himself in the crowd.

But perhaps more importantly, this abortive attempt of the beginning of a public ministry in His own hometown is illustrative of a major scriptural truth rejected by so many millions today: to wit, Jesus did not come to save the world then, and He is not setting His hand to save it now!

The concept held by the religious leaders of the day demanded a returning, conquering Messiah who would once again exalt the nation of Israel to its Davidic greatness, or the glitter of the reign of Solomon. They wanted a military king; one to overthrow the yoke of the Roman conquerors, and to so expand their own borders, commerce, domestic economy and social order that they once again became a great kingdom.

Many other examples in the four gospels illustrate the same point.

Jesus had said repeatedly, "Why do you call me Lord and yet do not the things which I say? Not everyone that says unto me, Lord, Lord, shall in anywise enter the kingdom of my Father."

"None can come to the son except the spirit of the Father draw him."

And, in answering His disciples' queries as to why He spoke in difficult-to-understand similes and parables, He plainly referred once again to a prophecy by Isaiah in which He instructed His disciples, "Because as Isaiah said their eyes are totally blinded and their ears are deafened and they stumble at my teaching, lest at any time they should turn and be converted and I should heal them."

Read the thirteenth chapter of Matthew and you will discover a profound truth which is rejected by most professing Christendom today—Jesus deliberately *concealed* His message from the majority, and *privately* taught it to a select hand-picked group of disciples for the purpose of raising them up as His immediate successors to form the human building blocks of the New Testament Church of God which He predicted would continue from that age to this.

Never at any time, not during the human lifespan of Jesus Christ of Nazareth when He with His own footsteps trod the pastures, orchards, and grainfields of Palestine, or throughout the intervening millennia, has the real Jesus set His hand to save the world!

Anyone who believes in the childish beddy-bye concept that Jesus has been trying to save the world must automatically believe, at the same time, that Satan's efforts are infinitely more powerful; that Jesus is weak and inept, and that God seemingly is losing the battle on all fronts.

Jesus' attitude throughout His life was not one of pomp and vanity. There was not one iota of braggadocio in the man—but there was a deepening awareness, especially following the frightening confrontation with Satan the Devil in the wilderness, that His public ministry would result in a growing hostility and resistance on the part of political and religious leaders.

Yet Jesus had the *faith* to see it through.

CHAPTER 12

Miracles and Healings—

Signs of His Messiahship

A miracle is a miracle is a miracle.

There is no such thing as "little miracles" or "big miracles." Jesus performed many miracles during the course of His ministry, and, may have performed, at least on rare occasions, private miracles for family members or perhaps a neighborhood friend.

However, to say He "performed" miracles is not quite so accurate as to say Jesus was the human instrument in the hands of His Father, God, who generated the miracles.

Jesus said, "The Father who lives in me, He is the one who is really doing this work."

He said repeatedly to His disciples that the miracles were evidence of His divine origins, His preexistent life with His Father, and His present divine calling and commission. Jesus never took any personal credit for "performing miracles," but insisted continually that it was the combination of the faith of the believer and the spirit of His Father from heaven that accomplished the miracles.

Most of the accounts of Jesus' healings are quiet, personal accounts of miraculous healings performed either out of great compassion or following an example of particular perseverence on the part of Jews as well as Gentiles.

Even though Jesus mostly healed privately and repeatedly told people not to tell anyone about it, and even though the Bible plainly records that the great healings during Jesus' time and the early years of the Church gradually waned and virtually disappeared even prior to the closing of the New Testament writings, yet many seem to believe that great healings or supernatural phenomena are the test of whether a church body is truly "of God" or not.

Of course, others doubt whether healing could take place today, or that it ever could have taken place in the past.

One of the most obvious, oft-repeated and sensationalized facts about Jesus was that He could really heal. He Himself, in telling the disciples of John that they should judge "by the fruits," pointed to healing as a demonstration of His Messiahship (Matt. 8:16-17, Matt. 11:2-6).

Immediately following the Sermon on the Mount (Matt. 5:7) there are many accounts of healings in the subsequent chapters.

Jesus was making His way down from the mountain, which had to be only a short distance from Capernaum, and therefore was probably one of the steep hills at the extreme northwestern corner of the Sea of Galilee, when a leper finally got close enough to Jesus to call out to Him.

No doubt the crowd following along and discussing what they had just heard, parted to allow the man access, giving him wide berth, for he had to follow the prescribed laws of shouting out, "leper," or perhaps even ringing a bell to warn of his approach. (Lepers were the "pariahs" of that society, looked upon with revulsion and distaste, as they still are in some societies today, and suffering a certain measure of isolation, though not necessarily placed in "colonies," as this account reveals.)

The leper finally called out to Jesus, "Lord, if you only will, you can make me clean"! Jesus then did something which must have appeared doubly remarkable to everyone around him, and something none of them would have dared do.

He put forth His hand and actually *touched* the leper and said, "I will—become clean"!

Miraculously, the pasty flesh tones became ruddy, the horrible open wounds and scars disappeared, the disfigurement vanished, and the man stood before Jesus whole!

There is no strong indication that dozens were surrounding Him at this moment; rather, it is more likely that many in the immediate vicinity actually fled the leper, and that Jesus was there with only a handful of His own disciples.

Otherwise, you could not understand why Jesus said to the

man, "See that you don't tell anybody about it, but go your way, be sure to show yourself to the priest and offer the gift just as required by the law of Moses, because this will be a testimony to the religious leaders."

Mark says the man almost instantly disobeyed Jesus' admonition because of his excitement and joy over being healed, and began to tell everybody in sight and "blaze abroad the matter," insomuch that Jesus could no more "openly enter into the city" because of the pressure of the crowds who were clamoring for the healing of their sick, or confirmation of the miracle (Mark 1:40-45).

Though it will anger some, it happens to be a simple fact that many others attempted to be healed by Christ but that He deliberately withdrew into a private place to pray. Mark says the pressure of the crowd seeking Him out to ask for healing for their own loved ones or themselves became so great that Jesus "could not enter into the city" and so went apart into a desert place nearby where no one knew where He was.

Later, Jesus was at home in Capernaum teaching many who had gathered to hear.

A particularly determined group of friends brought one of their buddies who was paralyzed, but they found they could not fight their way through the crowd with the poor guy lying there on a pallet. Every time they tried, they were jostled out of the way by all the people pressing around the door, filling up the foyer, standing, sitting all over the house, intently listening to what Jesus was saying.

With some risk and not a little ingenuity, they actually began to take up some of the stones or other roofing material on the roof. Those down below began to notice a crack and sliver of light, and then a lot of dust and mortar tumbling down, and perhaps any in the way stood up, and began brushing off their clothes and hair and began looking anxiously toward the ceiling. Jesus, a bit bewildered, probably stood up, pausing in the middle of the lesson He was giving to the others about, and watched with a combination of patience and bemusement as the hole got larger and larger.

Soon several faces probably peered in, disappeared, and then the light was blotted out while a pallet seemed to cover it. Finally, all noticed a paralyzed man slowly being lowered into the room!

Because of this audacious act of ingenuity, Jesus seized upon the opportunity to present a great lesson of compassion, and at the same time give a stinging rebuke to the religious leaders of the day as well as teach an important spiritual principle concerning the forgiveness of sins to the crowd.

The Bible says He saw *their faith* (including the buddies of the paralytic, and perhaps not even necessarily the paralytic's own faith) and so He said, "Your sins are forgiven."

After saying this and looking at the man for some moments, some audible arguments began to come from a nearby group of religious types whose garments identified them as leaders of the local synagogue. Immediately Jesus knew He was being judged and criticized for making such an outrageous statement; so He completed the act in two parts by saying, "But that you may understand that the Son of man has the authority on this earth to forgive sins, I'm telling you," and turning to the paralytic He said, "Get up from there, roll up your pallet and go home."

When the man did exactly that, a ripple of surprise echoed through the crowd, and the religious leaders took a step backward as if in utter shock, while Jesus' disciples looked around at the people, with Peter probably wearing that smug smile that said, "I told you so" to some of those who had been doubting Jesus' abilities a little earlier.

The forgiveness of the man's sins according to these accounts (Matt. 9:1-8; Mark 2:1-12; Luke 5:17-26) was separate from the healing, which was performed in two parts; the first was Christ's declaration that the man's sins had in fact been forgiven, and the second, after a brief explanation to the crowd and a rebuke of the religious leaders, was the actual command to the man to "get up, roll up your pallet and go on home."

Jesus' remarkable capacity for seeing, knowing, feeling and sensing that "other dimension" of His Father's spirit kingdom, the presence of powerful angels, and the ebb and flow of the power of God's Holy Spirit through Him, had given Him perfect faith so that in issuing such a command He knew it would be honored.

Both before and after the famous "Sermon on the Mount," Jesus healed many people who came to seek Him out from all over Judaea, from as far away as Jerusalem and Syria. His ministry began to be spread abroad in towns and cities for literally hundreds of miles, and in the early weeks of His Galilean ministry, He became one of the most famous individuals of that time. The crush of the crowds became so great on some occasions that He had to jump aboard a boat to avoid being crushed in the stampede.

Only a few ranks away from Jesus, in crowded marketplaces, in streets and along roadways, the hundreds of people thronging around could not even discern which one He was. In jumping up and down, looking over the shoulders and heads of others, trying to spot precisely where the center of action was, many of them pushed, jostled, shoved and elbowed one another. Jesus was no doubt afraid of personal injury, when from time to time He was caught in the midst of a mob. His escape to the top of a nearby mountain where the "Sermon on the Mount" was delivered was perhaps a sermon of *convenience,* as he sought to outdistance the crowd below. Jesus had to scramble up to a high place, possibly even having to *run,* in order to escape the crowds. His disciples came puffing up behind Him to likewise escape the crush of the crowd. As a result, these circumstances were to provide a mountain environment for the delivery of the most famous sermon in all of history (compare Matt. 4:24-25; Mark 3:7-13; Luke 6:17-19).

Jesus was no respecter of persons when it came to having compassion for people and reaching out into that "other dimension" of the spirit world for the power of His Father to heal.

A Roman officer, having authority over one hundred soldiers, came to Jesus begging Him to heal his slave who was near death. Many lessons can be gleaned from the account of the Roman soldier simply by wondering what Jesus did *not* say or do.

First, He did not scathingly indict the Roman soldier, standing there in his burnished breastplate, with his sword at his side, or his helmet in his hand. There was no bitter indictment about being in the military, no scathing denunciation because of the brutal Roman occupation of Jesus' homeland, and no contemptuous epithets because the Roman was of another race, from another country, and a stranger in Jesus' own country.

Next, even though the Roman plainly told Jesus his servant was a slave (all the Roman officers had both household slaves and personal slaves, and could from time to time commandeer additional help from other private citizens who were not necessarily indentured to them), Jesus did not enter into the internal politics of the land at the time by loudly condemning slavery, though this is not to imply by the remotest stretch of the imagination that His lack of stern condemnation represents, in an argument from silence, that He either condoned or approved the practice.

Perhaps Jesus was a little curious about where the Roman lived, and actually wanted to set the example of walking along the road with a Roman officer so others would notice the kind of companions He was willing to keep. In any event, He said, "Sure, I'll be glad to come and heal him—let's go."

The officer, startled, said, "I am not worthy to have you come under my roof; after all I'm an officer in the Roman army. I tell one of my troops to come here and he simply comes. I tell him to go and he goes. You are in total authority. All you need to do is give the word and I know my servant is going to be healed."

Jesus turned to those nearby and said, "I haven't found an example of faith like this among my own people throughout Israel!"

Turning to the Roman he said, "Go on home, and as you have believed and have faith, so will it be done to you exactly." When the officer arrived back home after a rapid ride over some rocky roads, clattering along in his chariot, it was to find some excited house servant telling him that his favorite slave had miraculously got on his feet, the fever had left him, and he was standing there looking wonderingly about.

The officer found out by a careful comparison of the amount of time it had taken him to ride home and the time the servant told him the slave had been healed, that it was right at the same hour when he had been in personal conversation with Jesus (Matt. 8:5-13, paraphrased).

Some time later, Jesus was staying in Peter's home, and after a brief journey from Capernaum down to Bethsaida walked into the house to find Peter's mother-in-law sick with a high fever.

Jesus felt bad; here He had arrived with a whole group of His disciples, expecting to spend some time (probably for Peter's own benefit, giving him a chance to visit his family and to be with his wife for a day or so), only to find Peter's wife's mother lying there grievously ill with a high fever.

Jesus, thinking of the vastly increased household chores which would immediately be forced upon her, of the throngs of the people who would be coming and going and the heightened activity in the house because of His presence there, let alone His immediate compassion because of the poor woman's condition and the close family relationship, reached out, took her hand, smiled into her face, and said that He was rebuking the fever.

She was healed instantly. Very shortly after sundown that day, evidently a Sabbath, other people from Capernaum had heard the news, and flocks of individuals, knowing that He was at Peter's home, came to Him to be healed. The gospel of Matthew says this helped fulfill Isaiah 53:4 ("He took our infirmities and bore our diseases," Matt. 8:17, RSV).

Sometimes, at a particular request, Jesus would be on the way to heal one person when someone else would come forward in the crowd and beg His attention. There were accounts of people pressing forward in the crush of the crowd and actually reaching out to touch His clothing and being healed. This was not only attested by three of the gospel writers, but it was said later by Luke that in the early days of the New Testament Church when the early apostles were so filled with zeal, with the newness and freshness of their conversion and their knowledge of God's Holy Spirit, that sick people lying in the streets were healed miraculously when the very shadow of Peter passed over them!

On one occasion, Jesus was on the way to heal a little girl that was near death, who happened to be the daughter of the ruler of the synagogue, named Jairus. (Actually, she died while Jairus was in the process of bringing Jesus to her.)

This was an especially important occasion, for Jesus would be visiting in the home of one of the important men of the local Jewish synagogue, a site of so many of His frequent confrontations with the religious leaders. Jesus was keenly aware of His need to show His deep outgoing concern, love and compassion toward people regardless of their background, religion, color, or nationality.

He was on His way to Jairus's home when, surging forward from among the mass of people crowding along behind Him, was a woman who had been plagued with a serious bleeding for twelve long years. The Bible says she had spent her whole living, going from one resort to another, trying everything imaginable from herbs, poultices, teas, baths, compresses; everything in the medicines available in that day, and was still not helped, but rather had become destitute because every bit of her savings was finally exhausted.

The story reveals another important item in Jesus' personal life. When the woman finally got close enough, she reached out, full of desire and faith, and touched the hem of Jesus' outer cloak.

The Bible says Jesus "felt virtue flow out of him." Jesus said, "Who touched me?" When all denied, Peter and they that were with him said, "Master, the multitude throng thee and press thee, and sayest thou, Who touched me?

"And Jesus said, Somebody hath touched me: for I perceive that virtue is gone out of me."

With the crowd there was curiosity, perhaps even suspicion and anger in some cases, but with the desperately afflicted woman, there was deep desire and strong confident faith. She *knew* that all she had to do was fight her way forward until she could *touch* that fabulous man. A spiritual contact was made. God actually healed the woman *through* Jesus' own body, even without Jesus' knowing to whom the healing had happened.

"And when the woman saw that she was not hid, she came trembling, and falling down before him, she declared unto him before all the people for what cause she had touched him, and how she was healed immediately. And he said unto her, Daughter, be of good comfort: thy faith hath made thee whole; go in peace" (Luke 8:43-48).

Jesus had *felt,* by an actual ebbing or draining of strength from Him, that a miracle had taken place. Without launching into speculations which border on the realm of ESP, or implying anything more than that which is stated, it is clear that Jesus could feel not only *physical* exhaustion, but could literally feel the surge and flow of *spiritual* power and strength. It is clearly shown that, in His lengthy 40-day fast, in order to gird His spiritual loins for the violent confrontation and matching of wills with Satan the Devil, that Jesus knew He had to be in exceedingly close contact with God, and filled with more spiritual energy than ever before.

On the occasion of praying so hard to select each of his 12 disciples, knowing both that the future of the Church depended on them and that one of them should betray Him, He prayed so earnestly that His brow was running with rivulets of sweat as if they were like "drops of blood splashing on the ground." When He told His disciples they couldn't cast out a demon because "this kind comes not out except through prayer and fasting," Jesus indicated there were moments when greater measures of spiritual power would be required to perform some miraculous act.

Thus, while it is impossible to "feel" the Holy Spirit in the sense of implying that the Holy Spirit impresses itself upon a human mind emotionally or through the sensory perceptions, Jesus, with His perfect mind and having the Holy Spirit poured out "without measure" upon Him, could actually be super-sensitized to the fact that a portion of God's own power had flowed through Him, almost as if He were a conductor of electricity, feeling the passing on of power.

He turned, saw the woman standing there, and said, "Good for you daughter; be of good cheer and take heart, because you had such faith, you are standing there well!" He smiled at her, turned around, and continued toward Jairus's home.

At this point, a weeping servant came running toward them, and seeing Jairus, reported to him in Jesus' hearing that it was too late and that Jairus's little girl was already dead. Jesus continued on into the house, stopping at the entry, and following the customary foot washing and slipping into household slippers, turned toward the sleeping quarters. He told the people crowding at the door and looking in with tears streaking their faces, "Don't worry about it, I'm sure she is only sleeping."

Hopelessly, with tears streaming down their faces, they looked at Him, and one or two even laughed bitterly, expressing their scorn and disbelief because by now her pulse and breathing had ceased. But you could imagine one of the more scornful present saying, "Are you kidding? Everyone knows she's dead. And I checked her pulse myself", as well as there being irate protests of "Who does he think he is? " coming from the crowd.

However, Jesus eventually got Jairus to clear the room, except for the immediate parents and Jesus' own closest disciples, and, after making sure the home was free of all outsiders, He went back into the bedroom, took the girl by the hand, and, praying fervently but quietly, called upon His Father in heaven who was so close to Him in that "other dimension" of the spirit world from whence He had come. With the supreme confidence coming only from the sure knowledge that His Father *had* heard, Jesus took the girl by the hand and lifted her up from the pallet where she lay.

Her mother and father immediately embraced her, and then

embraced Jesus, giving Him their thanks in tearful rejoicing. The only ones who saw the miracle were a few of His closest disciples, Jairus and his wife, but none of the household servants.

Jesus continually tried to perform these acts of great mercy and compassion in a private environment to avoid the wildfire tales which would be spread, including the bitterest accusations that He was using some sort of sorcery or witchcraft, which might bring about even more intense persecution, and plunge His whole ministry and the training of His disciples into a chaotic uproar far too early for His purposes.

But so many people had claimed to have seen the girl dead; for example, the household servants who were nearby had known of the girl's illness and that she had indeed apparently died.

Though totally divided in their opinions of just how He had done it, or whether she had, in fact, been dead or merely in a deep coma from which she had awakened, many people began widely spreading the account, and Jesus was made the more famous or infamous, depending upon the version of the story that was told.

It is obvious that Jesus had a distinct purpose in telling the people in advance, "Don't worry about it, she is only deeply asleep."

Jesus no doubt said that because He still wanted there to be sufficient room for doubt later on when they learned the girl was alive. He didn't want this great miracle of raising one from the dead to greatly disturb the local environment, or reach all the way to the Sanhedrin in Jerusalem because it could have precipitated a violent reaction bringing about a premature end of His public ministry.

Therefore, when he took the girl by the hand and raised her up from the bed, saying in Hebrew, "Get up, you're going to be all right," He turned to the disciples, the parents, and quietly told all of them, "Look, and I really mean this, I don't want you to noise this abroad. Be happy about it, and rejoice over it—but keep it quiet; let's keep it within our own closest circle of friends and the family."

But the Pharisees had begun spreading the story that Jesus was using trickery, by directly cooperating with demons. Jesus was alleged to be Satan's own cohort, so that He could make it appear, through allowing a demon to enter a person and then having evil power to make the spirit come out, that He was performing miracles and healings when in fact He was only doing it through "Beelzebub the prince of the demons."

Jesus had been healing a large number of people in some of the Gentile towns, probably in the Decapolis, where large crowds were following Him about, and He "healed them all" (Matt. 12:14-15). This fact is further proven by the statement of Matthew that this practice of Jesus asking people to keep silent about their healings "fulfilled" that which was spoken by Isaiah ("Behold my servant whom I have chosen, my beloved in whom my soul is well pleased; I will put my spirit upon him and he shall shew judgment to the Gentiles. He shall not strive, nor cry: neither shall any man hear his voice in the streets" (Matt. 12:18-19, taken from Isa. 42:1-3). This prophecy was beautifully fulfilled by Jesus, for He not only avoided large calamitous public confrontations in the main, but also continually charged those whom He healed not to make it known to others. Jesus' whole attitude was totally different in the accomplishing of His healings and miracles from what is imagined by many sincere, Bible-believing folk who have read all too casually the inspired accounts.

Not long after the many miraculous events around the Sea of Galilee, Jesus went back to Nazareth, where He had grown up.

The local religious leaders knew who He was—knew His family, and His trade, and knew that He was "Jesus, the son of Joseph." What they *didn't* know, or want to admit, was that He was also the Son of God.

Shortly after going back home to Nazareth, Jesus went into the synagogue, and began to teach. Here was this ordinary-looking, fairly stocky workman, who had been seen laboring in the sun of Nazareth for many years, suddenly speaking out in a voice ringing with authority about *how to live,* and about Bible prophecy, especially the predictions about the coming of the Messiah.

The Pharisees were outraged. (Being "outraged" has always been a popular religious pastime, it seems.) They used the shopworn old dodge, "Just who does this guy think he is?"

The illogicality of their charges didn't seem to occur to them. They couldn't gainsay the doctrines He taught. They couldn't withstand the authority with which He spoke. But the fact that it was *He*—a nondescript, unknown, average working man, whose father and brothers were laborers in the building trade, who was now the center of attention, who was now the subject of such excited conversation by all the people—*this* was particularly galling.

They said, illogically, "From whence has this man these things?" This plaintive question shows their consternation that Christ wasn't "accredited." He wasn't "approved" by any great rabbinical teacher. He was not a rabbi. He was not a graduate of any school.

They reasoned that it just wasn't "fair," all this success, power and attention coming Jesus' way. They said, "what wisdom is this which is given unto him [with sarcastic accent on the *him*!], that even such mighty works are wrought by his hands?"

No wonder Jesus taught that a "prophet has no honor in his own country, among his own relatives."

Healing was a testimony with two edges!

For one, it was a great witness to those who were healed and those who saw it that Jesus was in fact the Son of God, the Messiah and the Deliverer, that "Prophet" who was to come, a son of David and a son of Israel, and the soon coming King who would establish the kingdom of God on this earth.

These amazing, mind-boggling miracles were the clearest stamp of Jesus' authority, together with His teaching of God's law (as carefully prescribed by Deuteronomy 13:1-5).

Jesus insisted that the law must be obeyed in all its spiritual applications and intent. And having met the test not only of the dozens of prophecies surrounding His birth, His flight into Egypt, His boyhood in Nazareth, and the fact that He was able to perform powerful miracles, but also now that He taught *within God's law,* those whose hearts were willing could easily prove His Messiahship.

The opposite edge of Jesus' healings was a cutting indictment as a witness *against* doubters. They had no further reason to doubt. Some of them, even including Jewish leaders of leading synagogues, saw these miraculous events, and were blessed and touched by them in their own homes and lives.

Still, most rejected Him.

Thus, healing was never performed as a sensational act, never done in public before milling throngs and crowds to aggrandize Christ's position, never to exalt Him in the eyes of the people, nor to provide Him with some vehicle for egomania. Compare this, if you will, to some of the so-called healing campaigns and "special blessing nights."

I well remember one of the most (to me) obscene sights of my life.

When I was a very young man, my wife and I, with another couple, decided out of mere curiosity to go to one of these advertised "healing campaigns" in the southeastern part of Los Angeles, which was to be held under a great sprawling tent. I would prefer not to name the would-be faith healer who is no longer in the land of the living.

Fortunately, we were able to find seats well in the rear. During one session of the meeting (it seemed to go from one carefully rehearsed segment to the next, punctuated by three shockingly commercial offerings, which I will describe), the wildly waving, hoarse-voiced, colloquially accented Southern evangelist who claimed to be having almost daily communication with "the Lord," was calling upon personal testimonies from the audience. From time to time, a person (nearly always a woman it seemed to me) would rise, wave both arms, and scream out some unintelligible utterance. Some were actually speaking in a kind of babble which I took to be a combination of gibberish, tongue bitings, and suspected Spanish epithets. In any event, it seemed to be both enjoyable and intelligible to many others in the crowd because it would usually bring forth shrieks and moans of ecstatic agreement.

There was a group of teenagers sitting directly in front of us, and they seemed to be under the tutelage of an amply overstuffed older teenage girl who was urging her younger brother, "Go ahead, you can do it, there's nothing to it," and gave him an outpouring of other similar urgent instructions.

On a moment's sudden inspiration, and adding to our growing and acute discomforture, because suddenly all eyes were turned in our direction, the girl jiggled herself into position and springing onto the seat of her chair with all the grace of a rhinoceros began to wave her arms ecstatically in the air and shrieked a series of piercing "testimonies," interrupted by breathless screams of "Bless you Jesus! Praise you Jesus!" Then she said, and I do not even wish to repeat it that many times even in quotes, the name "Jesus" over and over again in mindless repetition!

Even though those of us sitting immediately behind her knew that all of this was a carefully contrived demonstration in which she hoped to encourage her younger brother to throw off whatever remaining constraints of etiquette and propriety he may have had (and I could not imagine that he could have retained very much beyond this point), the wildly gesticulating figure came to the immediate attention of the hoarse-voiced evangelist on the platform who then confidently affirmed in the loudest possible terms over his microphone that what was happening in our vicinity of the tent was in fact a "direct message from God!" Then, knowing that most eyes were turned in our direction, and with the supreme confidence of the circus barker in center ring, the evangelist proceeded to take off his jacket, loosen his tie, and help himself to a drink of water. (I was a little chagrined, for I felt he wasn't paying this message from God the kind of rapt attention it both deserved and demanded, especially when it appeared for a time as if the whole meeting was going to be taken away from him.)

Soon, it came time for the taking up of an offering. This was my first and only experience with what I heard described as a "silent offering."

The evangelist said he only wanted to hear the "whisper of bills." No vulgar, noisy, obscene jingling of change! He then gave a quick financial report which was delivered with the same fervor and intensity of portions of his sermon, punctuated by frequent references to "the Lord."

It seemed that "the Lord" had managed to send him head-over-heels in debt, and the evangelist then proceeded to enlighten us regarding exactly what the tent cost, what it cost to pack it up, store it and lug it from city to city in those huge trucks outside, what it cost for payments on his buses, trucks and other vehicles in the traveling caravan, and many other costs which soared up into the thousands of dollars.

Then followed the promise of yet stranger miracles. But these miracles were the other edge of the sword. Many of the devoted were warned with absolute assurance that if they held back their money, it was quite likely they would arrive home and find it in flames! They were threatened with head-on collisions at intersections, heart attacks, a telegram saying that mother had died, and everything from liver attacks to instant senility.

It must have frightened the daylights out of enough of them that they parted with a surprising amount of their money, but even this was insufficient, because after what was apparently one of the quickest tabulations in all the history of accounting procedures, the evangelist and his staff took up yet another collection a few moments later in which they demanded only $100 checks, stating that they were something in the neighborhood of $700 short, which meant that the evangelist had to convince only seven people in this vast crowd of thousands that God had especially called and appointed them for the purpose of providing his, the evangelist's, most urgently "required deliverance."

I was beginning to get a clue as to what was meant by "special blessing night" or "double portion night" or that we would "see miracles." The *evangelist* was receiving *very special* blessings, double and triple portions, and it surely was a miracle the way those people parted with their money.

Along about then, after uproarious applause would ripple through the tent at each hand that would be raised as the individual called an usher to him and deposited a $100 check into the coffers, the evangelist began a shouting, screaming, exposition the way he said the "Holy Spirit was moving in the tent just then," and claimed that his very hands were glistening with "holy oil."

I could see that his hands were glistening, even from my distant vantage point, but strongly suspected it was merely from the perspiration he had been fervently wiping from his brow. (Even if it were oil, I could not really testify there was anything especially "holy" about it.)

He then latched on to one scripture concerning the "living waters" and proceeded to pick up the pitcher of water which was on the pulpit, talked about "being filled with the Holy Spirit," and began splashing water all over the stage, himself and a couple of interested bystanders as he filled the glass brimful and over-flowing by pouring it in a substantial torrent from the mouth of the pitcher.

It was still later that we were told that a "noisy" offering was now going to be taken up, as the earlier contempt toward the terrible "jingle of change" voiced during the "silent offering" had somehow been miraculously cured. Now the people were urged to empty their pockets of whatever loose change they had. Our own nods of negation or raised shoulders of helplessness (not only were we unable, but quite unwilling) to add to these offerings brought hostile, level stares from the ushers who passed near us and now strongly suspected we were not quite part of the proceedings, since we had never once applauded, moaned, shrieked, wailed, given testimony, or stood on our chairs.

The procession of people, at the highlight of this very educational meeting, were pronounced to be healed of everything from "dropsy" to epilepsy. I never had an opportunity, and did not attempt to seize it, to talk to any of the alleged afflicted, either before or after they claimed to have been "healed."

But my wife and I and my friends left the meeting, I must admit, with a deepening impression we should omit the word "almost" from the statement "people will believe 'almost' anything."

There is not one subtle innuendo anywhere in the Bible that Jesus, the *real* Jesus, ever involved Himself during His earthly ministry in such charades, and there is ample proof and testimony that He was surely not involved in the one which we witnessed.

Though I cannot document it, I have heard tales that any number of simple folk have willingly paid a certain amount of money for a square inch of cloth, cut with pinking shears, from the shirt of one of these would-be healing evangelists following a particularly exhausting evening of performing "miracles and wonders." (What a blessing that *The Robe* is pure fiction. What a blessing that no one really knows what happened to the garments of Jesus after they were ripped off, gambled over, and later worn out by Roman soldiers. Can you imagine what a square inch of Jesus' own robe would be selling for today?)

Never did Jesus set up a large public meeting, announce that He had come to a city for the express purpose of healing the sick and proceed to hold a revival or a "healing meeting."

There were tens of thousands of bodies lying in graveyards which Jesus did not touch: thousands of lepers whom Jesus never cleansed; many thousands of deaf, blind, twisted, injured, or sick individuals whom Jesus never healed!

There were occasions when, to illustrate that He had been sent "to the lost sheep of the House of Israel," He would refuse to heal those of other races either in the midst of Israel or on their borders.

Some of the most outstanding cases of faith are in those events when Jesus was in the process of *refusing* to grant healing at the request of a Gentile person.

Look at the remarkable contrast between these biblical facts and the practice of "faith healing" as it has sometimes been sensationalized in our modern era.

The sick sought Jesus—He did not seek them.

Even in the beginning of His public ministry, Christ repeatedly warned those who were miraculously healed to "tell no man" but told them to comply with the religious order of the day, by going to the priest and making an offering as required by the rituals of cleansing.

Insight can be gained into the principle of healing, too, by understanding another point concerning Joseph.

It is universally accepted and everywhere obvious that by the time of the beginning of Jesus' public ministry Joseph had already died.

Though there is no sure method of determining Joseph's age, assuming that he was at least 40 by Jesus' birth, he would have been at least 70 by the beginning of Jesus' ministry, and though the cause of his death is not revealed, it is evident that Mary was alone through Jesus' ministry.

The point is that even though Jesus no doubt performed a select number of private miracles within the confines of His own family relating to injury, sickness or disease, He did *not* prevent Joseph's death from whatever "natural causes" when the man's lifespan and purpose in life had been fulfilled.

God's Word has never promised anyone eternal life in the flesh, and states, rather, "It is given to all men to die once."

The healings Jesus performed were merciful, loving, miraculous acts done out of the deepest feelings of compassion and concern toward the poor folk with whom He so closely empathized.

On the other hand, there are many examples in which Jesus did not necessarily grant the first request for healing. Some would keep asking Him along the way, and follow Him for some time until He finally arrived at His own home. Often, it was their mere perseverance and tenacity that impressed Him.

Sometimes He would ask, "Do you really believe that I am *able* to do this?" If they would affirm that He was He would then say, "According to your faith it will be done to you" meaning, that He was making a statement somewhat *less* authoritative than "rise and walk," but affirming that in exact proportion to their own faith and belief the miracle would or would not occur.

Once, some family members brought a deaf mute to Jesus. There is nothing said about the mute's own wishes in the matter. There is no indication at all that he was mentally alert enough because of the terrible affliction he suffered to do much more than to look wonderingly about him, and most certainly, even though his parents would have attempted sign language to indicate to him what they hoped to accomplish, it would have been quite difficult to have conveyed to him what was to happen.

(This example is a particularly touching one to me since I have two deaf sons.)

Jesus wanted the boy to be alone, just with Him; Jesus wanted to have no one else around, so the boy could overcome all embarrassment, and really concentrate without distraction on what Jesus would indicate to him.

So Jesus took him aside privately, and then, looking intently into his eyes, began to communicate with the lad through touch. He reached out and put both of His index fingers deeply into the lad's ears, nodding purposefully, and indicating a positive and encouraging attitude of faith toward the boy. This was Jesus' method, through touch and sign language, that He was about to remove the blockage from the boy's ears.

Then Jesus indicated that the growth that had fastened the boy's tongue so that he could not speak would be removed through the divine power of God. In an attempt to explain how this growth should be ejected from his mouth, Jesus turned, and with a meaningful look at the boy, spat on the ground. Then, Jesus pointedly looked up to heaven, to indicate to the boy that He was calling upon the divine power of God, and moving His lips so the boy could see, pronounced, "Be healed!"

The boy felt something in his mouth, turned, spat it out, and suddenly began to talk! And as he looked at Jesus, realized that he was hearing the sound of a bird in a nearby fig tree! He laughed, he thanked Jesus profusely, grabbed Him in an embrace, with tears filling his eyes, and went to tell his parents what had happened!

Jesus told the excited family and the boy to "keep it quiet" but they were too elated and ecstatic to obey, and this miraculous healing contributed further to His notoriety.

One of the strangest healings of all was in Bethsaida when a group of people brought a blind man to Jesus and begged Him to touch the man, firmly expecting that he would be healed and regain his sight.

Jesus looked at the man, and saw that the poor man's eyes were so hideously deformed that they shone like dull, whitish orbs, covered with dirt and dust.

Jesus was filled with pity for the man, but because He knew very few would understand what He was about to do, He decided to lead the blind man by the hand, walk out of the village of Bethsaida, and try to find a private place, alone. He either related this to His disciples or perhaps one or two of them went along, because only Mark, of all the gospel writers, tells the story.

Finally, after several occasions of quietly warning the man of steps, obstacles, or steep paths, Jesus brought him to a place away from the crowds conversing in their doorways and the public squares, or selling their wares along the roadsides, and stopping the man, turned to him and deliberately told him what He was about to do.

Then, lacking water, Jesus actually used saliva, gently applying it to the man's dust-filled, sightless eyes. He asked the man, "Do you see anything yet?"

The man looked, and seeing passersby walking through a nearby intersection, said, "Yes, I believe I see men, but they almost look like they were trees walking!" The second time, Jesus reached up and touched the man's eyes gently, and this time, the man's eyesight was restored fully.

Perhaps because of the unusual elements of the manner in which Jesus performed this two-part healing, He told the man, "Go ahead to your own home, and be careful not even to go back through the village we have just left, I don't want you to tell anyone about this just yet."

The man, no doubt overcome with emotion, grasped His hand and arm, and looking straight into His eyes, thanked Him profusely and assured Him he would do as He said. Jesus was extremely careful on this occasion, because He intended trying to ease the pressure during this phase of His ministry by going into what Bible scholars refer to as His "fourth retirement" in the area of the villages of Caesarea Philippi on the slopes of Mount Hermon, where no significant hostility against Jesus had yet developed, and where He could spend some months with His disciples teaching them quietly and privately without arousing public protest.

It was during this trip into the villages of Caesarea Philippi that Jesus began to wonder about His "press," and asked His disciples, "When you talk to people in the villages, who is it they tell you I am?"

Several of them began to answer, and Jesus, bemused, listened to different ones of His disciples, even including Thaddaeus, Bartholomew and Judas, agree together they had heard Him called everything from John the Baptist to Elijah or one of the other prophets.

After all of the strange tales had been related, with one story triggering the memory of another, bringing about amused smiles and perhaps even some roaring laughter from Jesus, He finally said, "All right, so much for all the stories. So they claim I am everybody from John the Baptist to Elijah. Who do *you* say I am?" Peter spoke up and said with the strongest assurance, "You are the Christ, the Messiah, the Son of the living God!"

Jesus said, "May the blessing of God rest upon you, Simon, the son of Jonah, because flesh and blood humans would not reveal this to you, but my Father who dwells in heaven, and I'm telling you that your name is *Peter* [*Petros*, a little stone or pebble] and upon this *rock* [*Petra*, a great craggy cliff referring to Christ Himself] I will build my church and the gates of the grave will never prevail against it."

All the disciples had gathered around and were hanging on every word by this time, as Jesus went on to say, "And I will give unto you the keys to the kingdom of heaven, and whatever you will decide as a binding decision upon this earth, will be backed up and bound in heaven. Whatever you decide, so long as it does not conflict with the laws of God, to loose on this earth, will be loosed in heaven."

Then He turned to all His disciples and told them again, "I am deeply pleased that you understand that I am the Christ, but I want to warn you again, do not be gossiping about this or telling people about it. It is important that my identity be kept quiet for the time being, and I don't want you to tell anyone that I am the Christ" (Matt. 16:13-20, paraphrased).

Jesus knew and understood that in the earlier months His

disciples had gone through periods of doubt. He understood deeply that they had become frustrated when in the first year or so of their continual devotion to Him, after being in a state of constant amazement about the miracles He had performed and about the teachings they heard, that He had failed to gather an army, and did not seem to be making any concerted effort to mobilize or to take direct command of all of the potential forces that were steadily gathering around Him.

Somehow, through the flurry of miracles that had occurred just prior to this brief vacation along the foothills of the slopes of Mount Hermon, and because of Jesus' opportunity to teach His disciples quietly, their faith had once again been shored up.

It was during this time that Jesus began to really unload upon His disciples what would eventually happen in Jerusalem. He began to show, from that time, that He was going to have to go to Jerusalem to face the chief priests (Sadducees), the scribes and Pharisees, government and military leaders, and finally that He would be arrested, tried illegally, horribly beaten, crucified and left to die.

Peter, after his statement of deep devotion and assurance to Jesus that he really felt Jesus was the Messiah the Christ, the very Son of the living God, grabbed Jesus by the shoulders and shook Him, and looking straight into His face, said, "Nonsense, Jesus! Don't talk this way! Nothing like that is ever going to happen to you! We won't let it happen, *I* won't let it happen!"

Jesus turned out of his grasp, and said, "Get behind me, Satan! You are not thinking in a spiritual dimension, about the things of God or heavenly things, but you're only thinking carnally, humanly, physically—the way men think. Peter, you are a trial and sometimes a stumbling block to me! Listen all of you, come here! I want to tell you something! If any man is going to truly come after me and follow me all the way, he is going to have to completely deny himself, and take up his heavy cross daily, and follow me. Anybody who attempts to save his life and place his false material values on this human experience is going to lose his life. Whoever will lose his life for my sake and for my cause and especially for the sake of the message I bring, will save it. What good does it do anyone even if he should gain the wealth of the whole world, and yet forfeit his very being? What could a man ever trade for his human potential of living forever?"

The disciples were all quite struck by these words, and Peter was especially chagrined.

Foreseeing what might occur later on when all the disciples would forsake Him and flee, and especially sensitive to Peter's own weakness in this direction, and foreseeing clearly that Peter himself would deny Him in the future, Jesus gave them all a lesson about being ashamed of Jesus, His message, and His personality.

He continued His sharp rebuke by saying, "I'll tell you this, whoever is ashamed of me in this adulterous and sinful generation, the Son of man will be ashamed of him when He returns to this earth in the glory of His Father and with holy angels accompaying Him.

"And I'll tell you something else and this is the truth, that there are some of you right here standing in front of me who will not die before you have had a dramatic insight into the kingdom of God, and you will see what it is like for the Son of man to come in His kingdom" (vv. 21-28).

Jesus continued to teach, as they went about the small villages of this area of the tetrachy of Herod Philip, and it was six days later that Jesus asked Peter, James and John to accompany Him into an especially high part of the mountain, leaving all of the others behind.

The journey of hard climbing and walking was two full days in duration until they reached a spectacular part of Mount Hermon, with a beautiful vista spreading in all directions. It was here that a fantastic miracle took place, and Peter, James and John all saw one of the most striking visions recorded in the ministry of Jesus. They were allowed to see Jesus' garments take on a glistening white shine that was dazzling.

As they shielded their eyes and squinted at Him, it appeared that He was speaking to two people.

It almost seemed they overheard voices, and Jesus identified them as being Moses and Elijah! They too were wearing garments which appeared to be shimmering and dazzling white, and even the very skin of Jesus was altered so that it appeared translucent, and beautifully shiny.

This probably had happened while Peter, James and John were asleep. They were awakened by the voices, and looked around them to see this bright light shining and discovered the men talking. As they listened, they heard a discussion of Jesus' impending death and many of the events which would yet transpire in Jerusalem, and, as a bright cloud suddenly overshadowed them, a voice came out of the cloud which said, "This is my beloved son in whom I am well pleased, my chosen, listen to Him"! After this booming voice came out of the cloud, the disciples immediately got down on their knees and put their hands and faces to the ground, being terribly afraid. Jesus came and touched each one of them saying, "Come on, get up and don't be afraid any more." They reluctantly looked up and around and saw only Jesus standing there, alone.

On their way back to join the other disciples, they paused for a rest after a number of hours of winding their way along narrow mountain trails. Jesus stopped them and told them, "You be sure you do not tell anyone at all about this vision that you saw, until after the Son of man has risen from the dead"! They nodded assent, but as they were talking during the remaining few days, they continually wondered about what this "rising from the dead" really meant (see Matt. 17:1-9).

But why did Jesus take only these three disciples; why not all of the main twelve?

On several occasions it is obvious Jesus singled out certain disciples for certain crucial lessons, important healings, or as in this case, this remarkable vision.

CHAPTER **13**

Demons

Shop around any bookstore and you can easily be convinced that the general public accepts the fact there is a devil, and demons too. Sometimes, it seems that whole sections of bookstores are given over to materials on witchcraft, demonism, satanism, demon possession, astrology, extraterrestrial phenomena, psychic phenomena, and every other assorted study of the supernatural.

The Bible is filled with many eyewitness accounts about Jesus' direct encounters with Satan himself as well as with many of his demons.

Jesus Christ of Nazareth not only came to this earth in human fleshly form in order to atone for the sins of His masterpiece of creation—humankind—but also to *qualify* for future world rulership.

To do so, He had to overcome the influence and the grip of the present evil world ruler, Satan the Devil. Satan is admitted throughout the pages of the New Testament, to be the "god of this world" (II Cor. 4:4), "the prince of the power of the world" (Eph. 2:2), and "a spirit of disobedience" that now works throughout human society.

Evil supernatural spirits *do exist.*

They are created beings, created out of *spiritual essence* and given spirit life through a divine act of the Creator God. They therefore will exist in perpetuity. The Bible reveals Satan is eternal, and will not be "destroyed" in the sense of human or physical destruction as we might conceive of it, but will apparently live on for all eternity in the "blackness of darkness forever."

As rebellious spirits who formerly were given the responsibility for the harmonious maintenance of the government of God on this earth, Satan and his followers seem to represent fully one-third of the angelic hosts originally created by the divine family of God. The Bible reveals only three names for those of "archangel" status: Lucifer, Michael and Gabriel.

When Jesus was emaciated to the point of near starvation, and had been praying many hours a day and fasting in His determined effort to grow ever closer to God so that He would be able to withstand the strongest imaginable temptations, He actually allowed Satan, who is called the prince of the power of the air, to literally convey His physical body from one place to another through the air. The Bible claims Jesus was actually picked up and taken to a pinnacle of one of the Temple buildings; that He was taken to the top of Mount Hermon, and that the encounter with Satan took place over an area of several hundreds of miles, ending finally "in the wilderness" (probably the Negev) where it had begun.

Throughout His ministry, Jesus continually encountered those who were afflicted, tormented, tortured, "bothered," or even possessed by Satan's demons. (Judas Iscariot allowed himself to be possessed of Satan *himself*; and this brought about Jesus' betrayal, arrest and crucifixion.)

Never once did Jesus "advertise" to the general public that He was coming to that village or this town for the purpose of casting out demons or performing great signs and wonders!

When Jesus' ministry was completed there were no doubt many people still possessed of demons in the land, as there were many who were sick, afflicted, maimed or injured.

From time to time, however, in the course of His ministry, individuals would come to Him seeking special favor and compassion because of a loved one who was grievously tormented by being possessed or influenced by one of these evil spirit beings.

Matthew tells of a time when a man came to him and dropped to his knees before him, saying, "Lord, please have mercy on my boy—because he is acting crazily, and is terribly bothered. Very often, he will fall into a fire, and oftentimes into the water; it seems the spirit that possesses him is trying to kill him. He will have these seizures, falling to the ground, literally foaming at the mouth until he is bruised and cut, and then will go into these long dark periods of time where he just lies there like a vegetable, following the fit. I desperately wanted him cured, so I brought him to your disciples, and they tried very hard to get the demon to leave, but they couldn't cast him out!" (See Matt. 17:14-21; Mark 9:17-29; Luke 9:38-42.)

Jesus sighed deeply, and said aloud to the disciples that were there, "O faithless generation, how long am I going to be with you—how long am I going to put up with you? Bring the boy to me!"

They brought the boy to him, and the instant the spirit saw Jesus, he recognized exactly who He was, and threw the boy into a particularly violent fit. It caused a huge ruckus, and people began running from all directions when they saw the young man suddenly flung on the ground, writhing and moaning, chewing on his tongue and frothing at the mouth.

An uglier scene cannot be imagined than a human being wallowing on the earth in terrible torment. Jesus asked the father, "How long ago did this spirit come into him?" The father answered, "When he was a child."

Jesus looked at the man and said, "If you can believe, all things are possible to a person who can believe!"

The father, terribly distraught and seeing the son on the ground, broke up and with tears in his eyes and trembling voice said, "Lord, I believe, *help me with my unbelief.*"

He did believe that Jesus had the power to heal the boy, but he recognized that the revolting physical spectacle represented pretty powerful testimony in itself, and he knew that there were certain waverings in the back of his mind; certain doubts nagging away at his consciousness, and that he was not near so faithful and strong in his conviction as he should have been.

His statement, while I do not wish to wax maudlin over it, is nevertheless a beautiful example for those who are willing to pray to God today, and who are not ashamed to call out to God and ask, "Help me with my unbelief!"

When Jesus saw the crowds gathering rapidly, He said, "You dumb and deaf spirit, I order you to come out of him, and never enter into him again!"

Even after this command, the spirit yelled loudly through the vehicle of the boy's own voice and threw him into an even more violent fit, and then left the boy lying on the ground as if in a total coma.

A lot of the people began to murmur that he was probably dead, but Jesus reached down and taking the boy by the hand, drew him to his feet—whereupon the boy seemed to stir, looked around wonderingly, and began to flex his muscles and straighten his clothes, brushing the dust and twigs from his garments and from his hair, no doubt wondering what in the world had taken place.

Later, in private, the disciples rather sheepishly wondered why they had not been able to cast the demon out. They were not about to confess this in public, and were no doubt chagrined when the father had said so openly that they had been unsuccessful in previous attempts to exorcise the spirit.

Jesus gently rebuked them by telling them there were some demons that were far more tenacious than others, thus illustrating that demons are individual creatures and spirit beings who have different kinds of personality and different degrees of stubbornness, and strength. He said, "this kind [of violent demon which is able not only to convulse the body, but also to cause the ears to be stopped up and the tongue to be blocked] will not be cast out except through prayer and fasting.

Even the use of the word "lunatic" in the old King James version shows the popular concept of the person who was "struck by the moon" or "moon struck" when he was mentally addled, thus believing the affliction was more from an astrological source, attributing certain mystical powers to the moon, than from a demon. (The Latin *luna* provides the etymological basis for "lunatic" and means "moon.")

On one occasion Jesus was up in the vicinity of Tyre and Sidon, along the Syrophoenician seacoast, when a woman of Canaan, a Greek-speaking native of the old Phoenician area, was pestering his disciples.

Perhaps they were walking along through a marketplace shopping for some food to eat to take along to the coast where they could sit down for a few hours' relaxation and casual conversation, listening to the boom of the surf, and enjoying the bright blue day, when a woman kept asking first one and then the other of the large group of men who were walking among the bazaars and shops of the marketplace, stopping to examine first this and then that article, "Which one is Jesus Christ of Nazareth, the one who is able to do all the healing—I am desperate, you have got to point him out to me, because I need help!"

"What do you want?" one of the disciples asked.

"My daughter is terribly tormented and I believe it is a demon, and I have got to get some help, she is suffering terribly."

Looking back over their shoulders, perhaps Peter, John and Andrew saw the growing mob of people around the loud protestations of the woman, and, knowing Jesus had come into the area for a much needed rest, probably tried to hustle Him along a little faster, saying, "Lord, let's get out of here. I think a crowd is gathering."

Finally, the woman managed to discern who Jesus was and began crying after Him very loudly.

The disciples said, "Lord, send her away, she's been nagging and crying around after us for a long time now. She is embarrassing the daylights out of us, making a public disturbance and causing everyone to think we are crazy."

Perhaps Peter told Him, "Lord don't listen to her, you know you came up here to get a rest, and there is no reason to get involved with these people or there is no telling what is going to happen. Let's wait until we get back down into Galilee before drawing any further attention to ourselves."

The woman said, "I know you. You must be the one who is the Jesus of Nazareth. You have got to help me! I am desperate. My daughter is terribly troubled with a demon!"

Jesus refused to answer the woman. He did not even look at her! (See Matt. 15:21-29, especially v. 23.)

The woman kept insisting, and finally Jesus turned to her and said, "I am sent only to the lost sheep of the House of Israel." This surely reinforced the disciples' attitude that she was nothing but a complete nuisance.

Yet she persisted.

Clutching at His garment she knelt before Him in worship, bowed her head, and said, "Lord, help me!" Jesus looked down at the woman, seeing her shaking shoulders, and said, "It isn't right to take the children's food, and cast it to the dogs!"

This eyewitness account *should* be shocking proof concerning the true character and identity of the real Jesus.

Jesus' refusal to even answer the woman goes squarely against the grain of those who, like Judas, wanted to create "Jesus" in their own image, a "Jesus" who would never refuse anybody anything. This "popular" Jesus would have emptied every graveyard in sight, healed every illness, cast out every demon, and would never have refused a single request for aid from anyone. Yet the real Jesus *did refuse* to even listen to the woman initially, and had it not been for her own tenacity, and especially her faithful answer to a question she was asked, the account in Matthew clearly indicated that Jesus would have stolidly refused to have helped the woman's daughter.

The Bible account says that's *exactly* what He did. First, He refused to answer her *at all*. She had had to fight her way forward through the disciples until she finally discovered which one was Jesus. Then, she had to kneel before Him and beg Him to help her.

Still, He refused.

Rather He gave her the statement that He was come only to the lost sheep of the House of Israel and then gave her the unpleasant analogy of taking the food from the table of the children of the household, and then instead of giving it to them, throwing it to the dogs.

Finally, the woman said, "That's true Lord; still, the dogs are able to eat the crumbs that fall from their master's table."

With a sigh, and knowing that it meant the end of His few days' enjoyable vacation where He was able to bask with his disciples in the anonymity of a strange area, unrecognized, untormented by the crowds, not being maligned, ridiculed or accused by the religious leaders, and be able to thoroughly enjoy their forays into the nearby countryside, their times on the beach together, their pleasant walks through the streets of Sidon and Tyre, Jesus nonetheless relented.

He said, "Why, lady, your faith is really great. It will be unto you exactly as you believe."

Matthew says that the woman's daughter was made whole "from that very hour." The mother, of course, didn't find out until later. When she arrived home, she found that the demon had indeed departed and her daughter was resting comfortably in bed.

No doubt she wasn't surprised at all. However, she did determine, from conversations with others at her home who were with her daughter, that her daughter had become sane and was no longer tormented by the demon within the exact same time frame when her encounter with Jesus had taken place.

Sure enough, that was the end of Jesus' few pleasant days on the Syrophoenician seacoast.

"Jesus departed from thence and came nigh unto the Sea of Galilee and went up into a mountain and sat down there" (Matt. 15:29).

The people living on the heights overlooking the Sea of Galilee had been telling stories for years about a "crazy man" who lived in a graveyard nearby.

When Jesus came into their country, He was to be confronted by this man who was known to be demon-possessed and who had been captured, tied, and even bound in chains several times previously by the local people.

Demons always recognized Christ immediately. As James says, "Thou believest that there is one God [or, "God is one"]; thou doest well: the devils [demons] also believe, and tremble" (James 2:19).

Even though they hated Him, these unseen spirit beings, able to speak through the voices and minds of their human hosts, knew they were totally subject to His divine authority, and that they had to obey Him.

In this case, the man was actually possessed by *many* different demons. "And when he had come out of the boat, there met him out of the tombs a man with an unclean spirit, who lived among the tombs; and no one could bind him any more, even with a chain; for he had often been bound with fetters and chains but the chains he wrenched apart, and the fetters he broke in pieces; and no one had the strength to subdue him.

"Night and day among the tombs and on the mountains he was always crying out, and bruising himself with stones. And when he saw Jesus from afar, he ran and worshiped him; and crying out with a loud voice, he said, What have you to do with me, Jesus, Son of the Most High God? I adjure you by God, do not torment me" (Mk. 5:2-7, RSV).

This was spoken in sarcasm—saucily and contemptuously—even though the demons were forced to admit Christ's true identity. Their sarcastic implication that Jesus would "torment" them was coupled with fear of being sent out of the country, or being commanded to go "out into the deep" (Luke 8:31).

Luke's account shows that Jesus had already commanded the demons to depart, and they began to bargain for some alternate hosts. Maybe it's spooky to think about, but Jesus plainly said, "When the unclean spirit is gone out of a man, he walketh through dry places seeking rest . . ." (Matt. 12:43).

Demons desperately want to possess and inhabit, like a spiritual parasite, either humans or animals.

Jesus asked the man, "What is thy name?" . "And he said, Legion, because many devils [demons] were entered into him. And they besought him that he would not command them to go out into the deep. And there was an herd of many swine feeding on the mountain: and they besought him that he would suffer them to enter into them. And he suffered [allowed] them. Then went the devils [demons] out of the man, and entered into the swine: and the herd ran violently down a steep place into the lake, and were choked" (Luke 8:30-33).

The demons tried to cause the man to destroy himself; and somehow, enough human mind was functioning to keep the man alive, even if in a wretched, bloody, virtually mindless state.

Not so with the pigs. Even though the demons begged Jesus not to send them "into the deep," their violent entry into the pigs caused such a stampede the demons couldn't control their new hosts—and immediately upon the death of the pigs were once again disembodied. (Another theory suggests that some demons want to die; that they are so perverted they are constantly in a suicidal state. Consequently, they try to kill whomever they possess. But, they themselves, being spirit, cannot die.)

The swineherds (pigs were unclean and not fit to eat according to God's laws and, therefore, were avoided by the Israelites) were upset by the loss of their livelihood—and they began spreading the word around the nearby villages.

Soon, some of the local citizens arrived at the scene, to see the well-known crazy man of the graveyard sitting calmly at Jesus' feet, fully clothed and in his right mind.

To these pagan people, Jesus had some mysterious powers of which they were terribly afraid. Instead of rejoicing that the poor demented man was healed, they begged Christ to leave the country. The man who had been demon-possessed asked to join

Christ—but He refused him, saying, "Return to your own house, and show how great things God has done unto you" (vv. 34-39).

Jesus Christ's confrontation with the demonic world projected a meaning far more important even than the helping of suffering human beings. His ability to command the evil demonic spirits, as demonstrated by His casting them out of human minds, witnesses to the fact that He, Jesus, is Lord and Ruler of even the spiritual world.

This once again reinforces the fact that in His prehuman life, the Personality Who became Jesus of Nazareth, the God of the Old Testament, was the very Creator Being who had originally created all the spirit beings. And Jesus' confrontation with demons during His physical life foreshadowed the time when He, as King of kings and Lord of lords, will take control of the entire earth and subject all the demons to His direct control, binding them with Satan for a thousand years.

CHAPTER 14

"That which is born
of the Spirit is Spirit"

Jesus' sensitive awareness of the spiritual dimension was constant, continual, all pervasive and perennial.

That the voices which Jesus and/or others heard on various occasions throughout His life and His ministry had to be the voices of heavenly messengers, or angels, was made very clear by Jesus himself when He said, "And the Father himself which hath sent me hath borne witness of me. Ye have neither *heard his voice at any time*, nor seen his shape" (John 5:37). Earlier, John had said, "No man hath seen God at any time" (John 1:18).

This awareness of the "other dimension" gave Jesus an insight into human nature that was the most fabulous in all of history. He knew that combination of instant appraisal of expression, body language, gestures, mannerisms and speech of individuals to the point that He quite literally could read their minds, and know exactly what they were thinking in any given situation.

The Bible says as much on several occasions. Especially interesting is an account following the first "cleansing of the Temple" when He threw the money changers out (there could have actually been two such occasions, although most people would never discover this in a quick reading of the gospels separately).

Jesus told the money changers, "Get these things out of here—and don't make my Father's house a house of merchandise."

Then some of the religious leaders demanded to know what

in the world He was doing and wanted Him to show "some sign." They, like many a religious fanatic today, were hung up on the idea of "supernatural signs."

On this occasion, He refused to give them an immediate sign. He said instead, "Destroy this temple, and in three days I will raise it up," referring to Christ's own forthcoming three-day-and-three-night period in the tomb. He was saying, very plainly, that some of these leaders were themselves guilty and coconspirators with others who were seeking any possible excuse to put Jesus to death. The obvious inference was that He was referring to His own body, and yet the Jews answered, "Forty-six years it took to build this temple and you say you are going to raise it up again in three days?"

But John said, "He spoke of the temple of His body," and went on to say that when Jesus was risen from the dead His disciples remembered that He had said this to them—and thereby believed all the more the Scriptures and the words which Jesus had said.

Then follows a verse which indicates how thoroughly Jesus understood the attitude of other human beings around Him. When He was in Jerusalem at the Passover, many believed in His name when they saw the miracles which He did. (Just how much "believing on Jesus," or "believing in His name" really means to people was exposed later when the same people took up stones to kill Him. Compare John 8:31 with 8:59.)

"But Jesus did not commit himself unto them because he *knew all men*—and needed not that any should testify of man: for *He knew what was in man*" (John 2:24-25).

Jesus did not "commit Himself unto them," meaning totally reveal who and what He was; nor did He place Himself in a position of compromise or jeopardy, because He knew very thoroughly how quickly those same individuals—who "believed in His name" because they saw miracles—could become so enraged they would become a mob and cry out for His blood. This actually happened on many occasions, until finally they succeeded.

Bearing this in mind, we can read with more understanding Jesus' own words to Nicodemus, who came to Him privately at night and entered into a conversation about Jesus' qualifications.

Though most professing religions cannot seem to accept these plain words without swallowing a tremendous amount of false doctrine, and completely altering the popular concept of the meaning of the words *"born again,"* the meaning is nevertheless plain.

John's account said that Nicodemus was a Pharisee and one of the "rulers of the Jews," who, because he feared his constituency, decided to talk to Jesus at night when there was less likelihood of being recognized.

When he was finally inside Jesus' quarters and began to talk, he admitted that Jesus had come from God, because he said, "No man can do these miracles that you do except that God would be with him."

Jesus earnestly told Nicodemus, "I'm telling you truthfully, that except a man be *born again,* he can't see the Kingdom of God!" (See John 3:3.)

Jesus may have spoken in the Greek language since He was in cosmopolitan Jerusalem; in any event the gospel uses the Greek word *gennao* which has no exact translation equivalent in the English language, since the word *gennao* in the Greek implies the entire process from conception to birth (parturition) and unlike the words in English "beget," "conceive," or "give birth," it can be used of both men and women.

Gennao can include the entire process from conception to birth, and it is clear from Nicodemus' startled response that *he* understood Jesus to mean the process of *being born* like the birth of a cow, an elephant, or a human being.

Nicodemus said, incredulously, "How can a man be born when he is old?" He made himself abundantly clear when he said, "Can he enter the second time into his mother's womb and be born?"

That retort was perhaps a little laden with sarcasm, as well as incredulity. Nicodemus had already compromised his position to the Pharisees by coming to Jesus in the first place—and by coming there after dark he in essence admitted to Jesus that he was afraid of his peers. He then further compromised himself by acknowledging plainly to Jesus that he knew that He, Jesus, had to be a man of God. Having seen Jesus personally on some occasions, and having heard all the rumors, Nicodemus seemingly wanted to be convinced further.

But here was this young leader of these hill-country disciples telling him an utterly impossible thing; and he chose to seemingly hurl the words back in Jesus' face with even a little ridicule or sarcasm thrown in, protesting that no adult human being could ever crawl up into his mother's womb and "be born again"!

Nicodemus plainly understood what Jesus meant as He went on to explain it.

He told Nicodemus "I'm telling you the truth—that except a man be born of water and of the spirit, he cannot enter into the Kingdom of God"!

(Water is used to symbolize several things: (1) it is the symbol of the ceremony of baptism, through which the old sinful self is discarded and a new man emerges in a type of death, burial and resurrection; (2) it also represents the "washing of the water by the word" (Eph. 5:26), showing the cleansing of the human mind and spirit by the imbibing of God's Word; (3) Jesus' own inference on many occasions to the Holy Spirit being typified by "rivers of living water".)

Jesus then said in John 3:6, one of the most important verses in the Bible, *"That which is born of the flesh is flesh; and that which is born of the Spirit is spirit."*

A simple observation—yet crucially foundational to the very essence of God's ultimate purpose for mankind.

You and I, lizards, turtles, rabbits, elephants and oxen were all "born of the flesh," and like all other creatures, you and I are composed of *flesh*—physical matter, a metabolic organism made up of cells, with functioning physiological systems.

We can easily understand that "that which is born of the flesh *is* flesh"—why then is it so difficult for some to understand that "that which is born of the spirit *is spirit*"?

For that's precisely what Jesus meant!

Even as He lived and moved in a "spirit world" consciousness, so He wanted Nicodemus to understand that a complete transformation from one *state of being* into a new and different *state of being* would actually have to take place before a person could inherit the Kingdom of God.

Jesus went on to explain. "Don't be puzzled that I'm telling you that you have to be born again. The wind blows randomly, and though you can hear its sound, you can't tell where it comes from or where it goes to, because you can't see it; that's the way it is with everyone who is born of the spirit!"

Nicodemus was almost equally confounded by Jesus' statement that an individual who was "born of the spirit" would actually *be* a "spirit" (become spirit essence, something extraphysical, extraterrestrial, having its being in the spiritual dimension rather than the physical).

Nicodemus said, "How can these things be?" Jesus then showed Nicodemus that He was using "earthly" examples and analogies, and asked, "If I have told you earthly things, and you don't believe, how can you believe if I tell you of heavenly things? And no man has ascended up to heaven, but He who came down from heaven, even the Son of man which is in heaven."

Surprisingly, many millions have never read these words, and even many who have, still do not understand them. Yet this conversation with Nicodemus leads directly into the "golden text" in John 3:16, so beloved and so oft quoted, "For God so loved the world, that he gave his only begotten Son, that whosoever believeth in him should not perish, but have everlasting life."

Few seem to know that statement is a part of the quotation Jesus spoke that night *to Nicodemus* and that Jesus was earnestly trying to communicate to Nicodemus some essential points about the gospel of the Kingdom; the hope and trust in Jesus as Messiah; the belief in the death, burial and resurrection of Jesus as a sacrifice for the sins of the world; the acceptance of Him as the risen Savior; the necessity to await for one's own personal resurrection at His second coming; and the fact that only when you are really born of the spirit and literally become spirit have you been fully "born again."

It's no wonder that later, Nicodemus, together with Joseph of Arimathaea, lovingly and carefully wrapped the body of Jesus in grave clothes and ointments, and helped lay Him in the tomb following His crucifixion.

Jesus had come from a spirit world, and confidently expected to overcome the flesh and once again to be "born into" that spirit world and return to the bosom of the Father. He was trying to explain to a human being, from His own unique perceptions of that "other dimension," what it would be like to actually become a spirit!

Rather than choosing electricity (for it had not been "invented" yet), nuclear energy, or any other more "modern" space-age analogy, Jesus chose the example of *air* as a physical substance which has weight, occupies space, and is familiar, in order to illustrate to this leader of the Jewish people that when a person is truly *born* of the "spirit," he is to *really* become spirit!

This fact is lost on many religious leaders, who cannot seem to accept the plain statement that Jesus became, following His Resurrection, the "first born among many brethren" (Rom. 8:29) and this "rebirth" was the act of being changed from human to divine, from physical to spiritual, from a fleshly body to a spiritual body.

I have been criticized for allegedly claiming that "Jesus had to be born again." These critics hope to convince anyone who will listen that I make the hideous mistake of claiming Jesus "was a *sinner!*" needed to repent, and therefore "had to be born again."

The confusion is quite understandable since these critics are so thoroughly confused about what being "born again" means. To them it is the *conversion experience*, the time when one repents, and accepts Christ as Savior. Of course, Jesus did *not* have to repent. He *never* sinned, and He surely *never* had to be born again in the sense normally (mis)understood by most religionists!

But Jesus was "born again" in the *biblical* meaning of the term: He was born of the spirit at His Resurrection and became spirit, just as will happen to us at our resurrection.

Cheap tracts, books, articles, letters, and protestations of modern-day religious leaders to the contrary, this Armstrong and his father believe with all of our hearts that Jesus Christ of Nazareth never committed one iota of sin, not even in a subconscious or unconscious thought; and yet we just as firmly believe with all of our being those statements in the opening chapters of John, as well as every other word of the Bible, that Jesus Himself was, in fact, "born again" by a resurrection from the dead, that He quite literally became *spirit*, precisely as He told Nicodemus all humanity could ultimately become.

That's why Jesus is called the "first born" of *many brethren.*

It's no wonder the Apostle Paul talked about the fact that at the last trumpet, at the time of the resurrection of the dead, "We shall all *be changed*," and that Job said he would wait in the grave "until my *change* come"!

CHAPTER 15

The Kingdom Parables

There is as much confusion surrounding the *message* Jesus brought as there is about the personality of the man Himself—which is to say that there is an enormous *lack* of true understanding.

Even the word *gospel* is usually misinterpreted or misunderstood—connoting to most minds something smacking of Bible-belt Christianity peculiar to that portion of the United States so named, or even referring to "gospel music" or any kind of evangelical fire-and-brimstone preaching (often times charismatic and accompanied by glossolalia or speaking in tongues).

To the average layman, the "gospel message" is merely "believe on the Lord Jesus Christ and thou shalt be saved," judging from the billboards, barn roofs, roadside rocks and bumper stickers one may encounter.

But if you were to see the analogy of Jesus as a true being from outer space who, born of the virgin Mary, trod this earth as a human being, but whose mind was totally attuned to the different dimension of the spirit world, who brought a message of a coming government which was to descend from the heavens above to quite literally conquer and rule over this entire earth, perhaps the "gospel" would take on an awesome new significance.

If there had been in some far corner of the world a strange cylindrical capsule which, according to the natives, had come plummeting down in the cockpit of a flying saucer, and which represented a space-age "cockpit voice recorder," perhaps people would honestly believe there had come a message from outer

133

space and an imminent attack from Martians, Venusians, or Plu-
tonians would soon take place.

Come to think of it, considering all of the many ideas about
strange places on the earth (such as Lost Valleys in which primor-
dial creatures still roam, the Bermuda Triangle, et al.), or the
many concepts concerning UFOs and extraterrestrial phenomena,
there are, no doubt, any number of people who believe just such
an attack might some day occur.

If, for the sake of argument or experimentation, Jesus could
be seen for a moment as one who came from outer space, bearing
a message of a future intervention of that spacial power which
would drastically alter the course of human civilizations, the
whole matter of the meaning of the gospel of the kingdom of God
could be cleared up once and for all.

Jesus plainly showed He was speaking of a future world-
ruling government. He was continually talking to His disciples
about positions of responsibility in that yet-future kingdom.

Jesus drew analogy after analogy concerning not only the
kind of Christian personality required to fulfill the final requirement of "enduring to the end" or qualifying to be one "who has
overcome," but also illustrating the extent of the kingdom, the
approximate time of its arrival, its inherent nature, the laws under
which its citizens will be governed, and the celestial and terrestrial
phenomena which will accompany its arrival.

The precepts of religious tradition are so manifold and so
laborious that trying to research the works of critics and scholars
who have researched the works of other critics and scholars
concerning their own concepts of the kingdom of God is not
unlike being lost in a labyrinth of caverns with no lights.

Some think the kingdom of God is a sentiment within a
human being. Others believe it was the ancient Roman Empire
finally "Christianized" by the Roman Catholic Church. Hitler
thought he was going to set it up. Some believe it is here now, but
only "ruling in the hearts of men" in some nebulous spiritual
sense, meaning that collective feeling of "pervasive goodness"
alleged to live in the hearts of Christians universally, be they
Catholic or any of the hundreds of Protestant denominations. (Of
course, according to "mainstream" evangelical theologians, this
would almost certainly exclude any members of the alleged
"sects" no matter how sincere or Bible-believing they may appear

to be, simply because they are not one of the more "respected" or "establishment" theological bodies.)

A simple perusal of what Jesus plainly *said* would clear up the matter for any questing mind once and for all. But it is necessary to go to the *source,* armed with the idea that Jesus, after all, *ought to know.* Since He was the advance emissary of the kingdom of God; the very Son of that God who sent Him to this earth, and the King of the coming kingdom, perhaps, after all, the one human individual more qualified than any other to know just precisely what *is* the kingdom of God is Jesus Christ Himself.

Jesus continually preached about the kingdom of God (Matthew's gospel calls it "kingdom of heaven").

He continually tells what the kingdom of God is like.

On one occasion He said it was like *leaven,* using this example in the 13th chapter of Matthew where leavening is a type of righteousness. This analogy shows the all-pervasiveness of the kingdom which will finally spread over the entirety of the earth at the second coming of Christ.

On another occasion, He talks about the kingdom being of such value it is like a "pearl of great price," or a great treasure a man found in a field which, once he had discovered it, leads him to sell every other earthly possession to purchase that one field.

Of course, every conceivable political organization, military movement, paramilitary group and/or theological organization has tried to utilize the teachings of Jesus to justify its doctrines.

Surprisingly, though most people feel communism and the Bible have nothing in common, the very word "common" appearing as it does, in connection with those believers who "sold their earthly goods in order to have all things common" could indicate an early attempt at communal living. (But put this together with one of Jesus' lessons about the kingdom and see how incongruous such a conclusion will become.)

There are three major parables, all involving money, that Jesus gives about the kingdom of God.

The first parable (in Matthew 20) is about the householder who hired laborers at different times during a day, yet paid them all the same wage at the end of the day.

The second parable (in Matthew 25) is about a man who travels to a far country and entrusts differing sums of money ("talents") to his servants in proportion to their different abilities.

The third parable (in Luke 19) is about a nobleman who went into a far country to receive a kingdom and gave each of his servants one "pound" asking them to gain as much as possible before he returned.

Each of these parables conveys a different aspect of the kingdom of God as its primary point, as well as some interesting secondary points.

Let us now discuss each of these parables in detail, looking for practical information about human business, politics, financial affairs, labor relations, etc., as well as for the primary illustrations regarding the kingdom of God and its judgments.

We find that Jesus' concepts of fairness would not be palatable to the labor unions and blue-collar workers of today.

We begin by quoting each.

Matthew 20:1-16: "For the kingdom of heaven is like unto a man that is an householder, which went out early in the morning to hire labourers into his vineyard. And when he had agreed with the labourers for a penny a day, he sent them into his vineyard. And he went out about the third hour, and saw others standing idle in the marketplace, and said unto them; Go ye also into the vineyard, and whatsoever is right I will give you. And they went their way. Again he went out about the sixth and ninth hour, and did likewise. And about the eleventh hour he went out, and found others standing idle, and saith unto them, Why stand ye here all the day idle? They say unto him, Because no man hath hired us. He saith unto them, Go ye also into the vineyard; and whatsoever is right, that shall ye receive.

"So when even was come, the lord of the vineyard saith unto his steward, Call the labourers, and give them their hire, beginning from the last unto the first. And when they came that were hired about the eleventh hour, they received every man a penny. But when the first came, they supposed that they should have received more; and they likewise received every man a penny. And when they had received it, they murmured against the goodman of the house, saying, These last have wrought but one hour, and thou hast made them equal unto us, which have borne the burden and heat of the day.

"But he answered one of them and said, Friend, I do thee no wrong: didst not thou agree with me for a penny? Take that thine is, and go thy way: I will give unto this last, even as unto thee. Is it not lawful for me to do what I will with mine own? Is thine eye evil, because I am good? So the last shall be first, and the first last: for many be called, but few chosen."

On this occasion, Jesus said the kingdom of heaven is like a man who is a householder or home owner who went out early in the morning to hire laborers for his vineyard.

When he had agreed with the laborers for a penny a day, he sent them into his vineyard to go to work. He went out again about 9:00 A.M. and saw others standing in the marketplace jobless and idle and he said, "You can also go to work in the vineyard, and whatever is right, whatever is a fair wage, I will give you."

The account says these jobless idlers were willing enough and went their way.

Again Jesus said the landowner went out about noon and 3:00 P.M. and did likewise. Again about 5:00 P.M. (or apparently an hour before quitting time) he went out and found others standing and he said to them, "Why do you stand here all day idle?" They answered, "Because no one has given us a job." He said, "Then go to work in my vineyard."

That evening, Jesus said that the master of the property called his foreman or his steward and said, "Call the laborers and pay them their wages, beginning from the last to the first." The account goes on to relate that all the laborers received exactly the same wages—even those who were hired at the very last moment; they all received a "penny" (the old King James English changes the Greek term *denarios* into a comparable sum in 1611). But when the first group came in—those who had been laboring all day long—they supposed they should receive more.

Rumors had by now traversed the line of laborers waiting for their pay that those at the head of the line, who had only worked for one hour, were receiving a full wage. As a result there is no doubt that the ones who had gone to work early in the morning were expecting they would receive three to five times as much.

However, astonishingly, they all received "every man a penny."

Jesus went on to explain that "when they received it, they murmured at the householder, 'These last have spent only an hour working in the field, and yet you made their wages equal to ours even though we have had to bear the burden of the day in this scorching heat."

The landowner then said, "Friend, I do you no harm or wrong: Didn't you agree with me to work for a penny? Take that which is yours, and go your way; for it is my determination to give to the last ones I hired, these that came into my vineyard at the eleventh hour, the same wages as I gave to you. Isn't it lawful for me to do what I want with that which is mine? Or is your eye evil—are you thinking malicious thoughts—because I am good to others?"

Jesus' example here is laden with important principles concerning the kingdom of God; and at the same time would be almost impossible for the average wage-earner in a socialized society to accept.

Jesus went on to conclude in this lesson given to His own disciples as well as to those who were standing, by saying, "The last shall be first and the first last."

The obvious spiritual meaning of the parable is that those who walk this earth today at the eleventh hour of man's experience are like those who labored in the vineyard for only the eleventh hour, while perhaps other individuals who have lived and died long ago could be compared to those who labored longer.

To students of eschatology, the immediate reference would be to the stated sequence of events in biblical prophecy which illustrate Jesus' final, famous statement that the "last shall be first, and the first last."

The miraculous conversion, explained in Revelation 7, of a vast number from nations all over the world called "an innumerable multitude," plus the miraculous conversion at the very last moment prior to Christ's arrival on this earth of 144,000, representing 12,000 from every tribe of Israel except Dan, with a double portion going to Joseph, would obviously be inferred from this story.

It illustrates the fact that while many will have been "enduring unto the end" and earning their righteousness "tried in the fire of tribulation" (Jesus said, "in the world ye shall have tribulation"), and will have been living lives of privation, hardship, persecution, and even martyrdom, there will, nevertheless, be hundreds of thousands of individuals who, within perhaps only a few weeks or even days of their conversion, will be inducted into God's kingdom.

Still, there is more to the analogy since each human individual is limited by his own life span, when he or she was called to God, the vastly differing trials of life, etc.

Therefore, in *any* normal life span, there will be some whose lives will be filled with enormous trials to take place over 70 or more years, while others will be converted in a very short period of time. Both groups will be fully born into God's Family and become eternal spirit beings and Sons of God, and although some will have understood God's truth and will have received the real Jesus Christ of Nazareth as their Savior for only weeks or even days, they will be just as much Sons of God with just as long eternal life.

A more practical application of Jesus' parable of the householder and his practice of hiring idle passersby into his vineyard could cause some problems. Try it out on the unions of today and see what a riot would result!

First, let's understand from this analogy that Jesus ratifies and supports the principle of private ownership of property, of success gained from one's own skills and effort, of the determination to set wages based upon mutually agreeable circumstances, and the right of a landowner to settle individual disputes on his own property, privately, between himself and his laborers.

Furthermore, notwithstanding the obvious prophetic import of this analogy, there is a great deal which can be gleaned about the personality of Jesus as well as the character of the kingdom over which He says He will rule.

Politically, it obviously suggests that the capitalistic system of competition and free enterprise is, as long as man-made governments endure, the best. It indicates, furthermore, that free enterprise will be part of the economic system in the millennial kingdom setup following Christ's second coming.

Old Testament laws and judgments, coupled with New Testament teaching and Jesus' own example, uphold hard, honest work, and remuneration for that work. Also supported and upheld are the private ownership of property and sole control over such property according to law; the enjoyment of the fruits of one's own labors; and the ability to "lay up for one's children," meaning leaving an inheritance to come without governmental restrictions which would deprive legal heirs of the substance of their father's and grandfather's labors.

Notice that there was no standardized wage forced upon employers and employees. Each made a private, separate agreement; each was paid exactly according to the stipulations of his own original agreement.

Can't you imagine the placards and signs of those who would picket a modern-day vineyard where a winemaker had followed such a practice?

Screams of outrage, the hurling of epithets, and the possible destruction of his property would surely result.

The whole concept goes totally against the grain of our own beliefs that it is simply "not fair" for one person to receive exactly the same wage for working for 11 or 12 hours as does another person for working only one hour.

Yet, Jesus makes the point that the vineyard owner had a perfect right to make different agreements with different people. He was in charge. The vineyard was his. The fruit of his own labor was his own home, lands, and crop.

The householder had the perfect right to make private and exclusive agreements with each group of laborers for a specific wage.

The householder was therefore his own employment agency, union, and arbiter in the case of disputes. Will there be unions, collective bargaining, etc., under the rule of Jesus Christ? This parable, at least, suggests not!

It's no wonder the bumper sticker says, "Jesus will make you mad."

Anyone who dares to pick up the unembellished gospels of Matthew, Mark, Luke and John and simply read them as they would any other textbook, though in modern, understandable English, could probably grow quite angry at the personality they discovered there. Especially anyone attempting to apply sociological principles revealed by Jesus Christ to the federalized, socialized, unionized welfare states of this modern world would soon find ample room for conflict.

Jesus' concept of fairness is utterly different from our own; that what a person has earned by his own honest work is perfectly proper in God's sight; that what one can accomplish through one's own acquired skills need not be subjected to the rules and regulations of others. Certainly, this parable of Jesus, while surely primarily applicable to explaining the kingdom of God, upholds some of the fundamental values of the capitalistic system of private ownership and individual initiative.

Matthew 25:14-30:

"For the kingdom of heaven is as a man traveling into a far country, who called his own servants, and delivered unto them his goods. And unto one he gave five talents, to another two, and to another one; to every man according to his several ability; and straightway took his journey. Then he that had received the five talents went and traded with the same, and made them other five talents. And likewise he that had received two, he also gained other two. But he that had received one went and digged in the earth, and hid his lord's money. After a long time the lord of those servants cometh, and reckoneth with them. And so he that had received five talents came and brought other five talents, saying, Lord, thou deliveredst unto me five talents: behold, I have gained beside them five talents more. His lord said unto him, Well done, thou good and faithful servant: thou hast been faithful over a few things, I will make thee ruler over many things: enter thou into the joy of thy lord. He also that had received two talents came and said, Lord, thou deliveredst unto me two talents: behold, I have gained two other talents beside them. His lord said unto him, Well done, good and faithful servant; thou hast been faithful over a few things, I will make thee ruler over many things: enter thou into the joy of thy lord. Then he which had received the one talent came and said, Lord, I knew thee that thou art an hard man, reaping where thou hast not sown, and gathering where thou hast not strawed: And I was afraid, and went and hid thy talent in the earth: lo, there thou has that is thine. His lord answered and said unto him, Thou wicked and slothful servant, thou knewest that I reap where I sowed not, and gather where I have not strawed: Thou oughtest therefore to have put my money to the exchangers, and then at my coming I should have received mine own with usury. Take therefore the talent from him, and give it unto him which hath ten talents. For unto every one that hath shall be given, and he shall have abundance: but from him that hath not shall be taken away even that which he hath. And cast ye the unprofitable servant into outer darkness: there shall be weeping and gnashing of teeth."

This second important parable has been called "the parable of the talents."

A talent was a great deal of money; it represented an ancient Greek unit of weight—the heaviest in use—both for monetary purposes and for commodities. (It is understood that our English-language use of the word "talent" to imply the general capacity for knowledge or ability came about directly as a result of Jesus' use of the term.)

As the heaviest unit of monetary weight, Jesus' example obviously means that the benefactor of the servants was investing a great deal of his own money.

In this case, the property owner appears as a person who is about to move into a different nation, and who calls his own servants and delivers into their hands much of his wealth. Jesus said, "to one he gave five talents, to another two, to another one; to each person, he gave according to his different abilities; and the property owner went on his journey" (paraphrased, and so throughout parable).

According to the analogy, the one who received the five talents went and traded with them, using the principle of making money with money, and increased his bankroll by five talents; this means he achieved a 100 percent rate of return on his investment and eventually accumulated *ten* talents all together.

Though starting with a lesser amount, two talents, and therefore representing by analogy an individual with somewhat less ability or "natural talent," the second servant also bartered with the money he had received and also increased his estate 100 percent, ending up with a total of *four*.

But the individual who began with the least ability was both fearful and security-minded. He was taking no chances. Jesus said, "But he that received the one went away and dug in the earth, and hid his lord's money."

As Jesus related the story, in due time the master returned home and asked for a reckoning.

He said, "And he that received the five talents came and brought five other talents, saying, Lord, you delivered unto me five talents; look—I have gained five more talents!" Jesus said the householder said to him, "Well done, good and faithful servant: you have been faithful over a few things, I will set you over many things; enter into the joy of your Lord."

This scripture has been used in hundreds of sermons to illustrate that ultimate statement which is the most prized to any human individual who is truly and sincerely seeking entry into God's Kingdom. To be told, "Well done, thou good and faithful servant," no matter the degree of inherent, beginning ability, is the most priceless pronouncement any person could ever hear. (Notice, as the account proceeds, that the householder said the identical words to the one who reported he also had doubled his talents—starting with two he ended up with four—even though this man had only 40 percent of the first servant's sum.)

Finally, Jesus said, "And he also that had received the one talent came and said, 'Lord I knew you were a very stern man; reaping where you do not sow and gathering where you did not scatter—taking what is not even yours—and I was afraid; so I went away and hid your sum of money in the earth. Here is what you gave me; I did not lose it.' "

But, Jesus said, the householder said to him, "You wicked and lazy servant—you understood that I am an investor; that I have used my money to increase my fortunes, and not always through my own human physical labor; at the very least, knowing this, you should have invested my money in the bank (for at least they know how to properly reinvest it), so that at my coming I could have received back that which was my own *with interest.*"

Note that, contrary to some superrighteous attitudes, there is no condemnation whatsoever of the wealthy homeowner who first gave private loans and then expected a reckoning, fully planning both to reward and punish accordingly. Notice also the obvious approval given for a financial system of money and banking much as we know it today.

Jesus illustrates that it is *not* wrong for money to "earn interest," notwithstanding the attitudes of some to the contrary; at the same time He gives divine approval to the principle of "making money with money," by providing the capital for would-be entrepreneurs whose successes are then shared by the investor or capitalist.

Again, notice how totally cross-grained is the statement of the individual who, terribly security-minded, thought to hide his money in a can underneath the chicken coop.

Jesus said that the householder said, "Take away the talent from him, and give it to him that has the ten! For to everyone who has shall be given, and he shall have *abundance;* but to him who has not [has earned nothing; increased nothing, overcome not at all] even that which he has [which wasn't his own in the beginning] shall be taken away."

Jesus then gave the antithesis of His statement, "Well done, thou good and faithful servant" spoken to the other two by saying, "Cast out the unprofitable servant into outer darkness; there shall be weeping and gnashing of teeth."

Then follows the account of the "sheep and the goats," with Jesus' statements concerning rewards and punishments in the kingdom—which has led many individuals to assume the judgment scene is like a great courtroom in the sky, with a magic lever automatically plunging the unfortunate "wicked servant" down into an everburning hell, and with a supercatapult poised toward heaven ready to spring the "good and faithful servant" into the beatific vision!

It seems lost on many that judgment is a *process* of separation; that the Bible plainly says, "Judgment must begin today" on the Church of God (those who are converted and baptized), and that the "Great White Throne Judgment" pictured in the Bible takes place over at least one lengthy lifespan, and is as much a "process" as any other lengthy assessment.

Unfortunately, few seem to realize that God's "judgment" is *not* a summary execution of punishments following an angelic indictment over dozens of filthy deeds done in this human life. God's righteous judgment is carried out *throughout* the span of life *following* repentance, the receiving of knowledge of God's truth and the begetting of His Holy Spirit.

You can forget the childish horror story of a harsh God who sits in long robes with white hair and beard, and with a huge gavel in His hand, waiting for that one moment of sadistic delight when He can crash His gavel down on the judgment bench, looking almost through you with piercing, ice-blue eyes, and say, *"Guilty!"*

These two examples—the laborers in the vineyard and the investor of large sums of money—illustrate very clearly that "the kingdom of heaven is like" both of these pragmatic analogies. Therefore, Jesus illustrates the fact that human individuals are judged according to their natural abilities; according to the exact degree of knowledge and understanding they possess, according, to use the vernacular, to "what they did with what they had to do with."

Luke 19:12-27:

"He said therefore, A certain nobleman went into a far country to receive for himself a kingdom, and to return. And he called his ten servants, and delivered them ten pounds, and said unto them, Occupy till I come. But his citizens hated him, and sent a message after him, saying, We will not have this man to reign over us. And it came to pass, that when he was returned, having received the kingdom, then he commanded these servants to be called unto him, to whom he had given the money, that he might know how much every man had gained by trading. Then came the first, saying, Lord, thy pound hath gained ten pounds. And he said unto him, Well, thou good servant: because thou hast been faithful in a very little, have thou authority over ten cities. And the second came, saying, Lord, thy pound hath gained five pounds. And he said likewise to him, Be thou also over five cities. And another came, saying, Lord, behold, here is thy pound, which I have kept laid up in a napkin: For I feared thee, because thou art an austere man: thou takest up that thou layedst not down, and reapest that thou didst not sow. And he saith unto him, Out of thine own mouth will I judge thee, thou wicked servant. Thou knewest that I was an austere man, taking up that I laid not down, and reaping that I did not sow: Wherefore then gavest not thou my money into the bank, that at my coming I might have required mine own with usury? And he said unto them that stood by, Take from him the pound, and give it to him that hath ten pounds. (And they said unto him, Lord, he hath ten pounds.) For I say unto you, That unto every one which hath shall be given; and from him that hath not, even that he hath shall be taken away from him. But those mine enemies, which would not that I should reign over them, bring hither, and slay them before me."

Some consider this final parable concerning money to be perhaps the most important of all.

The reason Jesus gave it was that many of His disciples were making the mistake tens of thousands of others have made all the way down through history, and are still making to some extent today: they thought the kingdom of God would immediately appear (Luke 19:11).

Some 150 years ago, sincere believers thought Napoleon was

the anti-Christ, and surely the kingdom was then coming soon. Others had thought the world could not grow any worse in the days of Martin Luther, and surely Christ had to come soon.

Whether it was during the Crusades, the Hundred Years War, the Black Death in Europe, or the Revolutionary War, there were many in every generation who confidently predicted the end of the world. During World War I, World War II, and during practically every other major global event before and since, there have always been those who claimed the "end" was near.

Supposed "anti-Christs" have included most major military figures of the past, practically every papal occupant, Hitler, Mussolini, various kings, prime ministers, presidents, even bankers and business leaders.

When He gave this parable to His disciples, Jesus was very close to Jerusalem; He was in Jericho, a short distance from the Jordan River valley, and was staying at the home of a very wealthy man named Zacchias who was the chief publican or tax-collector, but apparently a fair one.

Even though Zacchias had the reputation of being "a sinner" (the general populace remained terribly suspicious of, and virtually hated, all publicans), he was able to tell Jesus that he had actually given half his goods to the poor, never wrongfully extracted money from anyone, and would restore fourfold if and when a mistake was made.

Because they were close to Jerusalem, Jesus wanted to straighten the disciples out on the matter of whether He intended to go to Jerusalem in triumphal entry to bring about an earthly "kingdom" at that time.

He told them about a certain nobleman who went away into a far country to receive a kingdom for himself and return.

Jesus said, "He called his ten servants, gave each of them ten pounds, and instructed them each to conduct appropriate business with his investment until he returns" (paraphrased, and so throughout parable).

Jesus is obviously the "certain nobleman" who went away into a far country (the throne of His Father in heaven) and His servants are, by analogy, individual Christians on this earth who, though varying in basic talent and ability as well as individual responsibilities, are each given challenging commissions and responsibilities in this life.

In this case the British pound is the unit of money that is used by the King James translators. Jesus said that the servants were given the money (a pound sterling) to "trade with" until He returned.

The analogy continued, "But his citizens hated him, and sent a message after him, saying, We will not have this man reign over us." (This reminds me of the skid-row "wino" who, peering bleary-eyed through a wine-soaked fog at a would-be benefactor who is peeling off ten dollar bills into his outstretched hand, says, "Look, fella, just what is it you want from me?")

Jesus' analogy said, "And it came to pass, when he returned home, having received the kingdom, that he commanded these servants, to whom he had given the money, to be called to him, that he might know what they had gained by trading. And the first came before him, saying, Lord, your pound has made ten pounds more."

The man had increased 1000 percent! Again, the same wonderful words as were recorded in Matthew's account of the parable of the talents are said. The nobleman proclaimed, "Well done, you good and faithful servant; because you were faithful in a very little, you are to have authority over *ten cities.*"

The second servant came saying, "Your pound, Lord, has made five pounds." And he heard the identical words, though his reward was in exact proportion to the amount of increase, which in this case was 500 percent: "Be also over *five* cities."

Again, the reward was exactly commensurate with the *degree* of increase.

Inevitably, here came "Mr. Cautious" with his debilitating admixture of ignorance of "the system," fear and suspicion of those who were wealthy, and an unhealthy desire for security. All of this resulted in his saying, "Lord, here is your pound which I kept laid up in a napkin because I was afraid of you. I knew you were an austere person; you pick up that which you didn't lay down and reap what you did not sow." (Almost the identical words, though in a slightly different analogy than Jesus used in the parable of the talents.)

Jesus said that the nobleman replied, "Out of your own mouth will I judge you, you wicked servant. You knew that I am an austere man, picking up that which I did not lay down, and reaping that which I did not sow; then why didn't you at least put my money into the bank, so that at my return I could have at least received back what was mine *with interest."*

Jesus said, "Take the pound away from him, and give it to him who already has the ten pounds."

If this sounds strange to us today, it also sounded strange to those in the story Jesus related.

Those standing by, who now had been charged with this unpleasant task, said, "Lord he *already* has ten pounds! He doesn't need another one!"

Jesus answered, "I am telling you that to everyone that *has* shall be given [and the only reason he "has" is because he has diligently overcome, grown, developed, improved and increased; because he has followed every principle of success and endurance including sweating out the hardships which would always exist in such a success story], but from him that *has not* [has not increased, not overcome, not grown or developed at all], even that which he *has* (precious little, if any of his own) shall be taken away from him. But as for these enemies of mine who would not have me rule over them, fetch them here and execute them in my presence."

A rather chilling ending to an otherwise pleasant enough, though difficult to understand, analogy.

Christ is clearly the "young nobleman" who went away into a far country to be crowned king and return. The "citizens" do not embody any members of any particular race; but represent, collectively, that group of individuals who simply cannot stomach the thought of the Lord Jesus Christ as the Boss, Ruler and Master who dares to expect faithful obedience of His followers.

Modern people want to believe in a comfortable household god they can kick into a corner at will; a "Jesus" made in their own image who is a spiritual tranquilizer for their problems.

In this last parable, these people represent those individuals who, by their combination of life-styles, attitudes, approaches and religious precepts, are constantly sending a "message" to Jesus saying, "We are not about to submit to any arbitrary spiritual dictatorship!"

In these three major "money" parables, Jesus is obviously the one who is proportioning the reward: to the laborers in the vineyard, those who were given the heaviest unit of Greek money to invest, or those who were required to invest their pounds.

Human beings, all of whom are different in some way, and who have varying degrees of knowledge, understanding and some skill, are represented by those who began *equally,* yet overcame and developed to different degrees according to their own "several abilities."

The rewards, at the time of Christ's arrival in the power of His kingdom, are plainly stated to be rulership over "cities."

Practically no professing Christian really understands the full scope of these simple truths today. The plain scriptures on the subject, especially Revelation 2:26, 3:21 and 5:10, plainly state that co-rulership with Christ over the nations on earth is the reward of the saved.

What's wrong with this physical earth, after all? That's where all the problems and opportunities are!

CHAPTER 16

Confronting the Pharisees
and Sadducees

Spiritual awareness brings spiritual comparisons.

The Pharisees and Sadducees were rival religious organizations. Though normally deeply divided, they could find temporary alliance in their hatred of Jesus. His popularity with the common folk—made poignantly obvious by their own unpopularity—and the sensational size and growing scope of His ministry made Jesus a significant rival for the affections and admirations of the people.

These religious leaders, like most religious leaders in all religious groups from time immemorial, inspired more superstitious fear than sincere loyalty in their followers.

The religious situation in first-century Palestine was not that different from the way it is today.

Most people were not members of a religious group. The average Jew back then was like the average American, Briton, German, Frenchman now. He probably had a certain form of piety, attended the temple very occasionally at one of the festivals, and perhaps even tithed in a good year. But the average Jew was not a Pharisee, Sadducee, or Essene any more than the average Israeli is ultra-Orthodox.

This point becomes obvious when we compare the population of the country with the membership in the different religious groups.

A conservative estimate of the population of Palestine at the time is about half a million. According to Josephus there were approximately 4,000 Essenes for one period and about 6,000 Pharisees for another. We have no figures for the Sadducees, but

being a priestly group they probably had fewer. If we are generous, we still come up with probably quite a few short of 20,000 for
all the religious groups put together. This would make only about
one out of 25 a member of a formal religious organization. This is
conservative; it could have easily been one out of 30 or 40. This
means only about 4 percent *or less* of the population had any
specific affiliation with a religious group.

The average Jew was what later rabbinic literature referred to
rather disparagingly as an *am ha'arets,* "person of the land." He
was considered to have a certain small amount of religious piety
or scruples without being overbothered with religion. He had
some definite views about certain aspects of religion so long as it
didn't affect how he lived. After all, it wasn't easy to make a living
and, like all peoples at all times, a short weight or a little water in
the wine was easily overlooked. Of course, many were very honest
and conscientious individuals, yet still did not claim any religious
affiliation.

A certain amount of respect was paid to the priests and the
religious teachers. But this respect was no different from that of
the average layman today. They told jokes about the Pharisee
with the bloody nose because he so averted his eyes from looking
at an attractive girl that he didn't see the wall until too late. They
thought it was funny when the young bull got away and had to be
wrestled down by the priests in their robes before they could
sacrifice it. And the many street-corner preachers were considered
as much wild-eyed fanatics as they are today.

It has been a standard myth that the Pharisees were an
overwhelmingly dominant force in Palestine in Jesus' time. This
erroneous view is based on late rabbinic literature, but recent
studies—especially those by the well-known scholar Jacob Neusner—have shown that the situation was quite different after the
destruction of Jerusalem in A.D. 70 from what it was before.
Rabbinic Judaism was a post-A.D. 70 phenomenon which descended directly from the Pharisees and therefore tended to exaggerate their historical significance.

Judaism before A.D. 70 was much more pluralistic than is
commonly believed, with a variety of different groups and sects,
many of which disappeared in the Jewish war against the Romans.

In the decades following the destruction of Jerusalem, rabbinic Judaism was hammered out and became the dominant religious influence on Jews (though again the average Jew was still the *am ha'arets* who basically ignored the detailed regulations proclaimed by the rabbis). Later rabbinic Judaism was Torah centered. Study of the law and legal disputations were common activities of the rabbis and their disciples.

But Pharisaism differed in many ways from the later rabbinic Judaism. The Pharisees were not a group formed to study the Torah. They were an organization of laymen who agreed to observe certain *purity* laws so that they could imitate the priests in the temple.

In other words they tried to make their home into a model of the temple and their table into a model of the altar. They were a *table fellowship* group. Even though they were concerned about such things as Sabbath observance, the bulk of their concern was with laws relating to eating.

They washed pots and pans because that was necessary for ritual purity. They criticized the disciples of Jesus for eating with "unwashed" hands (Mark 7) because the disciples had not followed the purity regulations (regulations nowhere required in the Old Testament *except* for the priests in the temple). They were scrupulous about tithing, not because they were concerned about the priests, but because they could not eat something unless it had been properly tithed!

Naturally, this was so much nonsense to the average Jew. What was to be gained by imitating the temple priests? Even the priests did not observe these purity laws outside the temple in their own homes. It is not hard to see why there were only 6,000 members or so of this superstrict table fellowship group. One had to conduct his life with his mind constantly on minute regulations of ritual purity with no purpose other than the desire to be able to sit down at a table from which non-Pharisees were excluded.

The Sadducees were a group associated mainly with the priests (Acts 4:1). Their activities centered mainly around the temple, and this is why their influence on Judaism was totally finished when the temple was destroyed.

The main appeal of the Sadducees was to the upper classes. Consequently, they had less popular appeal than the Pharisees and others.

Yet many of the professional scribes were Sadducees. The scribes were a professional class roughly corresponding to the civil servant or bureaucrat of today. They were trained in the law (the term "scribe" is basically interchangeable with "lawyer") and the literature of the Jews. They held various administrative and educational posts. They were respected much as are the legal and medical professions today. So when Jesus said, "The scribes and Pharisees sit in Moses' seat," he was recognizing their prestige and authority as teachers. (But then He went on to condemn many of their practices and examples!—Matt. 23).

The third Judaic sect of the first century—the Essenes—is not mentioned in the New Testament. Most scholars feel the Qumran community—immortalized and popularized by the Dead Sea Scrolls—was a leading Essene center. Other writers indicate that Essenes also lived in various villages and cities throughout Palestine. They were very much a minor group, though, and probably kept somewhat separate because of their exclusivist attitudes.

The popular press has long engaged in speculation about Jesus being an Essene or associated with the Qumran community. Such absurdities have been almost universally rejected by Qumran specialists. There is no evidence that Jesus had anything to do with the Essenes and Qumran. As already mentioned, the Essenes are not even mentioned once in the entire New Testament.

The Pharisees in Jesus' time, obsessed with their own rules and traditions of religious ritual, were no better and no worse than any other religious group of any other time. It is a basic psychological trait of human beings that, as one becomes more convinced of his own spiritual purity, especially if it can be expressed through physical means, he simultaneously becomes less tolerant of others. In a word, he becomes *self*-righteous.

Self-righteousness is the antithesis of Godly righteousness. It can in fact become the most insidious of sins because it is the most difficult to recognize. It is not particularly hard for a prostitute to know what she is, or for a murderer, drunk or thief to know what he is. Perhaps it becomes progressively more troublesome for a liar and a covetous person to recognize his sins. But the self-righteous person, one who *thinks* that he has not committed any sins, *"knows"* he is righteous and he *"knows"* that he knows it, is in the gravest danger of insidious self-delusion and ultimate self-destruction.

Whatever is required, the self-righteous person *thinks* he does; whatever is forbidden, he *thinks* he eschews. Yet God states that *"all have sinned"* (Rom. 3:23), and that the personal recognition of one's own sinful nature, mind and heart is the *essential* first step in the conversion/salvation process. For the prostitute or murderer it can be easy, but for the self-righteous person this can be an intolerable stumbling block. It's no wonder that Jesus Christ reserved His fiercest attacks for the self-righteous religious leaders, who epitomized the attitude and approach of *all* religious leaders of *all* religions from all times (and do not represent just one persecuted race).

The Pharisees personified the concepts of spiritual rank, show, pecking order, and degree of sanctimoniousness. How all such self-righteous characters know how to hate! (Satan himself must become at least a little jealous over their vituperative musings; their filthy, lying, carnal-minded plots.)

A "righteous posture" is always center stage; all the lights are on—it's opening night, and all the critics are out there. Give it your best!

Religious folk have always taken themselves altogether too seriously, and the Pharisees were no different. But they, like all other people of past generations, are dead. *They* were religious fanatics. *They* were spiritually proud, while being morally corrupt. *They* were hypocrites. *They* persecuted Jesus and finally succeeded in killing Him.

But the "Jews" did *not!*

Oh, the Pharisees were Jews, all right, but then, *so were most if not all of the disciples* and *early apostles, and so were the great majority of all the converts during the early days of the church!*

And, to once again state the obvious, *so was Jesus Christ Himself.*

Consequently, to capitalize on and exploit the fact that the Jewish religious leaders were involved in the crucifixion and murder of Jesus in order to support even implicitly an anti-Semitic attitude is the height of historical absurdity, ludicrous in the extreme, and only serves to broadcast one's own ignorance. In fact, surely a far greater case could be made for a "pro-Semitic" attitude, based on the clear New Testament testimony that the leading apostles and disciples and the great majority of the early church in Judea, as well as the core members of the churches even in the Gentile world, were all Jewish!

An ultimate contradiction is to posture that one is wearing the cloak of "Christianity" (which says to resist not evil; turn the other cheek; pray for—and even love—your enemies) in order to *persecute* the Jews or, for that matter, any other group, creed, race, organization or individual).

After the miracles of the loaves and the fishes, a continual furor began in the towns and villages as leading Pharisees from Jerusalem began stirring up the crowds. The confrontation between these religious leaders and Jesus was easy to foretell, and His denunciation of them as "hypocrites," who honored Him with their lips but whose heart was far from Him, was stinging. Jesus said, "Howbeit in vain do they worship me, teaching for doctrines the commandments of men"—and thoroughly scolded them for their man-made traditions which He said made the Word of God of no effect.

Many falsely assume the religion of the Pharisees was the Old Testament religion, the religion of Moses.

No way. Even though Jesus said that they sat "in Moses' seat," recognizing their inheritance of the *authority* of Moses (in administering the law), He warned against the doctrine of the Pharisees, which He specifically called their "leaven."

The added corruptions; the repressive, restrictive, hyper-religious *customs* and *traditions* of these men were what Jesus attacked. They had made the Word of God, a *way of life* spelled out in the scriptures, of "no effect" by their *traditions*.

After all, very few even today figure their religion is any good to them if they can understand it, do they? Isn't it much better if it borders on the mysterious, the unknown, the obscure? Isn't it more effective to gaze in wonderment at bizarre, detailed, carefully arranged *rituals* performed by some person dressed in obvious "religious" garb, and vaguely "guess" this must be pleasing to some sort of divine being, than it is to observe and appreciate the practical, day-to-day *way of life* that God lays down in His Word?

The Pharisees decided it was holy to fast twice each week, as if on a righteously rigorous schedule. (You'd be a rich man if you could have a dollar for every day those pretending religious fanatics *failed* to *really* fast "twice in the week," even though they openly bragged about it.)

Jesus was well aware of the story about the Pharisee and the publican. He said, "Two men went up into the temple to pray; the one a Pharisee, and the other a publican. The Pharisee stood and prayed thus with himself, God, I thank thee, that I am not as other men are, extortioners, unjust, adulterers, or even as this publican. I fast twice in the week, I give tithes of all that I possess. And the publican, standing afar off, would not lift up so much as his eyes unto heaven, but smote upon his breast, saying, God be merciful to me a sinner. I tell you, this man went down to his house justified rather than the other: for every one that exalteth himself shall be abased; and he that humbleth himself shall be exalted" (Luke 18:10-14).

Here was the *attitude* of the Pharisees again: That of spiritual pride, vanity, ego, self-importance and hypocrisy! The publican (normally suspected to be a cheat by the illiterate masses) *knew* what he was, and was repenting of it. The Pharisee was only interested in what the *publican* was, and had absolutely no doubt of his own "righteousness." He could not admit that he had any of his own sins, and bragged he was entirely righteous.

Unfortunately, the "leaven" of the Pharisees is very much alive and active in too many religious folk. Spiritual pride, vanity, pretense, hypocrisy—these are blatantly obvious in many a posing, pompous, pseudo-spiritual person today.

Jesus told of the martyrdom of men of God in times past, and then indicted the Pharisees because they admitted to being *descendants* of those who had done such things.

The implication of Christ's words are clear: if the *Pharisees had lived during those earlier days, they would have perpetrated the same crimes!* Not only this, but Jesus also implied that they were plotting His own murder, and that some of them would remain alive to be involved, no doubt, in the murder of James, Zebedee's son; of Steven; and the attempts on the life of Paul!

There were those, Jesus said, who "worshipped" Him. That is, they "revered" and "adored" His person; they "believed on Him"! But He said, *"in vain do they worship me,* teaching for doctrines the commandments of men" (Matt. 15:9).

Worship?

How many who are professing Christians believe that today? After all, the very essence of "salvation" according to the way many look at it is to accept Christ as personal Savior, to *believe* on Him; to admit you are a sinner, and to *worship Jesus!*

"If you love the Lord, *honk!*" says the bumper sticker. The guy in the automobile can look pityingly on each unsaved sinner who passes without honking—because he thinks "loving the Lord" is the key to salvation.

"If you *believe*—you shall be saved!" is the popular belief. But the *demons* believe, James said—and demons aren't "saved." Jesus said belief can flower into *worship,* and still be done *in vain.*

To those who believe "on" Jesus—how about *believing what Jesus said?* It's possible to worship even the *real* Jesus, and still do it in vain—remember, those Pharisees and others were facing the *real Jesus* and blew it, where millions today only fantasize about a *fake* Jesus, a *counterfeit,* and so start off worse than the Pharisees!

Jesus could become very *angry* at the Pharisees, but His anger was not self-oriented; He wasn't mad because His own ego was bruised.

Jesus *directed* His anger through an outgoing spirit of *love,* coupled with grief toward human beings who were so bigoted and pig-headed they could not see the simple truths before their eyes. For example, read Mark's account of Jesus' healing of the man with the withered hand.

"Again he entered the synagogue, and a man was there who had a withered hand. And they watched him, to see whether he would heal on the Sabbath, so that they might accuse him" (Mark 3:1-2, RSV).

Notice, there was no doubt in these religious leaders' minds *whether* Jesus had the power to heal—they *knew* He had that power!

So why didn't they rejoice? As religious leaders whose primary job was to "feed the flock," and to be as gentle shepherds over the "little people" in their charge, why should they not have been deeply grateful for the miraculous power that Jesus exercised which brought such blessed relief from physical aches and pains, from blindness, deafness, dumbness, epilepsy, leprosy and all the other hideous diseases which afflicted a sick and poverty-stricken generation?

Strangely, since these murder-plotting Pharisees postured themselves to be religious leaders and the proprietors of the Holy Scriptures, they should have at least had full knowledge of the terrible penalties God would impose on any such individuals who were guilty of forming various clandestine alliances with other religious and philosophical organizations with which they normally would have had no relationship whatsoever.

Jesus was in the synagogue, and these religious leaders watched Him to see whether He would heal *on the Sabbath* so they might accuse Him!

Thus, Jesus was being baited. They almost expected, indeed *hoped and prayed,* that Jesus *would* heal on the Sabbath in order that they might have what they felt was tangible evidence that Jesus had done something wrong! Just a few verses earlier, the Pharisees had tried to accuse Jesus because His disciples were plucking ears of grain and eating them on the Sabbath day, and Jesus had to tell them of how David ate the shewbread, and remind them that the Sabbath was not a yoke of bondage and a burden, but "the Sabbath was made for man" not "man for the Sabbath; so the Son of man is Lord even of the Sabbath." (Strange, isn't the Sabbath the only day which is truly sanctified by God in the Bible?)

Jesus looked about Him and spied the man with the withered hand and said, "Come here." Then He said to the Pharisees, "Is it lawful on the Sabbath to do good or to harm, to save life or to kill?"

Again, that ringing voice of authority and that level gaze of conviction. combined with the logic of those words, were simply too much for these hypocritical charlatans. They simply had to shut their mouths in the face of such piercing logic. They couldn't answer either way. If they said, "Yes, it is lawful to do good," they would give full approval for Jesus' actions of healing on the Sabbath. If they said it was lawful to do harm, then this would be an obvious flagrant violation of the biblical principles for which they stood.

"And He looked around at them with anger."

That's right—Jesus was *mad.* After all, doesn't the Bible say, "Be ye angry and sin not"? (Eph. 4:26).

The Spirit of God helps an individual *control* and *direct* these emotions, so that they are not motivated from vanity and ego.

Jesus' anger had nothing to do with the relationship between *Himself* and the Pharisees! He was not "mad at them" in the way you or I might have been! Actually, He *loved them*—hoped the best for them, wanted to see as many of them as possible come to themselves and repent (though He knew according to the prophecies of the Old Testament this was exceedingly unlikely); Jesus expressed *outgoing concern* for them, all the while plainly calling the truth "true," labeling their attitudes and woeful lack of character for precisely what it was!

The Bible says, "And he looked around at them with anger, grieved at their hardness of heart, and said to the man, Stretch out your hand. He stretched it out, and his hand was restored" (Mark 3:5).

Notice, the Pharisees *saw* one of the most incredible miracles in all of history! It defied anything any human eye had ever seen before! They actually *saw* an emaciated, withered, shrunken limb, grotesque in its gnarled condition, extended out toward Jesus to gradually swell to individual fingers and assume full size with a normal, healthy skin color, able to grasp and reach and be utilized with the full capability of the marvelous human hand.

Instead of congratulating the man, receiving him joyously, clapping him on the back, and having the rewarding experiences of gathering around to give a good honest shake and grip to that newly restored hand, then turning to congratulate Jesus and thank Him for having so freed and healed a member of their own congregation, "the Pharisees went out, and immediately held counsel with the Herodians against him, how to destroy him."

Such is the shameful account of religious bigotry. Unfortunately, such bigotry is alive and well in many a human heart to this day!

The Sadducees and Pharisees, as true to form as all competing religious groups, were constantly battling one another.

Religious arguments on all matters great and small constantly seesawed back and forth between them. They no doubt allowed their bitter hatred for each other to occasionally overwhelm their hatred for Jesus, and this record has been preserved as a witness to the abject futility of religious bickering for all generations down through history.

The occasion of Jesus' last public teaching in Jerusalem was particularly meaningful. The ruling Sanhedrin had formally challenged Jesus' authority, demanding to know whether He was an accredited teacher or not. Mark, Matthew and Luke all record the challenge of the Jewish leader who asks Jesus, "Just who in the world gave you the authority to do these things here in the temple, teaching the people and saying the things you are saying—where does your authority come from?

Jesus said, "I will ask you one question—and if you can give me a straight answer, then I'll tell you the source of my authority.

"The baptism of John, did it come from heaven, or originate with men? Answer me!"

Dozens of people heard this rapid-fire exchange in the temple. Nobody ever talked that way to the esteemed religious leaders. What were they going to do! In a hastily huddled caucus, the Sanhedrin reasoned among themselves.

In hurried and nervous whispers, and with the curious gaze of their constituents fixed on the backs of their heads, they came to the awfully embarrassing conclusion that they were stuck: if they were to admit the baptism of John had come from a heavenly source, they knew Jesus' answer would have probably been, "Then why didn't you believe him?"

On the other hand, if they should claim John's ministry and baptismal practice came from only a human source, the rulers of the Sandhedrin "feared the people"; because everyone surely held "John to be a prophet."

One of their number, chosen to be the spokesman, finally gathered himself to his full height, arrayed in his robes and great dignity, and gave Jesus their studied opinion.

Perhaps he put it this way, "The full question of John's authority has not yet been formally brought before the Sanhedrin, and such an egregiously complex question, considering its enormous implications and ramifications, would demand thorough consideration. We would therefore require a great deal of further study and deliberation before we could ever attempt to answer such an impromptu matter: consequently, we would wish to make no comment on John's ministry and baptism at this time." (Or he might have just said, "We don't know!")

Jesus' conclusive statement twisted their consternation into knots, "Since you obviously can't answer me, neither will I answer you by what authority I am doing all these things."

Then followed three keenly incisive—and obvious—parables in which Jesus exposed the hypocritical leadership of the religious leaders: the parable of the two sons, the parable of the wicked husbandman, and the parable of the marriage feast for the king's son.

Matthew's account begins with the parable of the man who had two sons (see Matt. 21:28-46).

Jesus said, "What do you think about this? There was a man who had two boys and he came to the first and said, 'Son, I want you to go to work today in my vineyard,' and the boy said, 'I won't do it.' " But afterward he repented and went to work.

The father came to the second lad and said the same thing. And the boy answered, "Yes, sir, I am going," but he didn't go.

"Which of the two did the will of his father?" Jesus asked the leaders of the Sanhedrin.

They had to admit the obvious, which was "the first."

Then Jesus, speaking directly to their leaders, in the audible presence of dozens upon dozens of people in the immediate environment of the temple, said, "I'm telling you the truth: petty crooks and whores will enter into the kingdom of God before you—because John came to you preaching and following the right way of the law of God, and you didn't believe him!

"But the petty crooks and harlots of our society believed him! When you saw that happen, you still didn't repent. Even when you saw John's ministry changing human lives, you never opened your mind so that you could believe John's preaching.

"But, before you leave, let me give you another parable [Matthew, Mark and Luke all record it]: There was a man, a homeowner, who had planted a vineyard and had grown a protective hedge around it; he also had set up a wine press and built a tower for the production of wine. He then became an absentee landlord as he was forced to go away to another country.

"When the harvest time was near, he sent some of his servants to collect the profits from his vineyard. But the renters willfully and maliciously ambushed his servants—beat one of them, murdered another, and stoned a third. The injured ones came back to the landowner, and so he sent another servant, only to find that they did the same thing to him. They injured him badly, and threw him out.

"Seeing that he was totally failing by sending his servants, the landowner decided to send his own son, reasoning that they would revere him because after all, 'he is from my own family.' But when the renters saw the son, they conspired among themselves saying, 'Now this is our real opportunity: he is the heir of the property—let's kill him, take away his inheritance and claim it for

our own!' So they captured the son, threw him out of the vineyard, and killed him in a nearby lot."

Jesus then turned to the leader of the Sanhedrin and asked,
"When the lord of the vineyard shall return, what do you think he
will do to those renters of his property!"

The leaders answered, "No doubt he will utterly destroy such
miserable creatures, and turn around and find some new renters
who would give him the profits which are rightfully his when they
are due."

They had trapped themselves. They could give no other
logical answer in front of the crowd, despite their refusal to
answer concerning John's baptism.

Jesus then asked, "Why, have you never read in the scriptures" (an acid-laden question, for they were supposed to be the
most highly skilled in this business claiming to have known every
minute aspect and understanding), "the stone which the builders
rejected, that same stone is made the chief cornerstone. This was
the doing of the Lord, and it is wonderful in our eyes"? (See
Psalm 118:22, 23.)

"Therefore, I'm telling you, the kingdom of God is going to
be taken away from you, and will be given to a nation bringing
forth the fruits thereof. And anyone who falls on that chief
cornerstone is going to be smashed to pieces. But whoever it shall
fall upon, will be scattered as dust." (A veiled reference to Isa.
8:14-15.)

The chief priests and Pharisees did not need to be either
especially learned or bright to perceive that Jesus was talking
about them, and so in another whispered conspiracy, they frantically tried to find some method whereby they could arrest him.
But the crowd of excited, enthusiastic people milling all around
thought Jesus was a prophet, and the religious leaders were smart
enough to realize they were asking for big trouble—a potential riot
in an occupied city is inviting disaster—if they continued with
their plan to physically abuse Jesus. Their time would come; but
just now they feared the crowd—knowing that such a precipitous
act would be illegal. They felt totally thwarted and frustrated;
Jesus' popularity with the crowd, who obviously believed He was
a spiritual leader and a prophet, was growing.

Matthew's gospel then includes the next parable where Jesus
explained that the kingdom of heaven was "likened unto" a

certain king who decided to throw a big wedding feast for his son who was the prince, and so sent all of his servants out to call the invited guests to the marriage.

Unfortunately, and for whatever reason, all of those who had received formal announcements to the wedding refused to come. So the king sent other servants out telling those who had been invited, "Look, the feast is all ready, all the preparations are made, much hard work has been done, all the special foods and meats are here, the wines and drinks are the finest and have taken much time to order; the rooms are decorated and the musicians have been hired to entertain you—so won't you please come to the marriage feast for my son?"

But the guests ridiculed the king, his son, the marriage, the feast and especially the invitation. The last, in fact, became a common joke. Nobody would have shown up now, so they all scattered. One went to his own farm, another back to his business, while the remainder of them manhandled the servants, bruised and injured some, even murdering others.

When word filtered back to the king, he was furious. "Angry" was in fact much too calm a word to describe his feelings. He wasted little time in sending his military units to destroy the murderers, and burn their city to the ground.

Then the king got back to the matter of the feast; he told some other servants, "The wedding is ready and those whom I had invited earlier have proved unworthy to attend, so I want you to go out into the county roads and highways and collect as many people as you can find—I don't care who they are—and tell them that I want them to come to my son's wedding feast."

So the servants went out into all the towns, villages, highways and byways, gathering together as many as they could find, without respect to economic standing, social status or personal reputation; bad and good, the servants were not to discriminate or make value judgments as to who should, or should not, come to the king's feast. All were now to be invited, and finally the palace banquet table was filled with guests.

When the king entered and looked them over, he noticed one man who had not bothered to dress up in wedding attire. Apparently he did not appreciate or respect the magnificent opportunity he was being given.

The king then went up to him and asked him, "Friend, how

is it that you came in here not having a wedding garment on?"

The man was struck speechless; he couldn't answer. The king turned to his servants and said, "Tie him up hand and foot and cast him out into outer darkness, for there shall be weeping and gnashing of teeth—because many are called, or invited, but only very few are *chosen!*" (Matt. 22:1-14).

The meaning of this parable was transparent to all who heard it. There was no doubt that the religious leaders were the first guests who had scornfully rejected their own king's generous invitation. Their reward was swift.

But the story had another point, a final twist. One of the guests who, though not deserving it, was fortunate enough to receive such a priceless opportunity did not appreciate it. His end was the bitterest of all—he was so close, yet so far.

The Herodians and the Pharisees had conspired together to load each of Jesus' audience with a handful of spies who pretended they were believers, applauding Jesus' words, nodding and looking at Him with bright-eyed agreement, in order to trap Him in some error of speech, some illegal activity or some seditious plot. The whole idea was to be able to bring about Jesus' arrest and turn Him over to the authority of the governor (Luke 20:20).

Finally, this mixed group of Pharisees and Herodians had an opportunity to ask Him a question—so they gave their best shot: They wanted to force Jesus into a direct conflict with the Roman authorities. They sought to get Jesus to condemn Himself.

To the question they maliciously concocted, Jesus dared not give either a "yes" or a "no" answer. "Master [Teacher or Rabbi], we know that you are true and what you teach is true, that you do not seem to be a respecter of persons or play any favorites among those of different social standing, and that you are indeed teaching the way of God—so we would really appreciate it if you would answer this question.

"Is it lawful to pay Caesar tribute money or not?" (In other words, "Why should we have to pay taxes to this pagan, heathen warrior?")

Jesus knew their collusion; He could immediately sense their vicious, sneaky maneuver. Jesus knew they were a pack of hypocrites (Mark 12:15) and bluntly called it straight: "Why are you trying to tempt me, you pack of hypocrites? Show me a penny."

Someone dug into the fold of his robe and produced a

"penny" (*denarion* in the Greek language, which was a coin of considerably more value than a "penny" of today.) Then Jesus, understanding how they would respond no matter which way He answered, said, "Whose image and superscription is on the coin?" They answered, "Caesar's," and He said, "Fine, since you say it is Caesar's, why don't you give it to him. Since Caesar's picture is on it, it's his coin. So you should give to Caesar the things which are Caesar's, and you should likewise give to God the things which are God's!"

Everyone absolutely marveled at Jesus' deft ability to turn a dangerous and potential trap—He could have been arrested—into such a beautiful example. And the words of this powerful verse, which have been immortalized in the King James English, are worth repeating, "Render therefore unto Caesar the things which be Caesar's, and unto God the things which be God's" (see Matt. 22:16-22).

There was no other possible answer. If Jesus had played it "safe" and said, "Yes, it is lawful to pay tribute," the religious leaders would have no doubt accused Him of rejecting all of the common hopes and teachings of the future kingdom of Israel, the total sanctity of the law of Moses plus the authority of the Sanhedrin, and claimed that He was giving public recognition to a Gentile government, approving its domineering occupation of their homeland, and indeed almost paying homage and obeisance to a pagan idol.

If Jesus had answered, "No," they could have accused Him of being an illegal insurrectionist who was trying to bring about an uprising against the Roman state: they could have reported Him to the governor, who had had his hands full with similar situations over the past several years, as one false teacher after another had tried to incite followers into bringing about a revolution and wresting the rich kingdom of Judea away from the Roman armies.

Later, first the Sadducees and then the Pharisees were again totally silenced when they brought their favorite trick questions to Jesus.

The Sadducees did not believe in the resurrection of the dead, and so, in order to confuse the Pharisees' dogmatic assertion of this doctrine, contrived an absurdly elaborate situation involving seven marriages to the same woman.

This never failed to befuddle and silence the Pharisees, much to the Sadducees delight. They took the same question to Jesus. "Rabbi, Moses writes to us that if a man's brother dies and leaves a wife behind him, yet leaves no child, that it is the obligation of his brother to marry his widowed wife, and to raise up seed unto his brother that their name be preserved in Israel. Now it so happens that there were seven brothers we know about, and the first married, then died, having left no child. The second son recognized his obligation and married his dead brother's wife, and they didn't have any children, and he finally died. The third did the same thing, and finally all of them did the same thing and married the woman, clear up to the seventh, all of the brothers successively dying, yet no one ever managing to have a child. Finally, still childless, the woman also died. The question is, In the resurrection whose wife will she be, because all seven had her to wife?"

It was important for the sake of this story that the Sadducees explain that each of the seven successive brothers had no children, because if any child had been produced, it would have meant there was no further obligation for the next brother, even upon the death of the elder one, to marry the woman—for an heir would be living, and the name would be preserved.

The Pharisees habitually stumbled all over themselves in their ultralegalistic approach to the Scriptures, trying to ask all sorts of counterquestions: they probably tried to find out how old the parties were, how long they lived together, whether or not their marriage was successful, whether there might have been some "unseemly thing" or other problem which could have nulli-fied one or the other of the seven marriages, etc. But the whole futile exercise always ended up in hopeless confusion, with no one actually able to give the Sadducees a satisfactory answer.

Jesus turned this trick question into a positive lesson, not only against their hypocrisy, but as an opportunity to teach the truth about the nature of the Resurrection, which millions of people still refuse to believe today.

He said, "It's obvious you are making a big mistake, and don't even know the scriptures, or the power of God. Because when people rise from the dead, they will neither marry nor give away a daughter or son in marriage, but will be exactly as are the angels in heaven—not physical, but spirit beings—sons of God's, sons of the resurrection and therefore not subject to the laws of human marriage. But concerning the dead, and the fact of the resurrection, haven't you ever read in the book of Moses [Jesus' favorite "putdown"] in the place concerning the burning bush, how when God said, 'I am the God of Abraham and the God of Isaac and the God of Jacob'; that that God is not the God of the dead, but of the living? You have no idea how far afield you are from the truth of the scriptures!"

When the crowd around heard this incredible answer, they were absolutely astonished.

Several of the scribes—most likely Sadducees themselves—then had the intellectual honesty to say, "Master, you have certainly answered well"—though perhaps not yet the courage to admit how wrong they were or to repent of it (see vv. 23-33).

And Luke says that from that time on, the Sadducees dared not ask Him any further questions!

I don't blame them!

CHAPTER 17

Was Jesus a Lawbreaker?

It is almost universally assumed that Jesus was dedicated to the task of eradicating the harsh, brutal system of law which had been like a harsh taskmaster, a yoke of bondage, over the Israelitish people from the days of Moses.

Christ is seen as abrogating the Old Testament, and ushering in the New. Millions believe Him to be the very symbol of deliverance from the requirement to obey the Ten Commandments.

These concepts are all false.

As has been amply demonstrated, Jesus Christ of the New Testament was the very God of the Old Testament. He was the *Lawgiver*, that "Rock" that followed Israel in the wilderness. This was the same member of the God family, later to be born of the virgin Mary and become Jesus of Nazareth, the same Being who wrote the Ten Commandments with His own finger, and delivered them to Moses.

Jesus was a Jew.

As such, He studiously obeyed the laws of Moses throughout His entire life. Never once did He commit the slightest infraction either against the "letter of the law" and most specifically never against the intent or the spirit of the law.

But He did smash the traditions of men.

His obvious disregard for man-made traditions was used to great advantage in teaching His disciples the moral principles of the spirit of the law, while at the same time condemning the "straining at a gnat and swallowing of a camel" legalistic attitudes of the Pharisees.

As a lawkeeper, Jesus fulfilled every one of the Ten Commandments in their deepest spiritual application. As Lord of the Sabbath (Mk. 2:27) Jesus strove to teach His disciples that the "Sabbath was made for man," and instead of being a grievous yoke of bondage wherein an individual could be better advised to spend the day in a straitjacket so as to avoid even the slightest infraction which would bring about sure death, Jesus taught His disciples of the many "grievous burdens" added as humanly devised "do's and don'ts" to the original laws of Moses by the religious leaders of the day.

The Jewish leaders had added many restrictions to the original law of Moses. They attempted to "build a wall around the Torah" in order to prevent a person from ever getting even close to breaking the law.

All knew that ancient Israel had been sent into captivity for disregarding God's Law—especially the Sabbath. In the generations following their return from captivity, the religious leaders were determined not to allow the people to ever again break God's Sabbath. So they added many further restrictions to "insulate and protect" the actual law. It was as if a property owner would put "No Trespassing" signs far outside the actual boundaries of his property in order that no one would ever trespass.

Humanly speaking, the architects of this concept were sincere, God-fearing men, dedicated to God's Law. But with the passing years, as is common to all ideological movements, the pure ideals of the originators became structured into the rigorous regulations of the sustainers. It is impossible to legislate character, however.

From early boyhood, Jesus recognized how the religious leaders of His day had managed to so exaggerate, misapply, distort, traditionalize and embellish the original Mosaic code that it took, quite literally, experts in "the Law" to even interpret the system.

Some of these scholarly interpreters of the law were among those who Jesus encountered when He was 12 years of age in the temple. Even then, Jesus' considerable knowledge of the Scriptures, plus the dimension of God's Holy Spirit, enabled Him to ask such embarrassing questions concerning the stringencies of their traditional codes that they were amazed.

Throughout His life prior to His ministry, Jesus became increasingly aware of the terrible fear gripping the minds of many members of the local synagogues: that the traditional system of law which occupied their time was so unbelievably complex and rigorous that one could find himself nervous, frantic, fretting, questioning and guilty—all at the same time! One had to be seeking continual advice from the religious leaders about every conceivable human act in order to even have a chance to be "righteous."

Jesus saw this "fear of religion" as a bondage of the worst sort. He called this legalistic mixture of ritual adherence to the laws of Moses "grievous burdens and heavy to be borne." Because of His previous existence as Lawgiver to Israel, Jesus could see that God's Ten Commandments were not intended to be restrictive, negative, punitive or confining. Rather, He knew that God's Law was a great law of liberty (James 1:25), and that any nation which would observe, *even in the letter*, such a law, would literally ride the high places of the earth.

Back in Egypt the ancient Israelites had been long accustomed to ceremonial religion; religion involving ritual, religion which required the use of animals as "representations of gods" and therefore worthy of worship, and, in their most grievous sin of all during their sojourn in the wilderness, they made themselves a replica of one of the Egyptian gods by throwing all of their household jewelry into a common pot, and, finally seeing the creation of their own hands in the form of a golden bullock, disintegrated into an idolatrous "religious ceremony" which was nothing more than a frenzied orgy.

Jesus could recall how He had finally been forced to "give them [ancient Israel] over" to a system of sacrifices in order to teach them certain lessons.

Repeatedly, in His prehuman form, He had inspired the prophets to explain that the sacrifices were not God's most perfect desire; that they only were able to provide a carnal, profane people with a "system" of ritual which accomplished two basic purposes: (1) It kept ancient Israel, at least from time to time and not perfectly, from embracing the idolatrous customs of heathen nations around them, some of whom practiced infanticide and other forms of human sacrifice; (2) in the slaying of lambs, goats, bullocks, and the offering of turtle doves, there was always the reminder that the wages of sin was death, as well as a shadowy type of the future sacrifice of a Savior.

Jesus inspired His disciples with His own deepest devotion to the Ten Commandments, not only in their letter but in their spiritual intent. He also inspired continual amazement at His almost casual disregard for the terribly complex system of rigorous legalism which had been attached to the divinely revealed law. By the time Jesus walked the earth as a boy and later as a man in His ministry, the religious system of the times represented not only the original Ten Commandments with all of the statutes and judgments given in the wilderness, not only all of the "morning and evening sacrifices" in the temple, including special sacrifices on annual high days and on each weekly Sabbath, but also included hundreds of additional restrictions, taboos, observations, judgments, regulations, ordinances, and legalistic requirements.

Thus, eventually, though perhaps after Jesus' day, the question had finally been brought to some particularly meticulous religious leader about what one should do if a flea were crawling on you during the incantation in the synagogue. It may have taken months to resolve this huge difficulty, but when it was finally resolved, the regulation handed down was that it would surely break the Sabbath to go to the "work" of picking the flea from your person and casting it away or attempting to crush it between your fingernails, but that if you observed carefully, and it actually *bit you*, then and only then were you permitted to kill the little beast!

From the very earliest moments of His ministry, Jesus had taught the broad spiritual principles of God's Law, applying them to human action and thought, while at the same time almost casually disregarding the added legalistic rituals.

This is why, in the first of His dissertations recorded, "The Sermon on the Mount," Jesus had to use the language He did.

He could easily have said to His disciples, "As you know, I have come to be the finest example of lawkeeping the world has ever seen!"

But He didn't.

Instead, He said, *"Don't think that I am come to destroy the law, or the prophets: I did not come to destroy them but to fulfill* [fill them up to the brim]" (Matt. 5:17).

Obviously then, people had thought—and perhaps His own

disciples were among them—that Jesus *was* breaking God's Law. He was *not,* and so had to remind everyone of this absolute fact.

("I am telling you the truth; till heaven and earth pass away, not one period, or one crossing of the *t* will in any way pass away from the law till everyone everywhere is fulfilling it.

"Whoever it is, therefore, who would break one of the very least of the commandments [whichever one he would hold to be least] and would teach others to do likewise, he will be called the very least in the kingdom of heaven: but whosoever shall do and teach them, that person will be called great in the kingdom of heaven." vv. 18, 19, paraphrased.)

Therefore, He said, *"Don't think that I am come to destroy the law."*

In a broader sense, Jesus was also referring to the two major sections of the Old Testament! They are referred to in the Bible as "the Law, the Prophets and the Psalms." The "Law" is taken by many scholars to mean the "Torah," or the first five books of the Bible from Genesis to Deuteronomy. In a more restrictive sense, it includes the Ten Commandments, the statutes and judgments.

Following this statement about law, Jesus explained in great detail what He meant.

He said, "Because I am telling you, that except your righteous deeds and acts would be even more righteous than those of the Scribes and Pharisees, there is no way you are going to enter into the kingdom of heaven."

This was a shocking statement. Everyone held that the religious hierarchy were the "most righteous," and their titles, albeit in a different language and a different religious system than that extant in most of our Western world today, were probably quite similar. There may have been "Right Reverend" this and the "Most Reverend" that, meaning holier than thou and practically everybody else.

To allege that a person could live a more righteous life than a posturing Pharisee was like throwing a brick through a stained-glass window!

The masses would have thought it impossible, because they assumed "Righteous Joe Pharisee" was living so perfectly and so close to God there was virtually no room for improvement.

This portion of the Sermon on the Mount, however, continues to explain in great length by using one example after another right out of the Ten Commandments how Jesus meant to magnify the law.

Isaiah had prophesied that the Messiah would "magnify the law, and make it honorable" (Isaiah 42:21). So Jesus began to extrapolate the Ten Commandments from what they had always heard into the broad, spiritual principles that God had originally intended.

Jesus said, "You have heard that it was said by them of old time, You shall not kill and whosoever shall kill shall be in danger of the judgment." (The original commandment against killing meant, from wording and context, "You shall do no murder.")

"But I say unto you that whoever is angry with his brother shall be in danger of the judgment day, and whoever would say to his brother, 'You vain, empty useless thing,' shall be in danger of the Sanhedrin, but whosoever shall say, 'You idiot, you fool,' shall be in danger of Gehenna."

Thus Jesus illustrates three steps of human contemptuousness toward a fellow human being. The first—anger, irritation, and "being mad" at someone—brings a person in danger of being judged of God for his anger. The second—hurling an epithet and calling another human being empty, purposeless, wasted and totally useless—would bring about a further degree of stern judgment; in this case being hailed before the council of the Sanhedrin or, in Jesus' broader terms, standing before the spiritual council of God, and giving account for every word that was spoken. The third—to commit the most serious act of actual seething hatred to the depths of one's heart, of wishing another human being *dead*—would bring about, unless it was repented of, loss of eternal life by being thrown into the Gehenna fire Jesus spoke of.

It was then, right in the midst of these examples of the magnification of the basic points of the Ten Commandments and applying them to broader spiritual purposes, that Jesus showed both His disciples and any other interested listeners that He was both *upholding* the law of Moses and *adding* to the practice of formal worship revolving around the temple, spiritual and godly elements of forgiveness and love toward a fellow human being.

Jesus said, "Therefore, if you bring your gift to the altar, and while you are offering it you remember that you have a contention against a brother, leave the gift there before the altar, and go back about your business. First, be reconciled to your brother, and then come back and offer your gift."

Jesus showed it does no good whatsoever to perform some sanctimonious religious act in a spiritualistic ritual, so long as the human *heart* is tainted with contempt, anger, or hostility toward one's fellow man.

He said, "Agree with your adversary quickly, whenever you are in contention with him; lest at any time the adversary deliver you to the judge, and the judge deliver you to the officer, and you be cast into prison. I am telling you the truth, you will not come out of there until you have paid the uttermost part of your fine" [served the final day of your sentence].

Again, Jesus showed that it made no sense to fight false battles for false purposes. In this case, "your adversary" was obviously able to make a legal case against you, no matter the moral or spiritual right or wrong of the matter.

Jesus showed His own disciples that a true Christian spirit should be willing to suffer abuse, even if in the right. Jesus taught His disciples to agree with an "adversary" knowing that they would be gaining spiritual riches and that such adversaries, given the smug satisfaction they had won a battle, "had their reward" here and now.

Again, Jesus upholds due process of law! He points out that the system of that time—and to a large measure the system of our time—required that a person judged guilty by the court be delivered to an officer of that court so that the proper sentence could be carried out.

Considering the obvious upholding of even these minor points of law, Jesus could never have been accused by His words in the Sermon on the Mount of being a "lawbreaker"!

If He could have been, *if* Jesus was advocating the breaking of the law, then the giving of this sermon could have meant the precipitous end to His ministry prior to ever coming down from the mountain!

Never, throughout the three-and-one-half years of His ministry, *in spite of* His casual disregard of ritualistic rigorism, could Jesus be arrested on the basis of supposedly "lawbreaking"!

Yet, this was the most intense area of concentration surrounding His ministry. Continually, Pharisees and Sadducees and other religious groups came to His disciples and plaintively whimpered, "Why does your teacher break every tradition of the elders?" Continually, they challenged Jesus on one or another of the finer points of religious ritualism. But never were they able to convict Him of a single "lawbreaking" act! Always He made it very clear there was a vast distinction between humanly devised religious traditions, and the divinely revealed will and law of God.

Jesus addressed Himself directly to one of the Ten Commandments when He said, "You have heard that it was said by them of old time, you shall not commit adultery: but I am telling you, that whoever looks on a woman to lust after her, has already committed adultery with her *in his mind*" (v. 28). Thus, Jesus upheld the original law against adultery, but vastly magnified and made more binding the implication of the law by stating it was just as great a sin in the sight of God to sexually "lust" after a human being as it was to literally complete the act.

The religious leadership of the time had taken every single point of the Ten Commandments, and added dozens of legalistic addenda.

However, they had also allowed to creep into their theological system various direct and flagrant violations of the spiritual intent of the first three commandments, by allowing various forms of "oath taking," "swearings," and affirmations of truth which were actually outside the bounds of God's Law.

Therefore, Jesus said, "Again, you have heard that it has been said by them of old time, you are not to foreswear yourself, but shall perform unto the Eternal all your vows."

"But I am telling you, do not swear at all! Don't swear by heaven because it is God's throne; don't swear by the earth; because it is His footstool; don't swear by Jerusalem because it is the city of the great king!" (Jesus knew that it was a series of oaths which could be taken in legal or religious proceedings which might embody the use of the heavens, or even the earth, as well as the city of Jerusalem, and addressed Himself not only to these legal applications of "swearing," but also managed to show that the casual use of seemingly harmless "by-words"—meaning "by-this" or "by-that" as used in a common form of swearing—were also contrary to God's expressed will.)

Even during Jesus' day, people were probably saying, "Merciful heavens." "For heaven's sake," "Good heavens," and similar exclamations. In every language, you will find those same expressions today, from one so-called Christian society to another.

Most people would see no harm in these expressions, and millions of good "Christian" folk, who would never think of "cussing" or using the language of restroom graffiti, will nevertheless use, quite freely and liberally, expressions which Jesus condemned.

Jesus said, "Neither shall you swear by your head, because you cannot make one hair white or black. But let your communication be Yes, yes or No, no, for whatsoever is more than these is from the evil one."

To a person who is *absolutely truthful*, Jesus explained, there is no need whatever for additional embellishments to impress the hearer. To a converted Christian who will not lie, a simple "yes" is sufficient. That "yes," based upon the Christian's perceptions of God's Word and the fact of the Ten Commandments of God as magnified by Jesus in the Sermon on the Mount and throughout His life, means far more than all of the oaths taken by every person who has ever entered a courtroom, and should be far more valuable than any number of swearings, oath takings, or promises made on the proverbial "stack of Bibles."

Next, Jesus addressed Himself to the section of the law of Moses in which certain penalties were prescribed for certain actions.

He said, "You have heard that it has been said an eye for an eye, and a tooth for a tooth." While not quoting the rest of it, Jesus knew it also said, "Hand for hand, foot for foot, burning for burning, and wound for wound, and stripe for stripe" (Ex. 21:24, 25).

But addressing Himself to the entire principle of meting out exact punishment commensurate with the injury, Jesus said, "But I say unto you, that you resist not those who are evil: but whoever will smite you on your right cheek, turn to him the other also. And if any man will sue you in the courts, and take away your coat, let him have your cloak also.

"And whoever compels you to go with him a mile [this happened from time to time when Roman mail carriers would impose burdens upon hapless passersby and make them carry their own loads] go with him two miles.

"Give to those who ask of you, and from him who would borrow from you, do not turn him away."

The principle of "give"—of forgiveness, loving, sharing—was what Jesus preached and practiced. But never did Jesus intend to imply that a Christian under His New Testament teachings was not obligated to *obey God,* and to obey the commandments which He, Jesus, in His preexistent state, had written with His own finger!

Later on in this same sermon, following His outline of a prayer, comments on fasting and seeking the kingdom of God over materialistic values, Jesus said, "Therefore, everything you want other men to do to you, you ought to do to them! Because this is the whole meaning of the law and the prophets!" Again, Jesus is *upholding* the law, magnifying and making it "honorable" by lifting it to the much higher plateau of spiritual application.

The traditional perception of Jesus is that He was anti-Jewish, having done away with the Old Testament and the law of Moses. The common reasoning behind this conclusion is *circular:* since Christianity is opposed to Judaism as a concept, and since Christians do not observe the Jewish Sabbath, Holy Days, etc., then *Jesus Christ* Himself must have been anti-Jewish and opposed to the Old Testament law. Of course, the erroneousness of the conclusion is only exceeded by the absurdity of the logic.

There are many features about Jesus in the New Testament that stamp Him as indisputably Jewish. His ancestry is traced back to David in two separate accounts (Matt. 1 and Luke 3). He was circumcised as the law stated (Luke 2:21).

Yet some have seemed to think that His Jewish heritage was only forced upon Him by quirk of birth—and He abrogated the Jewish law the first chance He had. This assumption is based on several falsehoods: (1) reading the practice, belief and biblical understandings of the later Catholic Church *into* the gospels, and (2) reading the gospels as if all the Jewish laws and customs being discussed were those perpetuated into modern times by the later rabbinic Judaism.

Rabbinic Judaism is a post-A.D. 70 phenomenon derived from Pharisaism, but with a strong infusion of other elements as well. However, Judaism *before* A.D. 70 was a much more diverse and pluralistic entity. The average Jew was not a member of a religious party even though he may have been more or less pious.

This is important to recognize because many people read Jesus' statements to isolated sectarians, such as the Pharisees, as if Jesus were speaking to all the Jews. Jesus condemned sin in any form, but He especially scourged the hypocrisy and duplicity of those who claimed to be religious teachers yet denied with their own lives the very platitudes they voiced. (This does not mean that every Pharisee or religious proponent was a hypocrite; rather, it is reasonable to require that those who set themselves up as teachers deserve the greater condemnation when they fail to attain their own standards.) Jesus felt only compassion for the poor sinner—the average Jew—who acknowledged his guilt and asked in humility for God's forgiveness and help (Luke 18:9-14).

Jesus was an ordinary Jew in a Jewish society. As such His associations were primarily with Jews. Far from being a stand-offish or a piously aloof individual, Jesus was criticized by religious sectarians on a number of occasions for associating with "sinners." Were these all Gentiles or lepers? By no means.

Jesus was willing to go to all levels of the Jewish community where He could help, whether it meant associating with the wealthy ruling class at banquets and feasts or with prostitutes and their customers at the lower edge of society.

Some of the Pharisees and Scribes who belonged to the Pharisaic sect thought it was quite a scandalous situation when Jesus and His disciples were willing to sit down at the same table with such people. In fact one of His disciples whom He had just called (Matthew, or Levi) was a tax collector. ("Tax collector" was, in the common parlance of the day, a synonym for "sinner." They ranked along with harlots, whoremongers, traitors; they were looked upon as crooks even though they might be very wealthy and "respectable." This was an outgrowth of the society of Jesus' own day; there was nothing in the Old Testament forbidding association with such individuals.) When Jesus was asked about this, He replied, "Those who are well have no need of a physician but those who are sick. Learn what it means by, 'I desire mercy and not sacrifice.' I have not come to call the righteous but sinners to repentance."

Jesus minced no words about the sins of the priests any more than He did about those of the Pharisees and others. Yet He very much respected and upheld the functions of the Old Testament priesthood. On a number of occasions, after He had healed a leper of this loathsome disease, He told him to report to the priest for the proper temple ritual and official pronouncement of cleanliness (Matt. 8:1-4; Mark 1:40-45; Luke 5:12-14; 17:12-14). Jesus in fact paid the temple tax even though He was legitimately exempt from it (Matt. 17:24-27).

Continually, people cite the cases of Jesus chasing the cattle and money changers out of the temple, believing this to be an example of lawbreaking on Christ's part. Apparently, they have never read the scriptural account; or, if they did, they read it only cursorily, and without real understanding.

You'll find the account in Matthew 21:12-16; Mark 11:15-18; Luke 19:45-47, and John 2:14-17.

Here, Jesus appears, not as a "vagabond" or "wayfarer" who is causing a disturbance against established authority, but as the *proprietor* of the temple, and the direct representative of its ultimate owner, God the Father. He said, "It is written," thus citing the greatest law common to them all, that of the Word of God, "My house shall be called the house of prayer, but you have made it a den of thieves." (In that day Roman money had to be changed into Jewish, in which temple contributions were collected, and no doubt shortchanging occurred, considering the differences in value of the two types of coins and the general tendency of human greed!)

Christ was in authority here, not a casual visitor. Not once did the money changers, nor the owners of the cattle, nor the Jewish religious leaders, say one word about anything "unlawful."

If He broke the law, why not arrest Him? But no law was broken; it was being *upheld.* Christ *cited* the law, when He quoted Isaiah 56:7. He, then, was a representative, both of the property (the temple), and the law.

Remember, too, that even when false witnesses were being bribed to bring false charges against Him during His trial, not once did anyone bring up the issue of Christ chasing the cattle and money changers out of the temple—even though He did so *twice,* about two years apart.

Jesus' *respect* for the temple is perhaps nowhere better illustrated than by these two cleansings of the temple. As soon as Jesus reached Jerusalem, He had a look around the temple, illustrating

His concern for it (Mark 11:11). The next day He returned and entered into it in wrath to clean it of the gross disrespect being shown by the business dealings in the temple precinct. He was determined that the temple, which He regarded as His Father's house, would not become a robbers' nest while He was around in the flesh. He even prevented people from carrying things through the temple area (Mark 11:16). Could Jesus have therefore regarded the temple as an obsolete vestige of an antiquated religion? His intense concern, risking bodily harm, demonstrates just the opposite!

Throughout His ministry, Jesus is described as teaching in the synagogues (Matt. 4:23; 9:35; 12:9; 13:54: John 6:59: 18:20), as well as other places, such as His house. Although we are not told of His years before His ministry, we may safely conclude that He regularly attended the synagogue and participated in the weekly Sabbath services (Luke 4:16). He caused astonishment by His bold teaching in Capernaum (Mark 1:21-22; Luke 4:31-32). In His own home city, Jesus attended the synagogue on the Sabbath day "as was His custom."

Jesus' relationship to the Sabbath has confused many people, most especially the vast majority of the Christian world who are determined to cast Him as a Sabbath breaker Himself and a Sabbath destroyer for everyone else.

But Jesus' sayings about, and actions on, the Sabbath have to be read in the proper context both of the gospel accounts and of the Sabbath beliefs of the Jews of the time. Without the proper cultural background some have twisted the Scriptures in order to justify their own personal convictions, traditions or desires.

Sabbath keeping was a practice among all Jews, both those in Palestine and in the Diaspora. In fact, Sabbath observance was very widely known in the Roman world as a whole even among non-Jews. This is clear from the number of references in various writers in the first centuries B.C. and A.D., including Josephus.

Sabbath observance was so important in the Jewish religion that there are statements in Talmudic literature to the effect that Sabbath observance is equivalent to the Abrahamic Covenant, and that the *law of the Sabbath was said to be equal to all the other laws and commandments in the Torah! (Mekhilta* 62; *Pesikta Rabbati* 23; Palestinian Talmud *Berachot* 3; *Nedarim* 38; *Exodus Rabba* 25). This is an incredible concept and highly relevant for achieving an accurate understanding of the teaching of the New Testament regarding Sabbath observance for the Christian.

The enormous importance of the Sabbath in Judaism—said to actually be the equivalent of *all the other laws* of God—is powerful corroboratory evidence that neither Jesus nor any of the following apostles ever "did away" with Sabbath observance as the day God created for rest and worship. The few scriptures (primarily in Paul's writings), often quoted in an attempt to end the obligation of Christians to keep the Sabbath pale by comparison with the overwhelming significance of the Sabbath. If the apostles had dared to eliminate the Sabbath, surely a gargantuan conflict would have exploded into the New Testament record. Compare, for example, the major controversy in the New Testament Church over circumcision (Acts 15), which was declared to be unnecessary or optional for Christians, with the *relatively* minor controversy over *how a Christian should observe* the Sabbath (in contradistinction to the customary rigorous regulations of common Jewish law).

Since the Sabbath was considered by the Jews to be so important—as important as all the rest of the law put together in some circles—*if* Jesus and His apostles had taught and practiced the total abrogation of the Sabbath commandment as is claimed by professing Christianity, then the religious controversy and disputations would had to have filled the gospels, the book of Acts and all the epistles! There was no such enormous controversy in the New Testament church because the Sabbath was not "done away"!

Why then do we not find repeated reaffirmations of the Sabbath as a command of God? It is mentioned, of course (e.g., Acts 13:42; 17:2 etc.), but everybody in the New Testament world already knew about or already believed in the importance of the Sabbath. There was no doubt or uncertainty. To have emphasized Sabbath keeping in the New Testament would have been like the proverbial carrying coals to Newcastle or taking ice to Eskimos. The issue that Jews (and later the apostles) addressed was *not whether* to observe the Sabbath—it was always revered as the fourth of the Ten Commandments; the issue was rather *how* to observe the Sabbath in light of the repressive, restrictive concepts of the day.

The Jewish reverence for the Sabbath developed during the

exilic period—because the Jews realized that the careless or flagrant desecration of the Sabbath was one of the major causes of
their captivity. This profound Sabbath concern continued strong
throughout the intertestamental period. During the persecutions
of Antiochus IV (Epiphanes), one group of devout Jews refused to
defend themselves on the Sabbath and was slaughtered (I Macc.
2:33 ff.). Therefore, Mattathias and his followers determined to
fight in self-defense on the Sabbath. But even then they would not
take the offensive on that day (II Macc. 8:26 ff.).

The Book of Jubilees, a midrash (extended paraphrase and
commentary) on Genesis, gives some detailed laws on Sabbath
observance. While the book itself may have arisen in sectarian
circles, it concurs with the general Jewish views of the time as
known from other sources. (It is generally dated to the second
century B.C.) Among its regulations are not to prepare any food
or drink, carry any burden in or out not already prepared before
the Sabbath, take anything between houses, or draw water (2:29-
30). Other rules include not lighting a fire, riding on an animal or
ship, catching and/or killing an animal, fasting, making war, or
having sexual relations (50:8, 12).

The Qumran community, generally identified with the Essenes, preserved similar regulations. Forbidden are going more
than a thousand cubits from one's town or lifting an animal from
a pit or helping it give birth, as well as a number of the regulations
mentioned in Jubilees. One is apparently allowed to save a
human from water or fire, though use of an instrument to do so
seems prohibited (*Damascus Covenant* x. 14-xi. 18).

When we turn to the rabbinic literature, we find that 39 kinds
of things were forbidden on the Sabbath (Mishah *Shabbath* 7.2).
One cannot automatically project the statements of later rabbinic
literature back into Palestine before A.D. 70. Recent research has
shown that much of the rabbinic material was derived in shape
and detail from post-A.D. 70 times (see the works of Jacob
Neusner). However, many of the kinds of things prohibited by the
Mishnah are borne out by New Testament examples as being
genuine practices in the time of Jesus.

By comparing the regulations of the Mishnah and later literature with the intertestamental and New Testament writings, there
also seems even to have been a gradual relaxing of strictness. G.
F. Moore writes, "Where the Sabbath observance in these [earlier]

writings differs substantially from the Tannaite Halakah [later rabbinic teachings], it is generally in the direction of greater strictness' (*Judaism*, II, 27). Billerbeck agrees "that there was a more rigorous administration of Sabbath observance in the days of Jesus than in the time during which the regulations of the Mishnah arose" (*Kommentar*, II, 819). If one thinks that the later proverbial talmud of Sabbath laws espoused by rabbinic Judaism was burdensome, they were still less exacting than many in Jesus' own time.

Therefore, when Jesus was called into account for doing certain things on the Sabbath, it was certainly *not* for violating specific *Old Testament* prohibitions. Rather, Jesus was ignoring the rigorous Sabbath regulations devised by sincere, though misguided, men. The Old Testament did not forbid one to pick ears of grain on the Sabbath and then eat them on the spot. Yet when Jesus and His disciples did this (Mark 2:23; Matt. 12:1; Luke 6:1), He was called to account and severely chastised, because this was classified as reaping, and their rubbing loose the grain into their hands as threshing. Similarly, it was forbidden to treat a sickness when the sick person's life was in no immediate danger. Jesus' healing of the man with the withered arm was a violation of this rule. (The incident immediately follows the one just mentioned in each of the gospels.) Many regulations—some early and some late—are given in the tractate *Shabbath* in the Mishnah and especially the two Talmuds.

The Pharisees and Scribes were watching Jesus to see whether He would heal on the Sabbath (Matt. 12:9-14; Mark 3:1-6; Luke 6:6-11). Note the analogy that Jesus used of pulling a sheep out of a pit on the Sabbath. Which was worth more, was the biting rhetorical question, a sheep or a man?

Was it lawful to do good on the Sabbath? Of course. And to prove it, Jesus healed the man. By using the analogy that He did, Jesus clearly showed that He was not breaking the Sabbath; Jesus was, in fact, upholding the purity and holiness of the Sabbath, doing what was quite consistent with its original purpose. To do good, to relieve another from suffering, was not only *not* a violation of the Sabbath, it was actually perfectly fulfilling its profound spiritual meaning that God created for man (Mark 2:26).

After Jesus healed a cripple of 38 years, He told him to take up his pallet and walk (John 5:5-9). The man had been sitting on a pallet to protect him from the stone floor. He was not lying on a queen-size four-poster bed or a king-size water bed. Therefore, when he carried his pallet away, as told by Jesus, he was hardly violating the law against bearing a burden on the Sabbath (Jer. 17:21, 22, 27). Therefore, the statement, "This was why the Jews sought all the more to kill him, because he not only broke the Sabbath but also called God his Father," can in no way be taken as even an indirect statement that Jesus broke the Sabbath. Only in the *opinion* of the onlooking Jews, steeped in their own restrictive regulations, had He violated the Sabbath.

Several other healings are mentioned as taking place on the Sabbath. In several cases Jesus had to defend Himself and used an argument similar to the one already mentioned. Diseases healed included blindness (John 9), a crooked back (Luke 13:10-13), and dropsy (Luke 14:1-6). Once again, the fundamental point being made is a reaffirmation by Jesus of why He had created the Sabbath, what its purpose was, and how it was a great blessing to man.

Josephus reports that the Essenes were so strict they would not even relieve themselves on the Sabbath (*War* 2.8.9). (It seems that more effort would have been exerted to wait than to go!) Whether Josephus can be trusted in this is not certain, but it does help illustrate the strictness with which many kept the Sabbath.

Jesus did not violate the principles of the Old Testament Sabbath; He showed the correct spirit in which it should be kept. Jesus was a Sabbath keeper, not a Sabbath breaker.

Just as He kept the weekly Sabbath, Jesus also kept the annual feast days. It was quite customary for Him to be in Jerusalem at the time. It was so expected that people waited to see whether He would come when his life was in danger (John 7:11; 11:55-57).

The final feast Jesus attended was the Passover, of course. But He came to Jerusalem at the Passover time on at least another occasion (John 2:13). He also spent one Passover in the region of Galilee (John 6:1-4).

John 4:45 mentions that Jesus had been to Jerusalem at "the feast." John 5:1 also mentions a "feast." In neither passage is the exact festival designated. It was likely that it was the spring or fall festival since these seem to have been the major times for one to go to Jerusalem. John 7 describes the Feast of Tabernacles (especially v. 2).

Jesus also observed at least one festival which was unique to the Jews and not given in the Old Testament. This was the Feast of Dedication or, as it is usually called today, Hanukkah. It was a festival of eight days, ending on Kislev 25 (i.e., sometime in December usually). Jesus may have had other reasons for being in Jerusalem, but it is especially noted that He was in the temple on this festival (John 10:22-23).

Another passage which has often been misunderstood concerns the disciples' not washing their hands (Matt. 15:1-20; Mark 7:1-23; Luke 11:34-41). The scribes and Pharisees were astonished at this. Was it because the disciples were unhygienic? No, because the washing is linked to the "traditions of the elders" (Mark 7:3-4). The subject was not cleanliness *per se* but *ritual* cleanliness or purity.

As Jesus showed, a person is not "defiled" by anything physical. A person can become ritually unclean; he can even kill himself by eating poison. But this is not defilement in its spiritual meaning. Only those sins committed by "coming out" of an individual truly defile him. What if he eats a bit of dirt? What if he even eats something unclean according to Old Testament law? It is not good for him but he is still not spiritually defiled.

Jesus was not opposing the Old Testament laws of purity. He was opposing the "traditions of the elders" because they were so much nonsense, holding up to ridicule the original instructions of God to Israel. Yet most of all, Jesus was showing that the real concern of the individual should be for spiritual and moral issues. Ritual purity without these was nothing. These without ritual purity could make one righteous before God even if not "perfect."

There is no hint that Jesus Himself violated any of the Old Testament laws of purity. We can be sure that He kept them in every detail. The only fault found with Him was that of not observing the "traditions of the elders." But as He showed, these became an excuse to overturn the very heart of Old Testament laws, such as honor and respect of parents.

As already mentioned, Jesus did not in any way dishonor the temple. On the contrary, He upheld the proper respect for it. Among the regulations relating to the temple were the laws of tithing. The well-known passage in Matthew 23:23 shows that He *commanded tithing*—even in a rather unnecessarily minute fash-

ion—so long as the weightier matters of the law were not overlooked.

Another example is that of the poor widow who put in only
two copper coins (given the value of the English coin "mite" in
the King James translation). Jesus emphasized the greatness of
her sacrifice in comparison to some who gave much more (Mark
12:41-44; Luke 21:1-4). However, something often not noticed is
that the money was being contributed to the temple treasure.
Furthermore, Jesus commended the widow's sacrifice for the sake
of the temple. This is certainly not the attitude of one who
considers the temple of no value.

During the middle of the Feast of Tabernacles, Jesus went up
into the temple, openly, and began teaching a sizable crowd of
people, bringing up another of His examples about the law.

He said, "I have done one work, and you all marvel. Moses
gave circumcision and so you practice circumcision even on the
Sabbath day (not because Moses was the one who gave it but
because it came from the Father long before Moses' time).

"If a man is to receive circumcision on the Sabbath day, in order
that you avoid breaking the law of Moses, the way you look at it, why
should you be angry at me, because I have made a man every bit
whole on the Sabbath day?

"Don't judge according to appearance, leaping to conclusions
when you don't have the facts; judge *righteous* judgment!" (John
7:21-24, paraphrased.)

What an indictment!

As He did throughout His ministry, Jesus pointed up once
again the ridiculousness of religious ceremony which so perverted
true religion that it became a legal system of do's and don'ts, a
ritual of exacting, constricted practice which totally ignored the
great spiritual values of love, joy, peace, forgiveness, deliverance,
tenderness and compassion.

Just after the Feast, Jesus had another opportunity to put the
religious leaders to shame, and to show the difference between
ritualistic legalism and the carrying out of prescribed penalties of
the law in the letter, as opposed to mercy and forgiveness.

Early in the morning a few days later, He was again in the
temple teaching a group of people when the Scribes and Pharisees
heard about it.

They were right in the process of questioning a woman who

had been caught while in the very act of adultery. Why they couldn't catch the man is obscure. At any rate, the poor woman, terrified, knew she was as good as dead. They thoroughly intended to stone her to death that very same day. However, a new thought arose. Here, it seemed, was a marvelous opportunity to take the woman directly to Jesus, and see if He would defy the prescribed penalty according to the law of Moses.

If He did, they thought they might be able to have legal excuse for stoning Him to death right along with the woman.

If they could make Him even appear to be an accomplice to adultery, a person who would condone the deed, it would degrade Jesus and be better for them.

Dragging the woman along with them, they finally came to the temple, and pushed their way forward until they brought the woman directly before Jesus.

"Teacher, this woman was caught in adultery, during the very act. There is no question about it, there are sufficient witnesses, and she is guilty.

"Now, Moses in the law strictly commands us that such a person should be stoned to death, but what do you say about it?"

The temple's floor was dusty in this large court from so many feet moving about in a public place, but the stones were highly polished and very smooth. Without a word, but with tension sparking the electrified air, Jesus stooped down, and appeared to begin writing characters on the dust of the stones with his finger. He kept writing for a few moments, with head down, arm and hand moving rapidly over the stones of the floor. Then Jesus stood up, took a couple of steps back, and looked at them and said, "Whoever among you has never committed any sin whatsoever, be sure you are the one to throw the first rock at this woman, will you?"

After saying this, He looked at them meaningfully, stooped on the ground, and began to write again where He had left off.

They rigorously adhered to their "pecking order" of religious rank, and one by one, beginning with the eldest, filed up near to Jesus to look over His shoulders on the ground. What they saw is obvious from the account.

How many of them were adulterers? How many were thieves? How many were liars, cheats and hypocrites? How many were "abusers of themselves with mankind"?

There is no way of knowing. However, what Jesus wrote was so sufficiently shameful, and so obviously dealt with their own personal, private sins, that their glass houses came suddenly shattering apart. Each, in his turn, walked by Jesus' shoulders and read very clearly what Jesus' own finger had written on the dusty, polished marble floor. Was it a series of names? Were their names attached to two or three words which convicted each, in his own turn?

We can only speculate, but the account in John's eighth chapter is clear. Each was convicted by his own conscience. And each very quietly and embarrassedly shuffled right on by Jesus, head to the ground, looking neither left nor right, until he could find his way out of the group and outside of the temple.

The woman still stood by. Jesus arose, looked around, and saw the woman standing there with the group of people he had been teaching, including some of His disciples.

He said, "Woman where are all your accusers? Is no one going to stay around to condemn you?"

The woman said, "There is no one here."

However, the woman probably feared that Jesus, who so obviously seemed to be in authority on the occasion, could have had the power to condemn her. Her shame, torment, sorrow and fear shone clearly out of her eyes.

Jesus said, "Neither do I condemn thee: go and sin no more!"

Jesus was not condoning sin; he was offering *forgiveness* for sin, and the opportunity to repent and "sin no more."

Time and again Jesus ripped away this facade and let the people and His disciples see the futility in believing God is appeased by repetitive mouthings and posturings.

Jesus showed it makes no difference if men turn around in circles, stand on this foot or that, raise this hand or the other, wear this cloak or the other, carefully pronounce this word or the other, sprinkle salt, tinkle bells, light candles, thump Bibles, talk out of the side of their mouths in colloquial accents, butcher and slaughter sheep, cattle, goats and oxen by the thousands, rotate prayer wheels, swallow wafers, smudge ashes on their foreheads, wave palm fronds about in the air, stare at the sun while it rises, squat, stoop, kneel, splash water, dab, leap over chairs, grovel on the ground, babble in gibberish, walk with half steps, bob and weave, peep and mutter, cry genuine tears, sing beautiful songs, smile beatific smiles, grow beards, shave beards, wear uniforms, eschew uniforms, drive automobiles or shun automobiles, repeat the Lord's Prayer endlessly, or softly intone, "Bless you Jesus," until the words lose meaning!

None of this appeases, satisfies, moves, or mollifies God!

But giving, serving, sharing, forgiving, healing, helping—that's what Jesus said God's true religion is all about.

Jesus fully supported the Sabbath and Holy Days of the Old Testament. He had created them as God. He observed them Himself as a man; and He taught His disciples to teach their disciples that all men should keep these God-ordained laws.

CHAPTER **18**

Satan and Judas—
the Mental Perversion

Satan was totally obsessed with the destruction of Jesus. First, he had influenced Herod in an attempt to kill Jesus shortly after His birth. Satan had no doubt also desperately tried to destroy Jesus on many other unrecorded occasions during His young babyhood, and growing years. Satan again tried to destroy Jesus following His 40-day fast and near-starvation at the beginning of His ministry. On several other occasions throughout His ministry, by influencing the minds of religious leaders and others either directly or through his demonic kingdom, the devil tried to have Christ murdered by the hands of His critics and detractors.

Satan finally managed to accomplish his purpose—and he found his opening, a weak link, right in the immediate personal entourage of Christ—Judas Iscariot. So Satan continually influenced Judas, and was able to take complete possession of his mind at the betrayal, thus finally bringing about Christ's death.

How utterly frustrating it must have been for Satan to eventually realize that in accomplishing his own malevolent objective, he had only facilitated the magnificent plan of God. Satan had always done only what God had allowed, and on each of these abortive occasions, his best efforts to destroy Jesus only resulted in the further fulfillment of God's master plan. Even Satan's alleged master maneuver, his final "success" in destroying the physical life that was Jesus Christ—the Son of Joseph and Mary, human being, planet Earth—who was also the Son of God, only succeeded in bringing about that final stroke of absolute divine genius: presenting to the world the resurrected, living Savior who would now ascend to the right hand of God in heaven to make daily intercession for those of His brethren who would acknowledge Him.

Almost instantly, Satan tried to destroy the fledgling New Testament Church of God—and has been attacking, maligning, criticizing, ridiculing, persecuting, and attempting to destroy it down through the ages ever since by every means at his disposal: organized religion, civil government, police states, pogroms, martyrdoms and persecutions of every sort. But Satan's most diabolically effective weapons have continued to be the same old reliable ones he has always used since the days of Judas—destroy from within, cause dissension and doubt, stir one against the other, destroy the credibility of the leadership, accuse the brethren, divide and conquer.

Jesus "knew who it was who should betray Him" from the very beginning!

God's Holy Spirit had revealed to Him the deep character flaw in Judas, and in His dozens of hours of intensive prayer in close personal communication with His Father in heaven, Jesus understood thoroughly that there would be one of His own immediate disciples who would eventually fulfill the prophecies. Judas' covetousness for money, his betrayal of Jesus, the thirty pieces of silver, and Judas' burial in the potter's field were all known to Jesus well in advance.

Was there anything to the story that Judas came from the south of Palestine, from the area of "Kerioth," hence the derivation of "Judas Iscariot," and the tale which would be written in an alleged "gospel" later that Judas and Jesus had met in a chance encounter when they were yet boys, and Judas had been possessed of a "biting demon" (was this the reason for the "kiss"?) which had fled from Judas upon seeing the boy Jesus?

These and other tales, including the complete rejection of Judas Iscariot as being a historically real person, but merely representing the symbolic rejection of Jesus by "His own," were to be told and retold in the centuries that followed.

However, there is no personal eyewitness testimony from any of the four gospel writers as to Judas's origins, boyhood, or the allegations of an earlier demonic possession.

Don't assume for one moment that Judas was unpopular with

the disciples; that he was a known "outcast" from the very beginning.

It is very much more likely that Judas was a pleasant enough
personality, and that he would have drawn close to any number of
the disciples.

For slightly more than a three-and-one-half-year period,
from the time of his first eager acceptance of Jesus' call, and his
determination to remain a loyal member of Christ's own closest
disciples, Judas, as any other human being, would have drawn
closer to a particular group of the twelve.

In any group of a dozen human beings, there will grow and
develop certain close personal associations, and certain vague but
polite discomfitures and animosities. Each man was a strikingly
different and unique personality, and it is therefore natural that
different groups of two and three of the disciples would tend to
gravitate toward each other; there could not be an equal relationship between all of them like some synthetic homogenization of
human personalities.

There is no doubt that Judas' weakness for money was a
gradual problem which finally developed into an overt act of
thievery now and then which he had kept secret and quiet.

When did it begin?

There is no way to know—perhaps clear back in Judas'
childhood when he began to get away with petty stealing around
his own environment. Knowing the stiff penalties for theft during
that time, Judas was a person who was running a great risk, and,
therefore, became the more clever.

Perhaps, after the baptism of John, and his first joyous acceptance of Christ's call, Judas intended to turn over "a new leaf,"
and in order to prove it (possibly even to himself), probably
volunteered to carry "the bag" or the common purse for the
twelve, acting as their "secretary-treasurer." Judas may have had
special training from some of the professional scribes and could
have been the "financial genius" of the twelve.

Judas was probably a sharp barterer, and managed to stretch
the money they were given from time to time when some of the
people paid their tithes directly to Jesus and His disciples to show
their deepest belief that He was the Messiah, and their rejoicing
over His powerful and authoritative teachings, as well as His
miraculous healings of the sick and afflicted.

Judas no doubt formed a few fairly close attachments among the disciples. These are never mentioned after the original group of twelve was identified. But surely Judas was included when Jesus sent His disciples out on a brief evangelistic tour to give them experience in teaching others what Jesus had taught them, in learning the lessons of suffering, rejection and persecution in this or that town, and in having the courage to simply shake off the dust of their feet and go on to the next place.

Judas preached just as fervently as the rest of them, and who knows, may have been used in performing miracles.

But perhaps this is the way his road to infamy commenced:

The first time Judas managed to find a bargain for some foodstuffs and lie about the price, pocketing the difference, he probably felt terribly guilty.

Certainly, Jesus would know about anything like this from the very beginning, for He could literally read human minds and hearts by the power of God's Spirit; Jesus could see right through the agony of conscience Judas was suffering. The more deeply Judas became involved, the more the normal psychological reaction of anger toward Christ developed. Judas had utter contempt toward himself, and was tremendously jealous of Jesus' purity. These resentments smoldered and became twisted into the deepest sensitivity concerning his own "honesty" and "integrity" and into the deepest hostility concerning Jesus' "hypocrisy" and "egomania."

Probably, if any of the disciples had actually called Judas a thief (and that was exactly what he was—John 12:6), it would have resulted in an insane screaming tirade, probably even physical violence, and Judas would have quit on the spot!

Judas could have been as magnetic and charming a personality as any of the twelve, and perhaps was a little more so than most. As the months passed, and Judas continued to live the double life of petty pilferage whenever his lusts and appetites got the better of him, his growing irritation with Jesus' expenditures, personal tastes in clothing and foodstuffs, and most especially Christ's seeming inattention to the poor "suffering people" continued to wear on Judas's nerves.

Did Judas influence any of the other disciples in these attitudes?

Probably so.

It would be ridiculous to think that he held these opinions totally secret inside himself. There must have been times when groups of three or four in intense personal interrelationships would talk about the others who were not present, as often occurs in any other collection of carnal (or converted!) human beings.

There were minor personality clashes and arguments from time to time, and these were usually silenced by Jesus Himself, who would rebuke the disciples for their hurtful attitudes toward one another.

Some of the more violent arguments centered around the jealousies of those who were closest to Jesus. Proximity to the source of power in any human organization is always a subject of contention.

On occasion the disciples' own families became involved in the petty bickering. At such times, there was ample opportunity for a spate of self-pity; the description of how much they had "suffered" and how long they had endured; the hardships they had undergone, and the fact that Jesus didn't seem to be paying them enough attention. Attitudes of fierce family loyalties and mutual commiseration at these alleged slights finally became so intense that, on at least two occasions, there was open conflict about who would "sit on His right hand and on His left hand" when Jesus would set up His kingdom.

Though the disciples were probably well along in their twenties or even older, on at least one occasion one of their mothers could approach Jesus and beseech Him to bring an end to the agony of doubt and curiosity, and name who would be His chief lieutenants right away (see Matthew 20:21-28)!

Jesus would exclaim, "I'm sorry! That is not my decision; it is not my choice or my place to appoint who is going to be at my right hand or my left hand in the kingdom, but my Father's!"

Probably, there had been some frustration among family members because of the long absences, the tiresome journeys, and the personal hardships and sacrifices as the result of Jesus' travels.

Such feelings could have been expressed over and over again in a family environment about how much these poor men were suffering, and Jesus could have become the object of irritation because of His seeming aloofness to these alleged family grievances.

Jesus has to give the striking example concerning the giving up of family ties, homes, and human roots to settle an argument about the leadership in the kingdom, to reassure His disciples and their parents in the strongest terms that anyone who had given up homes, families, lands, positions, business, personal wealth or even loss of everything down to martyrdom would "inherit an hundredfold" in the kingdom.

Jesus wanted to get across the lesson that, when one became truly converted, even though his own personal family and friends might turn against him, he immediately became the "adopted son" of every other member of the body of Christ (which was to become the church) and in that sense, he immediately inherited hundreds upon hundreds of "fathers and mothers, brothers and sisters" in Christ; in the ultimate sense, of course, the actual kinship in the Family of God after the Resurrection would yield an infinite increase.

Gradually, though, Judas became Jesus' chief critic.

Jesus knew it, even though on a day-to-day basis in their "love-hate" relationship (Jesus doing all the loving, and Judas doing all the hating), there were pleasant enough exchanges and greetings.

Not only did Jesus know Judas was stealing, but Judas also began to suspect that Jesus knew it, and this further exacerbated his anxieties. It even brought forth from him open criticism in public meetings near the end of Christ's ministry.

Mary of Bethany understood even more vividly than some of Christ's own personal disciples that Jesus literally meant what He said about His impending persecution, crucifixion and burial.

Thus, Mary privately began buying a very expensive ointment she was going to keep until the time of His death so she could insure that she had the finest funeral possible. Mary had heard the tale of the town prostitute who had wiped Jesus' feet with her hair, splashing her own tears on His feet, and totally humiliating herself in abject worship because of the weight of her sins and her deepest desire for Christ's forgiveness.

During a large public dinner in Simon the Leper's house in Bethany, very near to Christ's last twenty-four hours on earth as a man, Mary was overcome with emotion and grief as a result of the heaviness she saw in Jesus' face and in His demeanor. She then knelt at His feet, and producing a box of very expensive spikenard, began to anoint His feet with it, crying, and using the hair of her own head to wipe them.

Judas probably looked around at the two or three of the disciples he had influenced the most heavily, and, nudging one with his elbow, said, "Look at that! There is another example of terrible extravagance! Why in the world doesn't Jesus tell the woman to get up and save that expensive ointment; it could be sold for a great deal of money, and we could give it to the poor [Mark 14:4-5]. That would make a far greater impression upon people of the kind of person Jesus seems to want to be than to allow Mary to waste all of that expensive ointment on Jesus at a time like this when we are in such financial trouble."

Judas was pleased to observe that several of the other disciples were equally "outraged" as Judas pretended to be. Judas had set them up for this attitude by a long process of insidious innuendo.

But Judas was, of course, the first to raise his voice about the alleged outrageous waste. John later recalled, and wrote, that Judas said, "Why wasn't this ointment sold for 300 pence and given to the poor?"

But John added, "He said this, not because he really cared for the poor, but because he happened to be a thief, and, having control of the common treasury, was constantly skimming from it" (John 12:6, paraphrased).

Jesus then made another of His "outrageous" statements, neither understood then even by many of His own disciples, nor understood by many who believe in the false Jesus of today: "What are you bothering this woman for? She has performed a fine thing for me—because there will always be poor people in every society and you *will always have poor folk with you;* and, hopefully, whenever you find opportunity, you should do good to them. But you will not always have me with you! And she understands what you don't seem to understand; and is anointing the hair of my head and my body in advance for my burying!

"And I'll tell you something else; wherever the gospel is preached throughout the whole world, then what this woman is doing for me here tonight will be spoken of her as a memorial."

Judas became terribly angry at this stinging public rebuke. His ego had been badly stung and his guilt, rising up like bile in his mouth, became so intense he simply had to choke it down.

The only method to quiet his own guilt was to pretend Jesus could not have known about it, and to rise up in righteous indignation against Jesus Christ, hardening his resolve to "get him" if the opportunity would ever present itself.

Judas didn't like the real Jesus very much. He would have far preferred to have seen a Jesus much closer to the type imagined in the minds of many professing Christians today! When Jesus would refuse to heal someone, not even bothering to answer them at first, and only healed on those occasions where outstanding examples of perseverance or faith were shown, it annoyed Judas!

He would do it differently!

Judas knew he could be a better Messiah than Jesus was. Judas reasoned that if only he had studied as hard in the Scriptures; if only he had that unique combination of personal magnetism, quick wit and incisive insight that would deftly turn a social disaster into a great spiritual and moral lesson; if only *he* could have that amazing power to produce signs, wonders, and miraculous healing—that he, Judas, could have been the real Christ instead of Jesus!

Probably, Judas came to the point where he honestly felt that he had influenced enough of the disciples so that more than a majority would follow him if he could overthrow Jesus. Actually, Judas' attempts to overthrow Jesus seem to have begun well over a year prior to Jesus' crucifixion, when he seized every opportunity he could to heavily influence as many disciples as possible, so that they would warm up toward him, listen to what he said, agree with his contentions, and join with him in his continual abrasive attitudes toward Jesus' "life-style," the decisions He made and the conduct of their day-to-day business.

Finally, when Judas knew that Jesus had really enraged the top leadership in Jerusalem, the time suddenly seemed to be right. He had toyed with the idea of betraying Jesus on many occasions prior to this time, but the pieces never fit together. Then, almost instantaneously, the proper chemical ingredients generated the sudden reaction—the time had finally arrived when Judas thought the time was ripe.

His constant murmuring concerning Jesus' personal tastes and habits had scored on a significant number of the disciples.

He reasoned he could easily neutralize Peter's bombast, and James and John were quieter, especially John, against whom several of the other disciples nursed jealousy anyway because of John's constant closeness with Jesus.

Judas's years' long campaign to disaffect as many of Jesus' top disciples as he could had come increasingly into the open in recent months. Now, a sufficient number of the disciples seemed to agree with Judas, and disagree with Jesus' statement about the poor.

His hatred became so intense—exactly proportionate to the degree of his deepest sense of personal guilt—that his mind was opened up to Satan the Devil.

As soon as he found opportunity, perhaps early the next morning, Judas, now literally possessed of Satan the Devil, sought out the leading Sadducees of the temple, and struck a deal with them. The main element of his agreement was that he acceded to their demands that he deliver Jesus at a time when no large crowds were present, because the Sadducees knew that most of the people looked upon Jesus as a prophet, and told Judas of the many times they themselves had tried to have Him arrested, only to be thwarted because He always seemed to be surrounded by such a large group of believing people.

Judas craftily asked, "Okay, how much are you willing to pay me?"

Perhaps one of the priests vaguely remembering Zechariah's 11th chapter and 12th verse which said, "If ye think good, give me my price; and if not, forbear. So they weighed for my price thirty pieces of silver." And, either as a lark, or even believing some twisted application of this scripture might in fact apply in the "cutting asunder" of a "foolish shepherd," suggested precisely that amount: thirty pieces of silver.

This was a substantial sum, easily comparable to several thousand dollars in today's economy, and Judas agreed without haggling.

Rejoining the group in Bethany, Judas was tingling with excitement, constantly scheming and thinking ahead, trying to think of a time when Jesus would be most vulnerable, away from at least most of the people, and perhaps even isolated from a few of His closest disciples, so he could inform on Him with as little risk to himself as possible.

Also, he fervently hoped that his campaign of feigned love toward Jesus had succeeded; so that, even in the event of the arrest itself, he could pose as being so deeply concerned over Jesus' alleged "illegal ways," that he could preside over the whole sordid scene with a supercilious righteousness, shaking his head sadly, grimacing as if in pain, yet glancing significantly at those few disciples over whom he had almost complete control, so that immediately upon Jesus' disappearance and either terrible castigation and/or even death, Judas himself could pick up the pieces of the organization and carry on.

In Judas's twisted mind, perhaps he even imagined that he was doing this "for Jesus' own good."

He would show Him.

Wouldn't it have been far easier on their entire ministry if Jesus had gone further out of His way to give to the poor? Couldn't they have won far more friends and influenced far more people, avoiding all of the persecution that continually came upon them and the constant rumors that followed Jesus throughout His ministry that He was "a gluttonous man and a winebibber," if Jesus could have avoided the appearance of profligacy?

Judas wanted Him constrained. He wanted Him contained, rebuked, punished. Perhaps, though maybe he couldn't even admit it to himself, he was entertaining thoughts such as, "We're not going to go anywhere with this whole setup as long as Jesus remains the boss."

In Judas' own mind, he felt Jesus' arrest by the civil authority would be the greatest event that could have occurred in these three-and-one-half years, releasing his own full potential for leadership. He, Judas, would then set about doing what Jesus seemed to always be so reluctant to accomplish: the setting up of the kingdom right here and now, by the secret recruitment of an army, the quick overthrow of the Roman forces occupying the country, in complete cooperation with the puppet king, and most especially of the religious and commercial leaders.

Judas felt totally vindicated!

In his own mind, he had so twisted his reasoning around that he actually saw Jesus as the one who was the extravagant thief, the one who was abusive and abrasive, the one with whom almost no one could get along, the one whom no one could please.

Judas so misinterpreted Jesus' motives that he came to believe he would be doing the world a favor if he could get rid of Jesus. All Israel would surely pay Judas great homage for ridding the country of this egomaniac who was about to cause great slaughter by inciting the Roman occupation army to counter the threats of insurrection. Of course, Judas did have an immediate second thought: he desperately wanted to take over the leadership of the twelve disciples for himself; and with Jesus out of the way there was nothing to stop him. He had the money, the personality and, soon, the public recognition and the support of the religious leadership as well. Perverted and ferociously misguided ambition had blinded Judas to reality.

How many countless hours had Judas daydreamed during the course of the last year and a half or so about the marvelous feeling it would be to see the crowd surrounding him! How many clever things he would say! Judas would immediately set up two or three of his closest confidants as the leading apostles, and most certainly, they would not be Peter, James or John! They were too attached to Jesus personally to be of any use in the future.

Judas would demote Peter, James and John to lesser positions in the group; probably, on second thought, he would have to get rid of them altogether and appoint some new disciples from a few friends he had bribed here and there along the way. Thus, Judas had probably planned to set up a new organization which would solve all of their present difficulties, be they religious, social, political or financial. Judas could virtually see himself, in his mind's eye, plunging along the road toward great success and greater glory! Perhaps he would be able to set up the kingdom right here and now! Surely the people were ready. But he would have to do it through wily cooperation with the present powers, and wait until he had gathered a small army of many hundreds of the key people in the main villages and towns before he could begin an underground recruiting program.

Judas thought he could amass thousands. He was certain he could do it! Jesus had fed the four thousand and then the five thousand, and, as Judas' shrewd mind began calculating the possible forces he could gather, he probably reasoned he could have at least fifty or sixty thousand troops ready in not much more than one year.

There was only one "if"—*if* he could get rid of Jesus, and be given full leadership without any constraints.

(The popular impression that Judas simply wanted the 30

pieces of silver may well be rather simple-minded. Judas was playing for much higher stakes.)

It is quite conceivable, however, that Judas did *not* want Jesus to be crucified and executed, for it was the actual condemnation of Jesus (Matt. 27:31) that rudely awakened Judas from his dream, shook him back to reality and triggered his suicide. Judas probably wanted only to get Jesus "out of the way" so that he could take over the leadership of the disciples; Judas perhaps also wanted to humiliate Jesus a little, "to give Him a taste of His own medicine," and "to teach Him a lesson."

But it got far out of hand. Once Judas had betrayed Jesus and turned Him over to the religious leaders, his role was finished—he could no longer control the situation.

Thus, his combination of vanity, ego, guilt and deep personal shame over his deceiving ways, the most vituperative resentment against any who would dare question his "highest moral integrity" and his megalomaniacal vision of his own importance, led Judas straight down the road into total Satanic possession and his own quick, self-imposed destruction.

When Judas finally came to his senses, when the devil had accomplished his task and left him, he was filled with a sickeningly intense self-revulsion. And in a mindless state of ever increasing self-hatred, Judas first tried to give the money back. Failing this, he simply cast it down in the temple where he thought he could at least partially return the money to its rightful owners. He then went out and hanged himself.

The ignominy of Judas's death was compounded when his swinging body, bloated and decaying, "burst asunder and all his bowels gushed out" in the very field bought by the religious leaders with Judas' own thirty pieces of silver.

What does the future hold for Judas? Did he commit the unpardonable sin? Is he heading for the Lake of Fire? Is he lost for all eternity?

Matthew reports that Judas *"repented himself"* (Matt. 27:3) right after Jesus was condemned and right before he committed suicide. What does "repented himself" mean? Was it only the carnal remorsefulness of masochistic self-pity following public failure and ego self-destruction?

It is impossible for any one man to read and know any other man's heart and mind; it is fruitless for any human being to try to fully appreciate the internal attitude and approach behind the external actions and deeds of any other human being. (It's hard enough to know one's own heart and mind!)

Only the God that created the heavens and the earth and all mankind will judge Judas Iscariot—and that's Jesus Christ Himself—the same fair and faithful and forgiving God who will ultimately judge us all.

CHAPTER 19

The Day the Earth Shook

It was the month of Nisan in the land of Palestine, and a prettier spring one could hardly remember.

This "beginning of months" in the Jewish calendar (corresponding roughly to the latter part of our March and the first of April) marked the end of three-and-one-half years of Jesus' ministry, and the approximate end of thirty-three-and-a-half years of His human, physical life.

It was the thirteenth of this first month, sometime during the day, when Jesus was asked by His disciples, "Where would you like to take the Passover this year?" (Mk. 14:12 ff.).

Always before, Jesus seemed to have known where they would partake of the Passover together, but this time His instructions were rather strange, even to those disciples who had long since overcome their constant surprise at the things Jesus would say and do.

He told Peter and John, always leaders in special circumstances, "I want you to go and get a place ready for us to partake of the Passover." They said, "Where do you want us to prepare this place?"

"Go on into Jerusalem, and you're going to see a man carrying a pitcher of water on his shoulder. I want you to follow him, and whichever house it is he shall enter, you ask for the owner of the home, and tell him, 'My Master [teacher] asks, Where is the best room where I can keep the Passover in your home with my disciples?'

"He will show you a large upper room at the rear of his

home, completely furnished. I want you to stay there and make all the necessary preparations."

Peter and John left Bethany, and went on to Jerusalem. Entering the city, they eagerly looked at the passersby up and down each street until at last they saw a man carrying a large jar of water on his shoulders.

Peter nudged John, and John, startled, saw the same thing, the two of them falling into cadence behind the man, a discreet distance away.

Twice, in the jostling throngs, they almost lost him, but finally succeeded in following him into a narrow side street, where he stopped to bang on a large door. Peter and John got close enough so that, when the door opened, they looked beyond the man and asked the servant at the door, "Could we see the master of the house, please. It's important!"

They repeated the statement as Jesus had instructed them, and were surprised to see the master of the house tell them happily, "Come in, come in. Yes, I've been expecting you!" Peter and John were led through the interior courtyard, through the kitchen at the rear, and up a flight of stairs to a large upper room where they saw tables and furniture easily able to accommodate Jesus and His disciples.

Why did this man expect Peter and John? Had an angel previously delivered the message? There is no record of it. Had Jesus Himself made arrangements a full year earlier, telling the man that He would send His disciples with such a message on the afternoon of the thirteenth? There is no way of knowing.

For about a month now the entire city had been in preparation for this most important of feasts. Bridges were repaired, walls whitewashed, sidewalks and drains repaired and replaced, decorative friezes painted, as the whole city took on an expectant, exciting pace.

Thousands of lambs were brought in from all parts of the countryside, and ceremonial preparations were underway in all homes for days in advance.

The priests would carefully select lambs "without blemish" out of the herds on the tenth day (about three days before Jesus sent Peter and John into Jerusalem to find their guest chambers) to be brought into the slaughtering places in the cities.

The candlelight searches were made through the nooks and

crannies of homes for leavening, and the scrubbing and washing
of utensils, pots and pans, the careful cleansing of silverware, the
collection of the bitter herbs and baking of unleavened cakes were
busily taking place throughout the city.

Citizens noted, with some chagrin, that the Roman legion
always sent additional concentrations of troops, both to remain
within the city and to bivouac in the nearby countryside, for they
always expected the possibility of an insurrection at this season,
when perhaps somewhere between one-and-a-half and two million
people would be thronging Jerusalem and its immediate environs
for the Passover. (Ancient writers such as Josephus indicate the
population of Jerusalem during the Passover season to be from
one to three million, though recent scholarship suggests this number could be exaggerated.)

Whose home was this where Jesus planned to take His last
supper?

The Bible does not say, but there may be reason to speculate
it could have been the home of Nicodemus, or the home of young
John Mark's father, or a large home rented for the purpose of the
Passover by Joseph of Arimathaea, a very wealthy man who
provided the tomb wherein Jesus was buried, and who actually
helped carry the body there.

In any event, Peter and John remained there for a time,
making sure all of the required rites for preparation of the Passover had been completed, that there was ample tableware and seat-
ing, and that other provisions had been made for the exact number
that Jesus would bring to this special Passover supper.

The servants couldn't understand it. The whole house was
thrown into an immediate uproar. Even though the master of the
home had tried to insure that all was in readiness, the household
help couldn't understand why in the world they were doing this
one day earlier.

For, notice carefully, Jesus intended sitting down to a
Paschal lamb supper *about 20 to 21 hours before all of the other
Jewish homes would be doing the same thing!*

Jesus intended eating the Passover supper early!

This truly was to be, then, a special "supper," later referred
to by the Apostle Paul as "the Lord's supper," and was taken
before the Jewish Passover! (See John 13:1.)

After sunset that evening, it was the beginning of the

fourteenth of Nisan, the day when the Israelites had been commanded to eat the Passover "between the two evenings."

Jesus' mind was almost continually fixed on that "other
dimension" now, and a great heaviness began to settle upon Him.
Still, it was mixed with the deepest sense of fulfillment, and even
personal satisfaction and warmth toward His disciples. Jesus knew
how much He really loved them, and how much spiritual information He wanted to convey to their minds during His last hours
on this earth, so that they themselves could give the greatest
witness possible at a later time.

We know from later Jewish sources that the Paschal supper
followed a rigorously exacting schedule, including specified
Psalms and prayers, four cups of red wine per person (which
would even require an individual who was too poor to afford it to
sign notes for future labor), plus the question and answer session
between father and son concerning the significance of the Passover in Egypt, and many other rites. Some sort of similar ceremony may have already been customary even at this time.

But Jesus' supper was far different. After they had all taken
their seats around the table, Jesus, having led them in prayer and
asking God's blessing on the food in a particularly moving manner, told them, 'I have had the deepest desire to eat this Passover
with you before I suffer. Because I'm telling you, this is the last
time I will eat it on this earth until it is fulfilled in the kingdom of
God."

The disciples were no doubt puzzled. They knew they were
sitting down to a lamb supper with the bitter herbs, unleavened
bread, the cups of wine; they knew that Jesus was particularly
heavy and seemingly serious and saddened; and they no doubt
expected that Jesus would be eating the regular Passover supper
with them either here or in some other place the following evening. Therefore, all the disciples were quite surprised when He
told them this was the *last* time He would eat of it until it was
fulfilled in the kingdom of God!

Suddenly, wild hope leaped into their breasts. They began to
talk excitedly among themselves, believing that true to the Romans' apprehensions, Christ was finally going to seize upon the
opportunity of the Passover *on the following night* to rally nearly
one-and-a-half million people around Him (probably by an
awesome series of miracles), simply overwhelm the Romans by

force of numbers, and establish a new kingdom of Israel right then and there!

Peter probably hastily excused himself during part of the noisy discussion that followed Jesus' sober words, and rushed downstairs to the foyer where they had left their outer cloaks, and retrieved his cherished Roman short-sword he had bought in a bazaar during their visit to the Syrophoenician coast.

While he was at it, he rummaged through the disciples' personal effects and found another sword hanging on a peg beneath a cloak. Expectancy and determination boiling up within him, he climbed back up the stairs and slid the swords under the mat on which he was sitting and rejoined the conversation.

The talk had turned to the deeds that had been done.

Peter could see Judas was getting in his licks down the table, and it seemed that Bartholomew, James, Alphaeus's son Thaddeus, and even Simon the Canaanite were nodding agreement.

Peter had been disgusted several times in the past over James's and John's constant discussions about who would "be the greatest" in the kingdom, and especially resented some of the interference of parents of some of the men, notably Zebedee's wife who had lobbied so heavily that "when Jesus came with His kingdom her boys ought to have the two top seats."

The talk swirled back and forth along the table, concentrating on certain qualities of character: who had been stronger in this or that confrontation, who had been used to cast out demons, who had attracted the largest crowds which had listened in this or that town during their earlier evangelistic campaign trips when Jesus had sent them out two by two. Finally, faces began to redden, voices raised a little, and a full-fledged argument seemed to be developing.

Jesus rapped for attention and said, "Now wait just a minute! You all know that the kings of Gentile nations exercise lordship over their subjects, and they that have authority over the people are usually called 'benefactors.' " (He said this somewhat sarcastically, for the record of bestial brutalities by Gentile kings, even including the oft-told tale of Herod's assassination of the children at Jesus' own birth, was well known.)

"But with you it will not be that way! He that is the greatest among you, let him become as if he were the youngest. And he that is the chief, as if he were a servant. For which is the greatest, he that sits at the table, partaking of the meat, or he that is doing the serving? Is it not he that is obviously sitting at his own table, partaking of his own meat? But I am in the midst of you as he *that serves*. But you right here are those special few that have continued with me in all of my temptations and trials; and I am appointing unto you a kingdom, just as my Father has appointed that kingdom unto me; that you will finally eat and drink at my table in my kingdom; and you will all sit on thrones judging the twelve tribes of Israel!"

They didn't understand this statement though we in retrospect can easily understand it today.

Jesus was showing the futility of reasoning carnally, bickering over special favors, and striving to use political methods and influence to gain prominence.

Rather, He reminded them how, just prior to the meal, He Himself had helped set it out, had arranged this or that place setting, had gone willingly to the kitchen to carry some of the food to the upstairs room, as He had always done; pitching in with His own hands to do task work. Jesus never followed the examples of the aloof Pharisees and Sadducees who loved to posture and flaunt their importance while they allowed others to wait on them hand and foot.

Judas, in lively discussion with several of the disciples whom he had greatly influenced, was seated close enough to Jesus that he could hear snatches of conversation between Jesus, John, James and Peter from time to time.

His mind was tormenting him. Was this the time? How could he slip out? Was there any way he could bribe a servant? He knew Peter had secretly stashed away a couple of swords, but he didn't feel this would be enough to resist an armed guard, arriving quickly and without announcement. Judas thought he had better bide his time—perhaps wait until the supper was over and maybe everyone would be asleep from the effects of the delicious meal and the few cups of wine.

But Judas used every opportunity during the lively discussion concerning rulership to get in telling blows about how he had saved them a great deal of money by his skillful financial transactions, and how much more popular he would prove to be with his deferential ways and especially his programs for the poor.

Judas seized what seemed to have been his best opportunity, with Jesus particularly preoccupied during the Passover supper, to launch into one of his longest and most emotionally intense accusations of Jesus.

Jesus had gotten up several times, but this time He returned to the table carrying some brazen pots and pans. When He had accumulated enough of them, Jesus stood up from the table, and began to take off His inner layer of garments until He was stripped to the waist, wearing only His loincloth. He then took a large towel and wrapped it around Himself, poured water into a large brass basin, and, beginning with one of the men at the end of the table, laid heavy emphasis on His words of a few moments before, "I am in the midst of you as one that serves," literally *acting out* His part of a "servant" by, of all things, beginning to wash the disciples' feet!

Bemused, Judas watched Jesus wash the feet of Thaddeus and Simon the Canaanite. When Jesus came to Judas, he probably rolled his eyes, winked significantly at a couple of people nearby, grimacing in hopelessness, as Jesus, with His head and shoulders bowed, washed Judas's feet.

Finally, it was Peter's turn. And Peter blustered.

He said, "Lord, what in the world do you think you're doing—are you going to try to wash *my feet?*"

Jesus looked at him and said, "What I am doing now, you don't understand, Peter, but you will understand afterward."

Peter couldn't stand all of this "serving" any further and so he said, "You're *never* going to wash my feet!"

Jesus smiled and said, "Peter, if I don't wash your feet, you won't have anything to do with me whatever."

Peter said, "Lord, you go right ahead—and don't wash just my feet, but wash my hands and my head as well!"

Jesus had to smile more broadly at this. "He that has had a bath does not need to wash anything but his feet, but is clean every bit. . . ." And, looking at all of them, while still noticing the glittering eyes of Judas, Jesus turned his statement into a direct and pointed lesson by saying, "And you are clean"—then with a glance in Judas's direction—"but not all of you." "Because," John added, "He knew who should betray him, therefore he said, 'You are not all clean.' "

Finally, He finished washing the feet of all twelve of them, replaced the basins, removed the water jars, swabbed up the remaining droplets of water with a towel, and, picking up His garments, got dressed.

He sat down again, then with voice rising above the hushed conversations he went on and said, "Do you know what I have done to you? You all refer to me as Master [teacher] and Lord and you say well, for so I am. If I, then, your Lord and your Master, have washed your feet, you also ought to wash one another's feet. Because I have given you an example, that you also should do as I have done unto you! In plain point of fact, I am telling you, that a servant is not greater than his lord; neither one who is commissioned or sent greater than the one who commissions or sends him.

"If you know these things, blessed are you if you do them! And I'm not talking of every one of you; I know each of you that I have chosen, and that the scriptures must be fulfilled that say, 'He that eats his bread with me lifted up his heel against me.' [Compare with Psalm 41:9] It is absolutely true that he who receives whomever I send is doing the same thing as receiving me; and he who receives me will receive Him who sent me!"

Only moments later, Jesus said loudly enough for several of the disciples to hear, "I am telling you the truth that one of you right here at this table is going to betray me! His hand is partaking of the food right here at the table, and that hand is going to betray me! But I'll tell you this, Woe be unto that man through whom I am betrayed!"

A deadly hush fell over the crowd.

Judas's face was sober. With widened eyes, he looked, with a combined pretense of shock and curiosity from one to another near him as if wondering which one of those other disciples could dare do such a thing.

A few tears sprang into a few eyes, and several of them were sorrowful.

Perhaps some few who had been influenced a great deal by Judas and had allowed themselves to criticize Jesus from time to time were suddenly conscience-stricken. Several of them had to take the opportunity to say, "Surely you don't think I would ever do a thing like that, do you, Jesus?" Jesus reaffirmed again, "It is one of you who is eating with me right out of this common bowl, who dips his bread in the dish and who will betray me. The Son of man will go through with all that is required and written of Him, so it is all predetermined; but woe unto that man through whom the Son of Man is betrayed! It would be better for that man if he had simply never been born!" John had had a moment to express himself to Jesus, and in a particularly moving moment leaned over and placed his head on Jesus' chest.

Peter thought John was whispering to Jesus, not recognizing that John was overcome with sympathy and compassion, or the emotion that he felt.

Peter crooked a finger at John and whispered in his ear, "Tell us, who is this he is speaking about?"

John leaned back a little further, and lifting his lips to Jesus' ear, said, "Lord, who is it?"

Jesus said quietly, but with a searching look at His three closest disciples near Him, John, Peter and James, "It's the one to whom I'm going to give this sop."

Picking up a piece of the bread, Jesus dipped it in the common vessel, picking up slivers of roast lamb with its juice, and purposefully leaned far over and gave it to Judas Iscariot.

Judas noticed that John's face whitened with shock, and suddenly Judas felt his body convulse with both rage and guilt.

Judas was thunderstruck. He sneered, "I suppose you think it is I, don't you Rabbi?" Jesus said, "Well, you said it."

This final, public break was more than Judas's tormented emotion could stand! His bitterness had grown in the recent days and weeks during the tortuous confrontations with the leadership in Jerusalem. And now, inside himself, his mind snapped and he lost all mental control.

While he probably couldn't really realize the enormity of the evil that was engulfing him, his hatred for Jesus became so fierce, so intense, that his normal reserves were destroyed.

Judas had become fair game for Satan the Devil!

Satan was always hovering near Judas in a constant attempt to get him to whisper in this or that ear, to influence this or that mind—all in order to bring about Jesus' degradation and death by any means possible. Judas's mental collapse was Satan's golden opportunity. He immediately took complete possession of Judas's mind, brain and body, entering directly into him so that he completely controlled his every act, word and thought.

Jesus was still looking at Judas, and recognizing with His

powerful perception of the spirit world that the glint in Judas's eye had suddenly taken on a wild demonic glaze, He spoke even more to Satan than He did to Judas: "Get on with it; whatever you intend doing, you'd better do it quickly!"

The other disciples all heard Jesus' words to Judas—yet none understood. They probably supposed Jesus was giving Judas a special commission to go out and strike some special deal for a specific purpose. Perhaps Jesus had asked Judas to buy some extra provisions for the Passover. Judas, after all, was still the treasurer of the group; and Jesus had often told Judas to go buy things that they needed or had urged him to give an offering to some poor person. Therefore, there was no special uproar at the table when Judas hurriedly gathered his garments, got to his feet, and went clattering down the stairs.

And so, while Jesus was still talking in calm tones to His disciples, Judas was cursing, flinging stones, and kicking at things in his path as he determined to seek out the officials and bring them back to Jesus to have Him arrested!

Instantly, after Judas had departed, Jesus said, "Now is the Son of man glorified, and God is glorified in him; and God will glorify him in himself." Jesus explained to them it was all going to come to a rapid head now, and began to urgently teach the disciples in a kindly but firm manner, words which seemed to recall for them the most striking example of Jesus' teachings they had ever heard, that time when they had slogged, lungs gasping for breath and foot-weary up to the heights of that mountain near Capernaum so long ago when Jesus had told them, "Blessed are the meek, for they shall inherit the earth."

Jesus now said, "Little children, I'm only going to be with you for a short while longer and then you're going to seek me, and as I have told the Jews, where I am going, you cannot come. so now I am telling you, A new commandment I give unto you that you love one another even as I have loved you, that you love one another in exactly that same way!

"So long as you do this, all men will know that you are my disciples. Your primary characteristic must be the love you show for one another!"

Jesus turned to Peter and said, "Simon, I'm telling you something; Satan the Devil has tried to get a hold of you, time and again, so he can sift you just like wheat; but I have been praying especially for you, that your faith will not fail! Even though I know all of you are going to be offended against me, because I remember what Zechariah wrote, 'I will smite the shepherd and the sheep will be scattered abroad.' But, nevertheless, after I am resurrected, I am going to precede you into Galilee."

Peter, having already asked Jesus, "Lord, where are you going to go?" said, "Lord, even though everybody else at this table would leave you, I never would! I am ready to go to jail with you, or to be killed!" Jesus said, "Really Peter? Are you really ready to lay down your life for me? I'm telling you the truth, that this very same night, before the cock crows two times, you are going to deny me three times!"

Peter raised his voice vehemently! Tears sprang into his eyes. Mortified, furious, indignant, and at the same time filled with an urgency to convince Jesus of his sincerity, Peter wondered why in the world Jesus would be talking this way when Peter himself was ready for the breathtaking announcement that the time had come to go out into the streets of Jerusalem and begin proclaiming the news that the Messiah was taking over and setting up His government.

Peter felt his whole life's calling disintegrating around his ankles. Searching wildly for what could possibly be behind Christ's words, he said again at the top of his lungs with tears filling his eyes, "Lord, even if I've got to stand there and die beside you, I will never deny you!" His speech was so moving that all of the other disciples were nodding their heads, with tears in their own eyes, and were saying the same thing!

"You bet!" "Yes!" "That's right!" "Me, too!" all of them said.

Jesus interrupted, "When I sent you out without a bag or a wallet, or without even extra sandals for your trip, did you lack anything?" They answered, "No, nothing." "Well, I'm telling you now, if you have a valise, you'd better take it, and likewise a wallet. And whoever has none, had better sell his cloak and buy a sword. Because I'm telling you that this which is written must be fulfilled in me [compare Isa. 53:12—"And he was reckoned among the transgressors"] so that everything which has been written of me will be completely fulfilled!"

That was more like it!

Now Jesus was making more sense, Peter thought. With alacrity, he reached under the mat, and pulled out the two swords. Several of the others had seen him bring them and, nodding their heads, backed up Peter when he said, "Lord, look! We've already got two swords!"

Jesus said, "That is quite enough!"

Peter had carried the sword in its sheath around his belt as a utilitarian utensil for a long time. With it he had done everything from severing fruits and vegetables, trimming and cleaning them, butchering and skinning animals, or wiping or scraping the mud off his shoes. He had kept the sword exceedingly sharp, for its manifold uses kept the edge somewhat dulled if he didn't see to it constantly.

Then, a new phase of the supper seemed to develop.

They had all commenced to eat again, when Jesus took a loaf of the flat bread, began to break it, and again fulfilling His servant's task work, "blessed" (asked God's blessing on it in a brief prayer), broke it, gave it to them, and said, "Take and eat of this, because this is my body which is given for you."

Jesus may have winced a little while completing the act of breaking the bread, for He knew that in only a few hours, His very flesh would be broken open in great wounds—that He would be fulfilling His role in this human life as a great sacrifice for the forgiveness of sins for those down through the ages who would believe in the symbol of "His body," broken through a vicious scourging and terrible wounds, as offered in sacrifice to fulfill the scripture, "by whose stripes are you healed" (I Pet. 2:24).

Later, He took the larger vessel of wine and poured it into individual cups, and after asking God's blessing, said, "Drink, all of you, because this cup is the New Covenant represented by my blood which is to be shed for many and which is poured out for you, for the remission of sins. Because I'm telling you I will not drink of the fruit of the vine from now on until the day that I drink it new with you in my Father's kingdom. Whenever you drink this cup, I want you to do it in remembrance of me, because whenever you eat this bread and drink this cup, you will be proclaiming the Lord's death until He comes again."

Paul would later be inspired to write, "Whenever you eat this [broken] bread, and drink this cup, you are portraying the Lord's death until the time He returns.

"Whoever eats this [broken] bread, and drinks of this cup of the Lord without really discerning the deep meaning of it, thus taking of the symbols unworthily, will be guilty of the body and the blood of the Lord.

"But let a person examine himself, and then let him eat of that [broken] bread, and drink of the cup.

"Because he that eats or drinks unworthily is condemning himself by eating and drinking these symbols; not clearly seeing the Lord's *body!* It is for this precise reason many are weak and sickly among you, and that many have died!" (cf. I Cor. 11:26-30).

Jesus knew His body was being offered in summation of all sacrifice; that every bullock, lamb, turtle dove or any other sacrifice was only a "schoolmaster" (Gal. 3:24) looking toward this one *great* sacrifice; the very body, in perfect physical condition, unblemished by any sin either in spiritual intent or through physical accident, and the blood of the Son of God!

By this institution of these New Testament symbols, Jesus was *changing* the character *and the time of observance* of the "Passover" for all Christians to observe hereafter. He was partaking of His own "supper" about 20 or so hours *before* the time of the Old Testament Passover, when the tens of thousands of families would be sitting down to their sacrificial roast lamb; and establishing *new* symbols which would look *back* to the reality of Christ's sacrifice of His broken body and shed blood, rather than *forward* (through the slaughter of animals) to the need for such sacrifice for sins!

No wonder He spoke with such fervor; no wonder He was so deeply profound!

One can imagine that, humanly, Jesus so wanted His disciples to "get" what was about to happen to Him! When we're distraught, fearful, or terribly shaken, our most urgent human need is for those we love the most to *understand!* Jesus was reaching out during this supper for the compassion and the empathy of His closest and dearest friends. Perhaps John alone, who was chosen to write almost all that Jesus spoke, and who leaned over against His shoulder in an expression of deep compassion, really came close to feeling the heaviness that was on Jesus—and managed to communicate his understanding.

Again, the disciples were both elated and puzzled. It seemed He was contradicting Himself time after time. First, He would send the wildest hopes to fill their breasts with a statement which seemed to imply He was virtually ready to rush out into the streets and begin His kingdom; and then He kept talking of His imminent death!

A gloom settled over the room again.

Peter was shaking his head in sorrow, wondering when they were going to get on with it. Others were deeply troubled.

Jesus then began to say, "Don't let your hearts trouble you. You believe in God; I want you to believe also in me. In my Father's house are many places and positions. If this were not true, I would have told you; because I go away to prepare a place for you, I will come again, and receive you myself, that where I am at that time, you can be there also!"

"And the place to which I go, I have shown you the way!"

Thomas, one of the skeptics of the twelve, piped up, "Lord, we don't know where in the world you are going, and not knowing this, how can we know the way?"

Jesus said, "I am the way, and the truth, and the life. No one can come unto the Father except through me. If you had known me, you would have known my Father also: And from now on you will come to know Him, because you have seen Him."

Philip responded, "Lord, show us the Father, and it will be sufficient."

Jesus retorted, "Have I been so long with you, Philip, and you still do not know me? He that has seen me has seen the Father. How can you say, Show us the Father? Don't you believe that I am in the Father and the Father in me? The words that I say unto you I do not speak from my own self, but the Father who abides in me accomplishes His works through me! Believe me, that I am in the Father and the Father is in me, or else believe me *for the very works' sake.* And truthfully, I am telling you, he that believes on me, the works that I do, he can do also; and even greater works than these can he do, because I will go to the Father.

"And whatsoever you shall ask in my name, that will I do, that the Father may be glorified in the Son. If you shall ask me anything in my name, that will I do!"

These lengthy, moving, final instructions to His disciples recorded in John 14-17 contain not only some of the most important doctrinal essentials of Jesus' teaching, but also graphic insight into His "other dimensional" awareness of precisely who He was, what He had come to accomplish, and where He was going.

This was the great God who had created the universe, trying to pack as much meaning into every word with His human disciples during these last moments on earth as He possibly could. This was the Son of Man, the Son of God, a member of the Divine Family, having changed Himself into a tiny collection of human cells, growing to be born of a virgin in Bethlehem, and living human life as it had never been lived before for thirty-three and-one-half years.

The final chapters were about to be written. His hour was coming, and He knew it.

With a profound resignation, knowing that He had conquered and overcome Satan the Devil and *could* have commanded him to come out of Judas, Jesus allowed the furious tide of onrushing events to carry Him along to the completion of His human destiny.

He reminded His disciples that soon another "Comforter," the very Spirit of God, would come, and would "bring to your remembrance everything I have told you"!

He chided them for not understanding much of what He had said; reminded them that He understood they didn't "get it," but gave them such a powerful discourse that His closest and most beloved disciple, John, was able to put in writing most of the essential words even some years later.

Jesus told them they could never bear fruit apart from remaining "in Him," and gave them the analogy of the branch of a vine which could never produce fruit except it remain joined to the major vine from which it received nourishment.

He told them, "Greater love has no man than this, that a man lay down his life for his friends. You are my friends, if you do those things which I command you!"

Jesus told them the world would hate them, even as the world had hated Him, and would hate their disciples on down through the ages to come.

He said, "If you were of the world [humanly devised societies] the world would love its own; but because you are not *of the world*, but I chose you out of the world, therefore, the world will hate you."

He told them some frightening things during this last "Lord's supper." He even warned them that the time would come when religious zealots would "put you out of the synagogue; yes, the hour will come that whoever kills you will think that he actually offers a special service to God!"

And then He made one of the strongest statements of all; that, even though He had told them that the cup was the "blood of the New Testament which was shed for them," the bread was "His body" which was offered for them, and sure martyrdom would come to them later, He said, "I have yet many things to say to you, but you couldn't stand to hear them now! However, when the spirit of truth has come, it will guide you into all the truth!"

Jesus well remembered that when He had previously given His larger group of disciples the teaching that He was "that bread which cometh down from heaven" and that "His flesh" was the "bread" they would have to eat, that many of them had left Him and refused to go along with Him any further (John 6:48-66).

He remembered even then how Peter had said, "Lord, to whom shall we go; you have the words to eternal life!"

Now He was telling His disciples even stronger things, if that were possible, and furthermore stating to them that many of the things He wanted to say were so strong they would not be able to understand and appreciate them at that time. Jesus reminded His disciples that God's Holy Spirit would lead them into greater understanding and into "all truth" at a later time!

He concluded a portion of the discourse by saying, "In a little while now and you will not be able to see me any more; then a little later, you will be able to see me!"

Some of the disciples began reasoning among themselves, and one asked, "What is this that He is telling us? Why is He telling us that in a little while you will not be able to see me, and then a little later and you will see me?" And, "What does He mean when He says, 'Because I go to the Father?' "

They said, "Just what in the world does He mean, 'In a little while?' We don't know what He is telling us."

But Jesus perceived they were desiring to ask Him and He said, "Don't reason around among yourselves about what I said, 'A little while and you won't be able to see me,' and then, 'A little later and you will see me.' I am telling you the truth that you will weep and lament, but the world will rejoice! You will be sorrowful but your sorrow shall be turned into joy!

"When a woman is giving birth she is full of pain because her time has come; but later when she has delivered the baby, she forgets all about the anguish, because of the joy that a child is born into the world!

"And you are growing sadder now, but I will see you again, and your heart will rejoice, and that joy no one can ever take away from you!"

These chapters of the book of John (14 through 17) are some of the most beautiful in all the Bible, especially the *real* Lord's prayer contained in the 17th chapter of John.

Finally, Jesus' lengthy discourse and prayer was over. Supper was finished now. It was a custom to sing hymns (from the *Psalms*) during the Jewish Passover observance, and Jesus wanted to sing a special hymn with His disciples prior to leaving the large upper room in which the lengthy dinner had been eaten.

They all stood, and Jesus leading in a clear voice, sang one of His favorite hymns. Probably it was one of the psalms, and one may speculate if it could have been the twenty-second and/or twenty-third psalm considering the former's application to Jesus' moments of agony on the tree, and especially the latter's promise of deliverance.

In any event, one can well imagine the emotions flowing through these men, after such a particularly heavy atmosphere during the lengthy meal, Jesus' very pointed statements and long discourse, and especially His tone of unusual finality in so much of what He had said.

Clearly, the disciples knew that something very unusual was about to occur.

They filed out of the room, and gathering their outer garments, after thanking the householder and the servants, went their way out into the streets of Jerusalem, down a steep slope, fording the brook Kidron which still ran full in those days, and began to walk along pathways winding up the opposite slope until they arrived at a beautiful arboretum and garden place which was named Gethsemane. There were benches and stones, and it was a site to which weary travelers could resort and enjoy the beauty of the plantings. Realizing the imminence of His situation, Jesus told the disciples, "Sit here while I go over there a little and pray."

As He had done so often, He took with Him the leading three disciples who had accompanied Him on so many special occasions in the past—including the transfiguration—Peter, and the two sons of Zebedee, James and John.

They noticed that a terrible troubled look had come over His face, and He turned to them and said, "I am terribly sorrowful, and deeply aching inside, to the point that I feel death upon me!"

He said, "Stay here and watch for me," and then, going forward a few more steps, about a stone's throw, dropped to the ground quickly, and even pressing His face forward on the ground, began to pray loudly enough that the three closest disciples could hear Him saying, "Father, Father, everything is possible with you! If there is any way to remove this cup from me . . . nevertheless, it is not my will that should be done, but your will!"

The prayer continued, Jesus being in an agony of intense communication with His Father, until, looking up, feeling a strong hand on His shoulder, He could see a powerful angel standing there to give Him encouragement and strength. It was as if He had received a direct communication that the turbulent events swirling about Him would continue exactly as they had been intended, and that there would be no respite from the suffering of the next few hours. After looking at the angel's face, He prayed even more earnestly, until He quite literally broke out into a sweat, with rivulets of perspiration falling from His nose and chin, dropping down on the ground.

He got up, wiping His face, and walked back and found the disciples curled up on the ground, asleep.

He grabbed Peter's shoulders and shook him, saying, "What! Couldn't you keep your eyes open and watch for me here for one hour? I'm telling you, watch and pray that you enter not into temptation; the spirit of course is always willing, but the flesh is weak."

Peter, James and John stumbled to their feet, rubbing their eyes and looking foolishly about. Then, after saying these words, Jesus groaned, turned away, and went back to His place of prayer a second time, dropping to the ground and praying the very same prayer again, begging His Father to "take the cup from Him" but quickly saying, "If this can't pass from me except I have to partake of it, then your will be done!"

After this second earnest prayer, He came back to this same area and found them sleeping again, because they couldn't keep their eyes open.

Again He rebuked them and told them they should be watching and praying with Him, and turning away for the third time, went back to the same place and began earnestly and intensively praying the same prayer.

As the being who was the God of the Old Testament, He knew the case of Elijah and the third request for the dead boy's life; Jesus was after all the very designer of numerical symbolism and its revelation to the prophets of old, and as surely as He had designed a seventh day for the perfection of the weekly cycle, knew that three represented finality. After He had prayed so movingly for the third time, Jesus knew He had His *final* answer. The original plan would continue.

Thus, returning after His third intensive prayer, Jesus said, "Well, go ahead and get what rest you can, then, because the hour is at hand, and the Son of Man is betrayed into the hands of sinners!"

As Jesus returned the third time, He heard the clatter of an approaching group, and saw the torches they carried as they forded the creek below. He cried, "Get up! We'd better be going, because the one who will betray me is right here!" He had no sooner finished the statement to Peter and John when Judas materialized out of the dancing light of the torches held by the nearest of the group, followed by a large number of others including the chief priests and elders, a number of soldiers, the officers of the temple, all of them obviously heavily armed, carrying the lengthy lances, Roman short-swords, and some wearing helmets and breastplates.

It was well known among the disciples that Jesus resorted to the area of Gethsemane, and Judas knew precisely where to find Him since he had heard Jesus discussing His plans for the later evening.

Jesus stepped out from the gloom into the flickering glare of the torches and lanterns and said, "Who are you looking for?"

Those in the nearest ranks answered, "Jesus of Nazareth."

Jesus said, "I am he!"

When these words came out of His mouth, the strangest phenomenon you could imagine occurred!

Several ranks of the group seemed to quickly stumble backward and actually toppled over and fell to the ground! A babble of excitement went rippling through the crowd as they tried to disengage themselves from each other. One or two leaped about, slapping wildly where a torch had touched their garments! They picked up their spears, readjusted their helmets and swords, as the whole group tried to create some semblance of dignity and order out of the chaos of the sudden, unexplained idiocy of those boobs up in the front rank leaning suddenly backward causing the whole group to lose their footing and fall over backward!

(Several cases in the Bible show that when a person is under demonic influence, he always "falls away backward," when confronted by the influence of God, or in the presence of an angelic messenger.)

While reasonable order was being restored to their ranks, Jesus waited; He then asked them again, "Who are you looking for?"

Again, one of them said loudly, "Jesus of Nazareth!"

"Fine!" he said, "I told you I am he, so if I'm the one you're looking for then let these others go," indicating His frightened disciples standing nearby. "Let these go their way." John later wrote that Jesus said this to fulfill the word that He had spoken in His prayer when He said, "Of those whom you had given me I lost not one."

About that time, Judas came directly up to Jesus and in the most cheerful possible fashion said, "Hello, Rabbi!" And, taking Him by the shoulders, kissed Him quickly on the cheek.

Jesus stood rigidly, looking at Judas in scorn and hurt, and said, "Judas, do you mean to tell me you would betray the Son of Man with a kiss?"

Peter and some of the other disciples had drawn protectively about Jesus, as if to try to conceal Him from the leaders of the mob; Peter said, "Lord, shall we attack them with these swords?"

Several of the soldiers leveled their pikes and spears, and one of the officers of the high priest made as if to seize Jesus. Peter took a step backward, and the whisper of his sword coming out of his sheath had barely been noticed when the flashing blade descended with a vicious arc through the air! The servant of the High Priest dodged nimbly, or Peter's Roman sword would have split his head open like a ripe melon! The priest's officer stumbled backward, and Peter's blade barely sliced through his ear, completely severing it from his head! Peter was raising the blade for a second blow as a wild yell went through the crowd behind.

Jesus quickly spoke with great authority, saying to Peter, "Put your sword away into its sheath! All those that take the sword will perish with the sword! Don't you think that I could turn to my Father and beseech Him and that He could send me more than twelve legions of angels?" Saying this, Jesus stooped down to the ground, picked up the officer's severed ear, and touching it to his head spoke briefly. The officer, amazed, put his hand to his ear and found it as whole as the other! Peter, mumbling, put away his sword and stepped back with the other disciples.

Jesus said, "Have you come out here to arrest me as if I were some robber; do you believe you have to be heavily armed with swords and spears to seize me? Here I was, sitting daily with you in the temple teaching and you didn't arrest me; but this is all being allowed to happen that the scriptures the prophets wrote might be fulfilled; but this is your hour and the power of darkness and desolation shall prevail. However, your time will be short."

The mob moved forward with several of the soldiers trotting quickly left and right with their spears at the trail, intending to surround the whole group. Quickly, the disciples all melted into the darkness, and fled as fast as they could.

Years later, young John Mark (the author of the second gospel) admitted that he had been among the group when he wrote about "a certain young man" who followed along after them, being clothed only with a linen cloth about his naked body, and when they mistook him for one of the disciples grabbing at his clothing, he left the linen cloth and fled away naked (Mark 14:51-52).

This took place probably either a little before or a little after the hour of midnight.

They bound Jesus, and, with significant jabs with the butt of their spears and wild talk among the officers and the chief priests about what would happen next, plus any number of threats that "we will finally find out about all of this" and "see just who is in authority here" and other threatening statements, they clattered their way along the trails back to the brook Kidron, and began to climb the other side.

The boisterous crowd took Jesus through the streets of Jerusalem, where the curious peered out of their upper windows at the throng going by at this ridiculously early time just before the Jews' Passover preparation. The noisy band finally came to the residence of Annas, who happened to be Caiaphas's father-in-law, the high priest for that year.

Caiaphas was the one who had given instructions to the Jews that it was expedient that one man should die for the people—little realizing the awesome spiritual significance of his remark.

At Annas's home, the high priest demanded to know of Jesus, "Now just who in the world do you think you are? What is all this teaching you have been bringing in the temple? Who are your disciples, and where are they from?"

Jesus answered, "I have spoken openly to the world; I continually taught in synagogues all up and down the country, and even in the temple, where all the Jews gather together. I have taught nothing in secret. Why are you asking me these questions? Ask those who have listened to me what I have taught them. Look! These people standing right here by you know exactly what I have said!"

At Jesus' sincere yet authoritative tone, one of the officers standing by slapped Him with a ringing blow to the head, saying, "Do you think you can talk to the high priest this way?"

Jesus, His ear ringing from the blow, turned to the man and said levelly, "If I have spoken evil, then accuse me of the evil deed; but if I have spoken well, why are you hitting me?"

The confrontation came to an end when Annas indicated they should leave Him bound, and take Him to Caiaphas's house where the scribes and the elders were gathering together in a "kangaroo court," having already sent runners far and wide to roust out of bed as many as they could recall who might have agreed in advance to bear false witness against Jesus.

Again, the noisy group clattered its way along the streets until it came to Caiaphas's house, where Jesus was held bound, while the final preparations were being conducted with the false witnesses.

One after another they whispered their stories in the high priest's ears, only to have them rejected because the high priest realized some of these wildly absurd tales would never stand up with the people.

Finally, however, two of the false witnesses agreed that Jesus had allegedly said, "I will destroy this temple, made with the hands of man, and then in three days, I will build another temple made without hands!"

Another said Jesus had actually claimed that He "would be able to destroy the temple of God and build it again in three days."

Jesus had been ushered into the presence of the high priest as these two false witnesses were making this statement, and it was then that the high priest stood up and said, "Do you have nothing whatsoever to say about this? What is this that these witnesses are telling against you?"

Jesus looked straight at the high priest, and didn't open His mouth.

The high priest, growing angrier by the moments said, "I adjure you by the living God [the words reassured him, and gave him a greater consciousness of his alleged godly authority] that you tell us whether you are the Christ, the Son of God?" Jesus said, "As you say, I am! And I am telling you you will see after this the Son of Man sitting at the right hand of power, and coming with the clouds of heaven!"

That did it!

The high priest was beside himself with rage! Furthermore, Jesus had finally spoken out so publicly and in such a super-charged environment with all of the essential leaders there, that the high priest could seize this opportunity to dispense with any need for further testimony from the false witnesses. Ripping at his garments so that he tore them (the habit of rending one's garments in the time of great emotional stress must have given deep emotional comfort to these posturers) in an anguished scream, the high priest exclaimed, "He blasphemes! What further need have we of witnesses? Listen all of you! You have heard that blasphemy yourselves! So what do you think we ought to do about it?"

The crowd began answering, "That demands the death penalty! He ought to be killed! He is worthy of death!"

Some of them walked near and began to spit in Jesus' face, while others slapped Him ringing blows across His cheeks, hitting Him about the head and ears, as the scene disintegrated into mob violence.

Here and there, one would reach over the outstretched arms and fists of others pummeling Him and shriek, "Prophesy! Who is this who just hit you?"

Of course, Jesus had been quickly blindfolded upon entering

into the house, so He could not recognize any of the witnesses who appeared against Him. This was done as a precaution in case this thing should get out of hand and develop in an unwanted direction, or if Jesus should prove to have so many sympathizers that for some reason the high priest and religious leaders could not execute their plan of getting rid of the man once and for all.

While He was both tied and blindfolded, these "courageous" religious leaders continued to beat Him on the face, shredding His lips against His teeth, opening up cuts with their bare knuckles, spitting on Him and saying, "Go ahead, prophet! Who is this hitting you? Tell me!"

Many were shrieking, "Bastard! False prophet! False teacher, friend of whores and harlots!" and other epithets of every sort.

Outside the high priest's home was the large outer court. After the clattering group with their flickering torches and lanterns had left the garden of Gethsemane, Peter picked himself up behind a large boulder where he had hidden, and stumbling along in the dark managed to parallel their course until they entered the city gate. He waited until they were sufficiently far ahead, and then followed along behind. Peter and John were both surprised to find each other in the streets as they were about to turn in to the court of the high priest. John had already entered the court, and was standing by a fire that had been hastily kindled so some of the officers and the soldiers could warm themselves.

John, wondering what was happening in the large lighted rooms, and waiting to see what would develop, noticed a furtive figure just outside the door, and in quick whispered consultation with one of the maids who guarded the door, asked if the man could be brought in.

She ran to do as John asked, and said, "Are you one of this man's disciples?" Peter said, "I most certainly am not!"

He then walked over to join John and the officers and some of the servants warming themselves by the brazier.

The girl wouldn't quit, it seemed. Standing across the fire, she gazed steadfastly at him and said, "I believe this man was with Jesus, that Galilean!"

Peter denied it again, saying loudly before all of them as they were murmuring about the events of the last hour or two and, looking now and then toward the lighted rooms where the screaming epithets were dimly heard, "Woman, I don't know what you're talking about! You don't know what you're saying! I most certainly was not one of his disciples. I don't even know who he is!"

Peter had to get away from this stupid girl, and so, leaving the warmth of the fire, went out on the porch.

As he arrived there, when it was just darkest before the dawn, he heard a rooster crow. Another of the female servants said to a group of the others standing there, "This fellow here was with Jesus the Nazarene!"

Peter cursed at this, and said, "I don't know the man!"

He began to use epithets and oaths, cursing and swearing, and saying, "I don't know what you're talking about! I have never seen him before!" But a relative of the servant of the high priest whom Peter's own sword had nearly killed, said, "Didn't I see you in the garden with him?" Peter continued to vehemently deny Jesus for the third time, and while the denial was still on his lips, heard the second crowing of a rooster nearby.

Peter could see the raised fists, hear the distant "smack" of the blows descending on Jesus just inside the lighted hall. From time to time, he thought he caught a glimpse of Jesus in the midst of His tormentors; then, shockingly, just as Peter finished his third loud cursing denial, a hush seemed to fall over the group inside. It seemed they had knocked Jesus' blindfold loose, and, quickly stooping to retrieve it lest He could identify all of them later, several bent to pick it up off the floor. Just then, in the hush, Jesus glanced Peter's way; and, just after the cock had crowed for the second time upon Peter's third denial, their eyes met. Jesus seemed to give a wan smile through pulped lips, just as His face was blotted from Peter's stricken gaze by those surrounding Him. (See Luke 22:60-61.)

Peter was thunderstruck.

Knowing that Jesus was inside the hall being treated like a common criminal while Peter was standing out here denying having ever seen Him, Peter threw himself down the steps into the streets, and finally leaned against a wall in the deserted darkness of predawn Jerusalem and sobbed until he thought his heart would break.

This was our Tuesday night, or by Jewish reckoning the nighttime part of Wednesday, the fourteenth of Nisan or Abib.

By the time it was daylight, the chief priests, elders and scribes dragged Jesus to the formal court of the Sanhedrin and demanded again to know "who he was," as part of their preconceived, carefully staged plot.

Earlier, while He was being kept bound and blindfolded, they had called a hasty consultation of the entire Sanhedrin, and agreed on a course of action that would surely result in His death.

True to their hopes, upon their repeated demand, "If you are the Christ, tell us!" Jesus answered, "If I tell you, you will not believe: and if I ask you, you will not answer.

"But I'll tell you this! From here after shall the Son of Man be seated on the right hand of the power of God!"

"Are you then the Son of God?" they sneered.

"You say that I am the Son of God!"

"What further need do we have of witnesses?" they shrieked. "We ourselves have heard this blasphemy from his own mouth."

To insure they had the complete approval of the top Roman governor, and to give the "kangaroo court" the semblance of legality, Jesus was secured in His bonds again, and led away to the residence of Pilate, the Governor.

At about this time, a servant came to some of the priests, and mentioned that a man was desperately wanting to see them on "a most urgent matter" concerning Jesus.

It was Judas. He said urgently, "I have sinned—I betrayed an innocent man!"

He thrust toward them the bag with 30 pieces of silver in it, and begged them to take it back.

The chief priests said, "Whose business is that? That's your problem!"

With that, Judas simply cast down the bag in the sanctuary, and left.

The chief priests gathered up the silver, and terribly careful to make sure they complied with Deuteronomy 23:18 said, "It isn't lawful to put this into the treasury, since it is the price of blood" and so decided after a hurried caucus to buy a potter's field to bury strangers in.

Even this fulfilled the prophecy of Jeremiah (see Jeremiah 18:2; 19:2; 32:6-15 with Zechariah 11:13). From that time on the field they bought with that money became known as the "Field of Blood."

John's account is particularly important at this point because he said that they led Jesus from Caiaphas into Pilate's palace while it was early "and they themselves entered not into the palace that they might not be defiled, *but might eat the* Passover"! (This passage absolutely *proves* that the Jews were going to eat the Passover later on in the afternoon of the fourteenth of Nisan or the early evening of the fifteenth as was their custom. Consequently, the supper Jesus had eaten with His disciples at the beginning of the fourteenth, called the Lord's supper by the Apostle Paul in I Corinthians the 11th chapter, was about 20 hours *earlier* than the Jewish Passover!)

Pilate wanted to know what the man was accused of, and the delegation said, "Obviously, if this man were not an evildoer we wouldn't be here with him! But we found him perverting our nation, forbidding us to give tribute to Caesar [all lies!] and even claiming that he himself is a king!"

Pilate said, "Fine. Do what you want. Take him yourselves and judge him according to your own law." But the religious leaders answered, "It is not lawful for us to put any man to death!" They knew they had to have the Roman governor's full permission before they could get away with their hasty "kangaroo court" and put Jesus to death.

Pilate relented and asked to see Jesus Himself. He knew the crafty dealings of these religious types. But he also knew their power over the people. So Pilate's curiosity was now really aroused. Who could possibly have elicited such feelings of jealousy and rivalry from these religious leaders?

In due time, Jesus was brought in, the blood-spattered garments and open cuts on His face, the spittle in His hair and His beard, testifying to the terrible treatment He had received.

Pilate asked Him, "So you are the one they are calling the king of the Jews?"

Jesus answered, "You are the one who is telling me! Are you saying this of yourself, or did others merely bring this story to you?" Pilate responded, "What am I, some Jew? It's your own people and the chief priests who have delivered you to me. Just what is it you have done?"

Jesus said, "My kingdom is not of this society. If my kingdom were of this time, then my servants would fight, I will assure you, that I should not be delivered to the Jews. But my kingdom is not of this time!"

"So you're a king?" Pilate asked.

Jesus said, "You claim I am a king. To this end have I been born, and for this purpose I came into the world, that I should bear witness unto the truth.

"Everyone that is of the truth hears my voice!"

Sighing, remembering his Roman education, and the teachings of some of the great philosophers, Pilate asked the age-old question still being repeated plaintively today, "So what is truth?"

Turning from Jesus, Pilate told the Jewish leaders, "I can't find any crime whatsoever in this man!"

The chief priests and Sadducees fell all over one another clamoring about the great crimes and sins Jesus was alleged to have committed.

Jesus, standing there, heard it all. Pilate turned to Him and said, "Won't you answer any of their accusations? Listen to how many things they are accusing you of!"

But Jesus stolidly refused to open His mouth in answer to the hideous tales they were telling, including everything from theft to adultery, robbery, a threatened destruction of the temple, insurrection, rebellion, refusal to pay taxes and every other crime and sin that they could imagine.

The more urgently they accused Him, the more Pilate marveled that Jesus would stand there quietly taking it, and never saying a word.

Hearing all these railing accusations, Pilate finally realized that the man was a Galilean and thought he could find a way to get out from under the calamitous insistence of the Jewish leaders in this riotous mess.

Obviously, the man belonged under Herod's jurisdiction, and Pilate, knowing Herod would be in Jerusalem for the feast, told them to take Him away to see Herod.

Herod was actually happy when he heard he would have an opportunity to interview Jesus, because he had heard about Him for a long time. Herod earnestly wanted to see Jesus privately, and had even hoped that maybe some miracle could be performed for him.

When Jesus was brought before Herod, it was much like the scenes at Annas's house, the house of Caiaphas, and the court of Pilate.

The chief priests and the scribes took turns vehemently accusing Him, with Herod sitting on his throne, the soldiers standing about, and all listening attentively.

Jesus repeatedly refused to answer. Question after question was hurled at Him; carefully worded, laboriously explained, doubly and trebly repeated accusations of the filthiest nature.

Herod thought he had found a way at last to build some bridges between himself and Pilate, with whom he had been having the coolest of relations.

If he could appear to be totally cooperative even with one of his own subjects in asking for Pilate's help, perhaps he could heal some of the wounds.

Seizing upon a ridiculous idea, knowing Pilate would appreciate his little joke, Herod decided to make a mock "king" out of Jesus.

He quickly gave some orders to his soldiers, who, searching through Herod's wardrobe, found a purple king's robe, together with all the other trappings of the royal attire, and hurriedly dressed Jesus, cackling and laughing in glee as they arranged the gorgeous apparel on him (see Luke 23:6-11).

When Herod was satisfied he had fully developed the charade and Jesus looked suitably attired to tickle Pilate's funnybone, he had the men take Jesus back to Pilate's residence.

It had been a custom for a long time for the governor of the province to grant a pardon for one leading prisoner as a sign of clemency at the time of the feast.

A very famous prisoner named Barabbas, a leader of a large group who had tried to overthrow the Roman government, was in jail. During the insurrections they had caused in this and that town, some had lost their lives, and Barabbas was up for murder. The early morning hours were waning by the time Pilate called together the chief priests and the rulers of the people. Finding Jesus had been delivered back to him from Herod again, Pilate said, "Look, you've brought back to me this man as if he were someone who is perverting and subverting the people. Now look, I have examined him before you, listening to everyone of the accusations you've brought, but I can find no fault in this man, and no corroboration for those things you accuse him of.

"Even Herod, when I sent him over there could find no fault in him, and has sent him back to me again. So far as I can tell, he has not done anything that would mean he is worthy of the death penalty. As you know, there is a custom that I should grant clemency to one prisoner at this time of the Passover."

Pilate hoped his words were scoring well with the Jewish leaders, for he seriously wanted to see Barabbas killed! The man had been the scourge of the countryside, and Pilate had had to send his legions clattering around in their chariots in fruitless searches here and there, but Barabbas had always eluded him until a fortuitous circumstance involving the bribery of a certain maid Barabbas was known to favor had delivered him into the hands of some of Pilate's more skilled lieutenants.

Pilate had no intention of seeing Barabbas get away this time, and was hoping that by making a public example of his death he could have a little peace for the next few months or so.

Therefore, he was sincerely hoping that these Jewish leaders, screaming for the death of Jesus, would listen to both the testimony of Herod and of Pilate himself, and would agree that Jesus had done nothing worthy of the death penalty, and conclude that Jesus was the one who should be released.

Pilate finished his speech, "Therefore, seeing that he has done nothing worthy of death, would you want me to release unto you this one who claims he is king of the Jews?"

Pilate had another very important reason for making this speech, because while he was sitting on the judgment seat during the very time Jesus was being interviewed by Herod, his wife had interrupted him, saying, "Don't have anything to do with that righteous man! I'm telling you I have suffered many things just last night in a vivid dream because of him!" She went on to tell her husband of some of the frightening things she had experienced in a very real vision, and urged him with all of her persuasive powers to see to it that he kept completely uninvolved

But his speech before the religious leaders was to no avail, and they began screaming that Jesus be crucified and Barabbas be the one released! Pilate asked, "Well, if I release Barabbas, then what am I supposed to do with this person you claim is the King of the Jews who is called Jesus the Christ?"

The mob screamed the louder, "*Crucify him, crucify him, crucify him!*"

It began to become a chant—surging, ebbing, flowing, growing increasingly louder! They began to stamp their feet in unison, jam the butts of spears on the court floor, some of them jumping up and down with rage as the chant grew ever louder, until it literally rang against the walls and echoed down the corridors of the governor's residence, *"Crucify him! Crucify him! Crucify him!"*

Finally, Pilate gained their attention by gesturing to the soldiers nearby, and when he had quieted the crowds, he said, "Why in the world should I do such a hideous thing as pass on him our Roman form of death sentence? What evil has he done?"

Jesus stood there with the blood draining out of the livid scratches and scars on His cheeks, His mock crown of thorns glistening wetly with the blood of His own head where it had been jammed cruelly down over His forehead and had gouged deeply into one eyelid. The gorgeous purple robes, so gleefully and playfully arranged by Herod, were now darkening with the drops of blood dripping out of His hair and from His beard. Pilate said, "Crucify him yourself! I can't find any crime in him whatsoever!"

One of the leaders finally gained Pilate's attention while he stood talking to the mob in the courtyard and said, "We have a law; and according to our laws that man ought to die, because he made himself the Son of God—and that is blasphemy!"

When Pilate heard these words, that the man had actually "made himself the Son of God," something struck his mind with a resounding jolt.

His wife's beseeching eyes and her urgent voice came to him, as did a great deal of his earlier teaching, and his own religious doubts.

He turned, went back into the palace again, and coming before Jesus who had been standing there with the drops of His own blood spattering the floor about Him, said, "Where did you come from?"

Again, Jesus did not move His lips; did not acknowledge Pilate's presence, and gave no answer.

Pilate, irritated, said, "Do you refuse to talk to me? Don't you know that I have the power to either release you, or the power to crucify you?"

At this, Jesus said, "You would have no power against me whatever, except it were allowed you from above. Therefore, because of this, those who delivered me unto you are guilty of the greater sin!"

That clinched it in Pilate's mind. A man who could speak this way, and act with this incredible dignity in the face of such a hideous death, saying such striking things in utter honesty, must not die. Pilate wanted very badly to release Him.

Returning to the men outside, Pilate again encouraged them to allow him to release Jesus. But they screamed the louder, saying, "If you release this man, you're going to be in terrible trouble with the Emperor! Everyone that makes himself a king is after all claiming to speak directly against Caesar!"

Pilate was perplexed. What should he do now? The Jews had scored a telling blow with this statement that any insurrectionist was actually looked upon as a direct rebel against Caesar's claim to divine powers himself. Pilate was in fact being blackmailed. He therefore decided to bring Jesus down to the judgment seat at a place on a wide courtyard called, The Pavement or in Hebrew *Gabbatha.*

John says, "Now it was the preparation of the Passover, about the sixth hour (by Roman reckoning probably 6:00 A.M.), and when Pilate had descended with Jesus to the courtyard where the mob stood, he said, 'Behold your king!' "

They screamed loudly again with the same chant, *"Crucify him! Crucify him! Crucify him!"*

Pilate shouted over their heads, "What? Am I supposed to crucify your very king?"

The high priest screamed, "We have no king but Caesar!"

Pilate sighed, realized he was getting nowhere, and that a riot was about to develop. So in the eyes of all, he called for a basin, dipped his hands, held them aloft so they could see the water, and went through the ceremony of handwashing, finally turning to the crowd and saying aloud, "You see it! I am washing my hands of it! I am proclaiming myself completely innocent of the blood of this righteous man. It's your problem, you see to it."

Willingly, the leaders screamed, "Fine! Let his blood be on us—and upon our children!"

Pilate, worried deeply about keeping his own office if this riotous tumult caused such an upset that it actually got all the way back to Rome, and recognizing he couldn't escape the full legal and even spiritual and moral responsibility for this surrender to the Jewish leaders, nevertheless couldn't seem to find any other way out. He desperately wanted to keep his own office, and had sincerely hoped that he could talk these rabid religionists into letting him release Jesus, and go ahead with his scourging and crucifixion of Barabbas. Instead, he found himself faced with the doubly obnoxious decision to release Barabbas, whom he knew assuredly would cause him terrible problems in the future, and to go through the brutal process of commanding his Roman soldiers to beat Jesus with a scourge, and lead Him out to be crucified.

Legionnaires in a Roman army were a motley collection from nations all over the Roman world; they came from Africa, from Germanic tribes on the continent, from faraway Spain, or even Gaul.

Most of them were totally illiterate save a few of their officers, and because of the harsh conditions under which they lived and fought, were wont to be as brutal as any soldiers at any time.

It was the soldiers who were finally given the nod at some-time between 6:00 and 9:00 A.M. in the morning on that Wednesday to lead Jesus away within the court (called the Praetorium). The Roman soldiers actually looked forward to venting their wrath and frustrations on this one man who claimed to be King of the Jews. What better way to attack this hated race than by scourging and crucifying their "king"!

The soldiers began by stripping Him of His blood-spattered clothing, finding a newer robe made of scarlet, and then, following the idea that Herod's own men had devised, jammed the crown of thorns back down on His head. They gave Him a useless reed for His right hand, and then, one by one came forward to do mock obeisance before Him, saying, "Hail, King of the Jews!"

As each leering soldier shuffled forward with his brawny forearms glistening with sweat, his leering, filthy face grinning in cruel expectancy, he would kneel before Jesus, grasp the rod (it was more like a cattle prod or a stick than a reed) out of His hand, and strike Him right across the top of the crown of thorns on the top of His head, saying, "Hail! King of the Jews!" Then, each one would hawk up a clot of spit and expectorate it fully into Jesus' face!

Finally, getting no response, save a wincing now and then, and the tightest shutting of His eyes, the Roman soldiers tired of their play, and took all of His garments away until He was naked.

The leader of the group grasped the heavy handle of his

scourge, letting the metal chunks grate ever so slightly on the polished floor, and, with a cruel leer at his fellow soldiers, his eyes feverishly glinting with a perverted bloodlust, he flailed at Christ's back with all his strength.

A scourge was the Roman version of the "cat-o'-nine-tails," and featured leather thongs with bits of metal wrapped in the ends of each one, fastened to a wooden or a heavy leather handle.

Oftentimes, a person who was so scourged died in the whipping, just as many seamen in the navies of the world, both then and in the generations thereafter, have died during a particularly vicious whipping on the gratings.

Jesus grunted in terrible pain, his back arching spasmodically, lips torn back from bleeding face and gums. The first blow had cut him deeply, splattering blood and chunks of flesh on those soldiers closest; they stepped back quickly, wiping at their faces and clothing.

"Chunk!" "Splat!" "Smack!" The raining blows continued; opening great gouges in his arms, chest, stomach, back, thighs and legs. The soldier's great chest heaved with his efforts; his companions laughed with perverted, bestial pleasure; Jesus' moans were becoming a dull sob, a bare whimper, until He almost fainted!

A splashing bucket of water in the face, and, jerking Him upright again, the hideous beating continued! Jesus was stark naked and terribly vulnerable; and the soldier now and then deliberately flayed the whip at his hips so as to strike out at his manhood.

The Roman soldiers, delighting in their animal-like bloodlust, took turns whipping Jesus' body until they quite literally laid open His flesh, exposing the ribs through the wounds, with chunks of lead and metal biting deeply into His body, and splattering the hall and the Romans themselves with His blood.

They beat Jesus until He fell, hauled Him to His feet, and beat Him until He fell again. Finally, they had to tie Him upright and continue the vicious beating until Jesus' head slumped down in total exhaustion and He had to be revived once again.

"Wait! Wait!" an officer cried out! "TenSHUN!" he screamed. The whip trailed bloodily on the floor. The soldier's face glistened with blood and sweat; his crazed eyes bulging with half-insane, animal-like incomprehension.

"You'll kill him, you fool!" the officer screamed! "If he dies here you'll be crucified in place of him, I assure you!" "Let's get on with the crucifixion. You two, pick him up; revive him, and let's get going—a huge crowd is gathering, and we may not be able to get him through it to the gate alive if we don't hurry! I'll want a triple guard, and a runner sent to the gate; we've got to keep this thing from getting out of hand!"

With a bitter glance at the still-dazed leader of the group carrying the whip, the officer said, "You stay here! I may have to talk to you later!"

With that, another bucket of water was splashed into Jesus' face, and they dragged the hideously deformed man to His feet. Quickly throwing His own clothes back on Him, they half-dragged, half-carried Him from the garrison room back to the street. They led Him out, and, holding up the heavy wooden beam He was to bear, slowly lowered it onto His hideously torn back. Then, urging Him on with whips, they began to lead the procession through the crowds.

By now, with His face a purpled, livid, blackened and bloody swollen mass, His eyes swollen nearly shut, one eyelid laid horribly back, huge open wounds in His scalp, shreds of skin and flesh openly exposed, Jesus would not survive much longer, the soldiers knew. So they hurried along the street, urging Jesus along when He stumbled and fell, inexorably moving toward the denouement of their bestial drama—crucifixion.

He could still speak even though His lips were torn and swollen twice to three times their normal size. As He felt His strength draining from Him, He knew He could not survive much longer. It was becoming increasingly difficult for Jesus, wracked with pain, to keep His mind focused on God and His own mission. But He prayed to God, utilizing all His mental efforts, and God gave Him the strength to continue.

When they first placed the heavy beam on Jesus' back, He trudged a few painful steps, and crying out in pain, stumbled and fell under the weight.

As the mob wound through the streets, they grabbed a man out of the crowd who happened to be Simon of Cyrene, a well-known older man, the father of Alexander and Rufus. The soldiers laid Jesus' stake on him, so he could trail along after Jesus. This cruel treatment of an elder, and a known person in the Jewish community, was only one more example of the utter contempt in which the Roman soldiers held the Jewish populace.

A large crowd began to gather, including dozens of women and men who were weeping and throwing dust in the air, sobbing aloud and letting out gasps of pity and remorse each time Jesus slipped and fell as the bedraggled figure lurched forward along the stony streets toward the gate of Jerusalem. On one occasion, Jesus turned to a group of the women and said, through thickened, swollen, purple and livid lips, "Daughters of Jerusalem—don't cry for me! Cry for yourselves and your children! I'm telling you that the days are coming in which they will say, 'Blessed are the barren and the wombs that never bore, and the breasts that were never nursed!'

"Then shall they begin to say to the mountains, 'Fall on us, and to the hills, cover us!' [Compare with Hosea 10:8.] Because if human beings can do these things in easy times, what will they do when terrible tribulation comes?"

The grisly procession continued out of the gate, turned slightly to its left and passing through a stony area where the herdsmen gathered their flocks for sale, descended along a pathway into a pleasant garden area bounded by a group of trees against the bluff of a large limestone outcropping.

Turning to the left, they started climbing this rocky hill, until they achieved the grassy slope atop it, and thus could look back at the city of Jerusalem only about two or three city blocks away from this height. The hollowed-out caves in the face of the limestone outcropping had given rise to its name, "the place of the skull," which was the meaning of its Hebrew name, *Golgotha.*

There the hole was dug for the stake, and Jesus' body was nailed to it, His arms wrenched over His head and driven firmly to the timber with a single spike through them, while His feet were fastened to the wood with a large spike driven between the bones of His toes.

Then He was hoisted in the air as the stake was jammed into the ground. A scream of sheer agony spasmodically burst forth from Jesus as the soldiers labored with shovels to insure that the stake was propped upright.

A carefully inscribed inscription had been arranged and had been tacked on the top of the stake. The inscription said, "This is Jesus of Nazareth, the King of the Jews."

Interestingly enough, Pilate himself composed the title

plainly stating that Jesus *was* the King of the Jews! (John 19:19).

Why? Was he being sarcastic? Was it a joke? An oversight? A mistake? Or just perhaps could he have begun to think that it might be true!

Seeing the inscription the priests and their officers were outraged. And panicked.

A delegation was quickly dispatched to Pilate's residence once more. Upon being admitted, they said, "The inscription is wrong! You should have put, 'This man *says* he is king of the Jews'; or '*claimed* to be King'; or even included the word 'impostor,' or 'pretender,' or 'criminal,' or 'fool,' or something. But you have said, 'This is Jesus of Nazareth, King of the Jews'!

"It is as though the sign is actually stating that Jesus is *in fact* the king of the Jews. This is disastrous. What will the people think? There are citizens here from all over the Roman Empire. We're all terribly embarrassed."

Pilate sighed wearily. It had been a long, hard night. First, these frenzied religious fanatics had roused him out of a sound sleep. Next, he had been involved in a political maneuver with Herod. Then, he had narrowly averted a riot in Jerusalem. Then he had been terribly bothered by his wife's dream.

Pilate's mind was plaguing him to death at the manner in which this person, Jesus, had allowed Himself to be manhandled, and at the strange answer He had given Pilate about being a "king" of some yet future, unknown kingdom.

"I have written what I have written," he said, eyes red-rimmed, heaving a weary breath, "and I'm not about to change it! The inscription stays!"

Muttering oaths to themselves under their breath while simperingly bowing, stepping backward, and, finding their way out to the street again, the tight-lipped group started back to Golgotha to report the bad news.

The inscription stayed as it was—well, he was still dying, wasn't he?

But the thought lingered: the inscription categorically stated that Jesus of Nazareth *was* the king of the Jews. It kept everybody on edge.

One of the soldiers had stripped Jesus' clothing from Him and another one of them reached up and tore the last of His garments off. Later, the Roman soldiers who had been sent to finish the whole sordid mess sat at the foot of the three stakes after they had finished hoisting each in place (including two criminals who were being crucified with Jesus) and began to gamble for His clothing (which was expensive).

Even this fulfilled a scripture (see Psalms 22:18) which said His garments would be parted among them, and "upon his vesture they would cast lots." John explains that Jesus' coat was "without seam, woven from the top throughout" and that the soldiers agreed that because of this it would be a shame to cut it into pieces.

By then it was about noon, but what was happening to the light? It seemed to be growing strangely dark!

Large crowds now had been informed of the proceedings, and they came by in the hundreds, reading the inscription, making their comments, wagging their heads, screaming epithets at Him, with each one trying to outdo the other with his bitterly clever invectives. One such person screamed, "Ha! Hey, you up there who claimed you could destroy our temple and then build it again in three days! If you are the Son of God, why don't you come down from that stake?"

The Scribes, elders and leaders of the people were standing around, so they could make comments to different ones who came by; their favorite chiding remark, repeated to many, was, "Sure! He claimed to have saved others, but he can't seem to save himself, can he?

"If he is the Christ, the King of Israel, then let's see him come down from that cross so everyone can believe on him!"

Finally, one of the dying criminals could stand it no longer, and turned to Jesus and said, "What is all this they are saying? You claim you are the Christ. If you are, for pity's sake, save us and yourself!"

The other thief said, "Shut your mouth! Even while you're dying, don't you have any fear of God, seeing you're in the same condemnation—and you and I are only paying for our own crimes which we deserve, but this man has done nothing!" Turning his head painfully he said to Jesus, "Remember me, please, when you come into your kingdom!" Jesus said, "Truthfully, I am going to tell you right now—you *will* be with me in paradise!"

It was indeed growing very dark now, and more torches and lanterns had been lit.

Mary, Jesus' mother, her sister, Mary the wife of Cleopas, and Mary Magdalene had managed to come forward in the crowd, weeping, looking with terrible anxiety and shock at the emaciated, disfigured, swollen, puffy, purple and livid figure, naked on the stake. Mary thought her heart would break. She didn't think she could stand it, but, unable to tear her eyes away, and yet seemingly unable to look, she stood aghast at this hideous spectacle who had been her firstborn, announced by angels, protected of God, and used to perform great miracles which she herself had seen, beginning in the household, from Cana of Galilee to the last moments of His teaching, just yesterday, here in Jerusalem.

Jesus opened His swollen eyes, and, blinking, saw His mother and John standing at the foot of His stake. Rousing Himself sufficiently that He could say in painful tones what He had in mind, knowing that their homes and properties would be seized by the leaders, that His brothers would be hunted and possibly even killed if they did not escape, that His disciples would disintegrate and flee back to their own businesses and into the security of anonymity, He said, "Woman, behold your son." Indicating John, He said, "Behold your mother!"

John got the message, as did Mary. John never left Mary from that moment on, and when they finally left the site of Jesus' death, John continued to stay right at Mary's side, taking her into his own home, and taking her with him on a trip which was to occur within a few months. (Could Mary have later gone with John to the Isle of Patmos?)

Gradually, everybody began to mutter in hushed and excited tones that something extraordinarily strange was happening!

"It's growing very dark, isn't it?" one or two began to exclaim. Others began to chime in about how dark it seemed to be getting, that the sun seemed to be growing dimmer, until finally it actually appeared as if a great eclipse or some terrible blackness was occurring. But this was unlike any eclipse they had ever heard of or seen before; it grew darker and darker until it was as black as midnight. It remained that way from after noon until 3:00 P.M. that afternoon! Torches in the streets were lit, and people were groping about because now it was completely dark!

During this time, Jesus was praying as hard as He could in His mind, calling out to His Father in heaven as He felt His life ebbing and seeping away from His body. From time to time, He saw visions of angels, knowing that powerful angels were all around Him, in the air over Him, at the foot of His stake, and there beside Him.

But suddenly, the angels were gone!

He felt a terrible cold blackness beginning to descend over His own mind and body. It was almost as if someone had put an impenetrable veil between Him and His heavenly Father.

Jesus was startled! This had never happened before. He was totally alone!

Something horrible had happened! Something completely unexpected. This wasn't part of their plan! Something had gone wrong!

Jesus, in constant prayer, had gained the spiritual strength and courage to stand the hideous beatings, the torment and torture. He had even been able to withstand the wrenching, shattering pain when the nails had been driven through His hands and feet and the stake jammed into the ground. Jesus had always been able to find methods of renewing His determination by His continual prayers to God the Father, and the feeling of God's Holy Spirit being renewed within Him was God's sure answer.

But now, suddenly, at the very time when He most needed comfort and sustenance, it was gone! Jesus looked out into space, as it were, and seemed to see the retreating back of God!

Jesus was cut off. Alone.

He couldn't believe it! It seemed that even His Father had now forsaken Him. He cried aloud, wanting desperately to see a strong angel standing by; remembering the time when at His very last moment of life in the wilderness with Satan to torment Him, He had been picked up by strong angelic hands and given nourishment and succor.

But now, *nothing.*

God the Father had placed the sins of all humanity on the body and being of Jesus.

Feeling the continual draining of His strength, and sensing the horror of His solitude, Jesus cried out in shock, pain and surprise, "MY GOD, MY GOD, WHY HAVE YOU FORSAKEN ME?!"

Because He said it in Aramaic, using the word *Eli* ("my God"), some of those nearby misheard and thought He was calling for the prophet Elijah.

Only a few moments had passed after Jesus, in great mental shock, cried out those terrible words—"My God, My God, why hast thou forsaken me!"—when, with His head bowed, He seemed to feel a moist, bitter softness pressed against His torn, terribly swollen lips and, stirring slightly, opened His dry, aching mouth and allowed a small trickle of the bilious mixture of vinegar and a strong soap-like cleansing agent made from a bitter plant called hyssop to pass His teeth. No sooner had this been done than the sponge was pulled away from His mouth and the soldier who had affixed it to the staff of his spear, reversed his spear, and, with a derisive laugh, thrust it into Jesus' side!

Screaming out in pain, Jesus' head hit the back of the stake with a solid whack, His body arched, His limbs straining against the large spikes pinning His members to the upright pale, and, muscles spasming and trembling, said, "Father, I commend my spirit into your hands!"

With this final soft utterance, the straining muscles relaxed, the bubbling stream of stomach fluids and blood running in a full rivulet down His hip, along His leg and dripping in a steady stream from His feet, gradually ebbed to a slow dribble, and His head lolled forward.

His body became pale, shockingly waxen beneath the livid blues and red of His dust-encrusted wounds, and looked even more grotesque in the flickering torchlight.

The blood dripped from His matted hair, from His nose, from His chin, and from the great gaping wounds up and down His body where the dull, yellowish color of blood and lymph could be seen here and there.

Isaiah's prophecies that He would "sprinkle all nations" with His own blood, thus providing one sacrifice for all sins, and that He would be so disfigured that He would no longer resemble a human being, had come to pass. So had the prophecies that not a bone of His body would be broken, and the graphic fulfillment of David's twenty-second psalm, in which, as Jesus had read and studied so many times as a young growing man and later had sung in hymns through His ministry, the very thoughts which went through His mind on the stake had been set to writing centuries before.

"My God, my God, why have you forsaken me! Why are you so far from helping me, and the words of my roaring. Oh my God, I cry in the daytime, but you do not answer; . . . I am a worm, and no man; a reproach of men, and despised of the people.

"All they that see me laugh me to scorn; they stick out their lower lip, they shake their head, saying, He trusted on the Lord that he would deliver him, so let him deliver him, seeing he delighted in him.

"But you were the God that took me safely out of the womb; protected me and gave me hope when I was a baby on my mother's breast. . . . You were my God from my mother's belly.

"Be not far from me; for trouble is all around me, and there is no one to help.

"Many bulls [*cherubim*] have compassed me, strong bulls of Bashan beset me around, and gape at me with their mouths as a ravening and roaring lion.

"I feel my strength pouring out like water, and all my bones are being pulled out of joint: my heart is like soft wax, it is melted in the midst of my innermost parts.

"My strength is drying up like a potsherd, and my tongue is stuck to my jaws; and you have brought me into the dust of death.

"Dogs have compassed me; the assembly of sinners have surrounded me; they have pierced my hands and my feet.

"Look! I can actually count my bones, my own bones seem to stare at me!

"They are parting my garments among them, and gambling over my clothing.

"Be not far from me, O Eternal, O my strength, hurry to help me."

This striking psalm of David, seemingly echoing the deepest and innermost thoughts of Jesus' own last moments on the stake, concludes with, "From one end of the world to the other they will finally remember and turn to God; all the people of all nations will worship before you!

"Because the kingdom is the Eternal's and he is the ruler among nations. It makes no difference whether they are healthy, successful and wealthy, every human being who goes back to the dust from which he came will finally bow before God, and no one can preserve his own life.

"They shall come and shall declare his righteousness unto generations not yet born, that God has done this."

Immediately afterward comes one of the most beautiful and most well-known of all the psalms and one that perhaps Jesus

Himself could well have repeated just before He perished!

"The Eternal is my shepherd, I will never lack anything.

"He makes me to lie down in green pastures, He leads me beside the restful waters; He restores my soul, He leads me in the paths of righteousness for His name's sake.

"Yes, even though I walk through the valley of the shadow of death, I will fear no evil, for you are with me; your rod and your staff they comfort me.

"You are preparing a table before me in the presence of my enemies; You anoint my head with oil; my cup runs over.

"Surely goodness and mercy will follow me all the days of my life—and I will dwell in the house of the Eternal forever!"

The moment Jesus died, a great earthquake rocked the land from one end to another; a deep subterranean noise rumbled like a thousand Niagaras, bricks and mortar began falling, people were knocked to the ground or swayed on their feet as they reached out for trees or walls to prevent them from toppling over.

Though not so great a quake as to lay waste the city, there was significant damage to any number of buildings. The shattering event was extremely frightening, especially on the heels of the mysterious blackness that had crept over the land beginning about noon and caused thousands upon thousands to drop to their knees, believing it was "the Day of the Lord" as Joel had prophesied!

"The end of the world, the end of the world!" some screamed and sobbed! John, Mary Magdalene, Mary the mother of James the Less and Joseph and Salome were standing a distance away from the stake when the earthquake struck. They had actually seen the soldier thrust his spear into Jesus' side, and had watched Him die.

Going back several minutes and shifting the scene to the center of Jerusalem, people could see the flickering torches which had been lit about noon to provide light in the temple court, where the thousands were going about the ritual of the slaughtering of the Paschal lambs.

Though they had to work by the light of hissing torches, flickering candles and glittering lanterns, the priests were determined to follow their prescribed rituals. The high priest, having been awake most of the night before planning Jesus' death and with Jesus' own testimony still ringing in his ears, had been terribly upset all morning. He couldn't keep his tormented mind and twisted emotions off that horrendously misleading and terribly embarrassing sign over the crucified Jesus which was still informing multiple thousands that Jesus of Nazareth was the King of the Jews!

But the high priest finally went through the prescribed washings and changed into his purest linen vestments with shaking hands, all the while looking over his shoulder at the black, lowering skies, and frantically trying to maintain some semblance of calm for the sake of all of the people who were nervously chattering, milling about, glancing around in apprehension, looking upward, or even praying quietly from time to time.

After all the required pronouncements and blessings had been completed, and amidst the leading families who had been admitted to the temple court with their lambs, the high priest approached the very first of the Paschal lambs to be slaughtered, held by two of his assistants a distance from the altar. Waiting in two lines were a group of priests with gold and silver bowls ready. The blood would be collected from the animals' throats, and passed hand over hand along the line of priests to be splashed at the base of the altar. The gleaming white marble columns led toward the entry to the Holy Place where the shewbread and the altar with its lamp of seven brazen pipes stood.

Beyond it, the veil—which was opened only once a year on the Day of Atonement (*Yom Kippur*)—was securely fastened. Behind the veil had once stood the ark of the Covenant; dully gleaming with its gold overlay, its two cherubim with wings outstretched almost touching over the mercy seat, with the sacred and prized jar of manna, along with the two tables of stone which Moses had put there so many centuries ago at Horeb. But this had been lost before the Exile, and the Holy of Holies now stood empty.

The formalities all finished, the high priest beckoned to all the people; and as a hush fell over the crowd, he raised the ceremonial knife high above his head.

It was then about three o'clock in the afternoon and the land had been engulfed in terrible darkness for almost three full hours.

The knife descended on the exposed throat of the lamb, and with a swift sure cut, the high priest slit the animal's throat. Just as the knife had accomplished its mission, a sudden dull, huge rumbling began to erupt from the bowels of the earth. The buildings and court of the temple began to slightly sway, some few people lost their balance as others clung to each other or grasped at a pillar or wall for support. The priest had to steady himself as he finished the sacrificing of the lamb. Screams, shrieks, cries and exclamations of dismay swept through the crowd and all over the city. Then an extraordinary sound was heard—as a large *tearing* noise from inside the Holy Place!

A servant, dispatched by the high priest, quickly ran to the entry, and face pale, came back to report, as the rumbling subsided and the first groups were catching the blood of the slaughtered animal in their ceremonial vessels, that "the veil that covered the Holy of Holies has been completely ripped from top to bottom!"

The high priest desperately tried to still the nagging voices of conscience plaguing his now tortured mind, and with the most urgent beckoning toward his assistant and the other priest, he indicated that the ceremony, already begun, should swiftly continue!

Nothing could prevent the precise timing of this centuries-old celebration of the Passover, the killing of the first ceremonial lamb, and then the swift butchering of the hundreds and thousands of additional lambs as each clan or large household came into the temple court to sacrifice its own lambs with the same ceremonies: the slitting of the throat, the passing of the blood, its dashing against the altar, the hanging of the lambs on pegs round about the walls or over strong men's shoulders while the viscera was dumped in a growing pile, the hides quickly stripped while the animal was still warm, and the fat thrown on a blazing pyre in offering.

What an incredible scene!

But the most incredible part of all was the ultimate spiritual significance that multiple millions of human beings would forever after understand was contained in those stupendous events. For little did the high priest realize that just as his ceremonial knife descended upon the exposed throat of the lamb, flashing with dull radiance in the flickering torchlight, so had a Roman soldier on a hill just outside Jerusalem quickly reversed the staff of his spear, shaken off the wet sponge with its bitter contents, and with a vicious laugh, thrust his spear into Christ's side!

Did Jesus of Nazareth die on the stake at the precise instant the sacrificial lamb died in the temple? Was Jesus Christ brutally slain at the exact moment of time when the *very same high priest who had just plotted His death* ritualistically slaughtered the un-blemished lamb?

Paul wrote that "Christ our Passover" is sacrificed for us (I Cor. 5:7). The Gospel accounts state that Jesus Christ died at the ninth hour, which was three o'clock in the afternoon of the fourteenth of Nisan.

The Jewish historian Josephus, who was born a few years after Jesus' death and lived throughout the last years of the temple in Jerusalem reports that the Passover lambs were sacrificed from 3:00 P.M. to 5:00 P.M. on the afternoon of the same fourteenth of Nisan!

"Accordingly, on the occasion of the feast called Passover, at which they sacrifice from the ninth to the eleventh hour [3:00 to 5:00 P.M.], and a little fraternity, as it were, gather round each sacrifice, of not fewer than ten persons" (*War* 6.9.3).

The indication from Josephus's description seems to be that *all* the Passover lambs from all the people were sacrificed within that two-hour time period. If this was indeed the case, the first unblemished lamb that had to be ceremonially sacrificed by the high priest had to have been scheduled for the beginning of the period, or precisely at 3:00 P.M. on the afternoon of Nisan 14th!

Independent confirmation of the approximate time of the Passover sacrifice comes from the *Book of Jubilees* (written in the second century B.C.) which gives a time between about 2:00 P.M. and 5:00 P.M.; and from early rabbinic literature (edited in the second century A.D.) which gives a time of sometime after 2:30 P.M.

If this temporal "coincidence" between the sacrifice of the Passover lamb and the sacrifice of Jesus Christ is striking, its spiritual implications are absolutely overwhelming.

The unblemished lamb that was required to be sacrificed every year by the high priest represented the recognition by Israel that death was the only way to absolve sin. This practice of sacrificing animals had been continuing from time immemorial. Yet it was really "not possible that the blood of bulls and goats should take away sin" (Heb. 10:4).

So God was now making a way to remove sin. God was raising the stakes of the sacrifice—infinitely!

Rather than offering the physical life of a lamb for the physical transgression of Israel, God the Father was now going to offer the life of His Son for the spiritual transgressions of all mankind (see Hebrews 9 and 10)!

The sacrifice of the lamb enabled human beings to live their physical lives forgiven from sin; the sacrifice of Jesus Christ would now enable human beings to attain a spiritual life—the promise of eternal inheritance—forgiven from sin (see Heb. 9:12-15).

God states that the wages of sin is death (Rom. 6:23). Consequently, it would take a death to pay the penalty for the sins of each and every human being. But God planned to offer in our place Jesus Christ, whose life, as Creator of the universe, was worth more then the combined lives of all mankind from all time put together. Christ would only have to die once (Heb. 9:26; 10:10-12), and through that death every man would have the chance to be justified before God and live forever.

Now what about Caiaphas, the high priest that year? It was his responsibility to sacrifice the unblemished lamb as an offering for all Israel. And he was also the very same person who plotted, organized and expedited the crucifixion of Jesus.

What powerful spiritual concepts are contained in Caiaphas's dual role that fateful year. The high priest symbolized all Israel when he ritualistically slaughtered the lamb as a sin offering to God. And this very same high priest just as surely symbolized all mankind when he accused and condemned Christ!

Then, bringing the overwhelming spiritual plan of God to its climactic point of spiritual impact, this same high priest slits the throat of the sacrificial lamb just as the Roman soldier spears the side of the sacrificed Christ!

Previously, Caiaphas had reasoned that it was "expedient that one man should die for the people" (John 18:14). What he had said was absolutely true—but in a way, and for a reason, incredibly beyond his limited and parochial understanding.

Caiaphas thought that Jesus was causing so much commotion among the people that the Roman authorities might use such crowd fervor as an excuse for a major attack on the population, even a pogrom. Therefore, to save the entire Jewish population from such possible atrocities, Jesus would have to die as a sacrifice.

Ironically, the high priest was right. More right than anyone could have ever even imagined. For it was now God's time to fulfill His plan formulated before the foundation of the world

(Heb. 9:26; Rev. 13:8). It was indeed absolutely essential that Jesus of Nazareth, Christ and Creator, would have to die as a sacrifice so that *all humanity could have the opportunity to live forever!*

Another spiritually startling revelation was that *direct contact* with God the Father was now for the first time available to all human beings. This was symbolized by the dramatic rip in the veil, which had previously concealed the Holy of Holies, at the precise instant of Jesus' death.

The spiritual significance of this tear in the sacred tapestry is enormous. The Holy of Holies represented God's Throne, and the access to it, under the Old Covenant, was restricted to one human being (the high priest once a year on the Day of Atonement). Other than this one occurrence, access to the Holy of Holies or, in its spiritual meaning, access to the throne of God, was completely concealed from mankind (Heb. 9:7-8). But the death of Christ ripped the veil apart—the Holy of Holies was literally revealed and direct access to God was now literally possible in personal prayer through the mediation of Jesus Christ.

The servants in the innermost sanctuary of the temple had felt a rumbling beneath their feet and had tried to grab hold of anything to keep themselves from toppling over. Brazen pots and pans were clattering about the floor, and dust was everywhere in the air when suddenly the veil which hid the Holy of Holies from the Holy Place in the temple had been split from the top to the bottom!

Thousands were thrown violently to the ground. Many were injured, some died. Nearby, those in the villages saw one of the most frightening spectacles in all of history, when stone tombs were jostled loose from the ground and virtually heaved upright, with their stone lids sliding loose in the enormous earthquake. (After Jesus' resurrection terrified citizens went screaming to tell their friends that some of these people had actually risen out of those tombs and had been seen walking!—Mat. 27:52, 53.)

Even the three stakes on the hill were swaying gently back and forth as the gradual rumbling of the great earthquake subsided in the land, still dark as if it were midnight.

Some Roman soldiers who were standing at the foot of the stake nervously jerked off their helmets, dropped to their knees on the dusty and bloody ground, and looking about them with fear, said, "Truly, this must *have* been the Son of God!"

Mary Magdalene, Mary, the mother of James the Less and of Joses and Salome, along with a number of other women who had been faithful servants of the disciples and Jesus were nearby when the earthquake struck, as were the mother of the sons of Zebedee and Mary, the mother of Jesus.

Gradually, as the dust began to settle, the shaking of the mortar, stones and bricks came to a stop, and as the rumble of the earthquake disappeared, it seemed to grow lighter. Bewildered people began picking themselves up where they had fallen; mobs of perplexed people came out from under trees where they had clung for stability to keep from being thrown to the ground, and everyone looked with fear at the cracks in some of the buildings as they went about the business of inspecting the amount of damage that had occurred.

It seemed that most of the large buildings and homes had survived. Thankfully, the temple was completely intact, though the veil separating the Holy of Holies had been split.

This caused some consternation. How could it be, some of the priests thought to themselves, that the temple was not damaged at all and yet that heavy veil was cleanly torn in two almost as if it were a deliberate act?

Still, there was much to be done, because it was the preparation for the Passover day. (John says that Sabbath was a high day—John 19:31.) The Jews therefore asked that the ghastly business be finished as quickly as possible, and that if the men weren't dead yet, the Roman soldiers should break their legs to hasten the process.

Pilate gave permission, and the soldiers came. They lifted up their heavy spear handles and smashed them into the shin bones of the first criminal, who screamed in pain. Now unable to keep heaving himself upward for desperately needed air, he kept gasping with painful exclamations until his gasps became weaker and weaker, and in the hideous agony of his inability to heave himself further upright on his shattered legbones, he finally died.

The soldier broke both criminals' legs, but when they came to Jesus and saw that He was dead already, they did not break His legs in order that additional scriptures could be fulfilled, "For these things came to pass that the scripture might be fulfilled." (Compare with Exodus 12:46; Numbers 9:12; Psalms 34:20;

Zechariah 12:10; Deuteronomy 21:22-23; —"a bone of him shall not be broken.")

As the land grew lighter and the sun seemed to gradually emerge from behind the dark veil which had been holding the land in its vise-like grip of blackness for over three hours, Joseph of Arimathaea, having seen Jesus' death throes, heard His cry from a distance, hurried down the hill, and half running, entered the city to proceed as quickly as he could to Pilate's governor's residence.

Upon being admitted, he was finally ushered into Pilate's presence. Pilate looked nervous and apprehensive. Repeatedly during the last three hours he had been going out on to his balcony above the courtyard of The Pavement where the terrible scene of the near riot had occurred some hours earlier, and he had finally been forced to turn around and ceremonially wash his hands of the whole incident. Still, the nagging doubts that had been assailing his mind like repeated hammer blows of a nine-pound maul would not let him alone. His wife's feverish warnings and anxious face kept coming back into his mind.

Joseph of Arimathaea told him Jesus was dead!

Pilate sighed. There *had* to be some connection between the most incredible phenomenon he had ever witnessed in all of his life—the blackness of the land for three hours and now the great rumbling earthquake.

Distraught, brushing a hand across haggard face and into unkempt hair, Pilate peered at Joseph with red-rimmed eyes and said "Yes, yes, you can have the body!" Gesturing for his servant, Pilate hastily wrote out the order and signing the short scroll with a sweaty hand, beckoned to the servant who dribbled the wax upon it and Pilate impressed it with his own ring.

Beckoning to a guard, one of Pilate's own private body-guards, he told the man to deliver the order to the centurion at Golgotha, and see to it that Joseph of Arimathaea was granted permission to bury the body.

Quickly, Joseph wound his way through the streets, back out the gate, and trotted along the way toward Golgotha. As he began climbing the low hill, he saw a figure toiling along ahead of him. Suddenly he recognized one of the most respected of the Jewish leaders—Nicodemus.

Nicodemus, together with his household servants, was laboring up the hill with several bundles. Joseph commented to him briefly, and Nicodemus said he was carrying about a hundred pounds of myrrh and aloes to use in the embalming procedures.

Joseph told him of Pilate's written order he carried, and Nicodemus, nodding, signaled to his servants to join those of Joseph of Arimathaea, and they went about the task together.

The Roman soldiers helped them dig around the base of the upright stake, and, lowering it to the ground, Nicodemus and Joseph began to gently detach the body from the stake. It was bitter, frightening, tearstained work as the men sought to pry the torn feet and hands from the spikes pinning them to the splintered wood without causing further damage.

Finally, rolling the body in a large wrapper, slinging it between two of the servants who carried a long stave, the procession started down the slopes, winding its way to the bottom, turning a sharp left until it came to a garden where Joseph had long since purchased a family tomb. The tomb was still being built; the workers had not yet completed the chambers Joseph had wanted for his entire family, but it would have to do.

The main feature of the tomb was that no other human being had ever been buried there; it was brand new, not even finished, and therefore totally clean. Further, Joseph had asked for a specific design which featured a deep trough running along the face of a sheer wall in front of the aperture, and a huge, round stone which was fixed in place at the upper level. When the chocks were taken out and the stone slowly set in motion, it would roll gradually along the narrowing trough until it would come to rest against a stone abutment and, by the force of its own weight, would wedge itself into the gradually narrowing trough so that it would have been impossible for anything short of a small army of men or several teams of mules to have dislodged it.

Now that it was growing lighter again, the party could proceed with the burial rites.

John, Mary, Mary Magdalene, and Zebedee's wife all joined with Joseph and Nicodemus and their household servants in washing and carefully cleansing the body, no doubt weeping with grief as they meticulously placed patches of skin or sections of flesh back in place, gently pouring or rubbing on the ointments and spices they had brought, until, gradually, with layer after layer of the finest linen cloth, they had succeeded in encasing the body so it appeared to be almost completely mummified.

There had been no chance for the women, in the sudden precipitousness of the events of the last hours, to have made preparation for such a burial, so they could only assist the servants of Nicodemus in the spreading of the myrrh and aloes they had brought. In a whispered conversation, the women determined to come back as soon as they could with additional spices and ointments, and sprinkle them over the body and about the tomb, for they wanted to ensure that this beloved man, and Mary's own son, had the finest possible burial.

Returning to their abode, they spent the last few hours on that Wednesday afternoon grinding up the leaves and the berries, working hard to prepare as much of the spices and ointments as they could. But at sunset on that fourteenth of Nisan, which brought on the fifteenth, they ceased from their work, for that Thursday was an annual Holy Day, the first day of Unleavened Bread, the first annual Sabbath of the sacred year (Luke 23:56; Mk. 16:1).

Pilate had spent a restive night. The next day, hoping that some sanity could return to the land, he requested that a quick damage report be given from all military installations in the area following the devastating earthquake of the afternoon before. But halfway through breakfast, he was interrupted by a servant who told him that a delegation of the chief priests and Pharisees were below wanting an audience.

Highly irritated, he wondered, "What could it be now?" as he stopped to pick up his official governor's robe.

The simpering voice said, "Sir, we remember that this deceiver, while he was still alive, said, 'After three days I will rise again.' We therefore respectfully request you to give an order that the sepulchre be made absolutely secure for that whole period of time, lest by any chance his disciples might steal away his body, and then claim to the people, 'He is risen from the dead.' Because if that should happen, it would be the last straw, and such a terrible mistake would be worse than all of this mess we have gone through in the last hours."

Pilate could immediately see the sense of that; the last thing he wanted on his hands in this hypersensitized region, following such remarkable phenomena and the restlessness of the crowds thronging Jerusalem, was a gigantic emotional uprising resulting from some contrived plot.

Therefore, he gave the order and wrote it out to make it official, saying, "I am going to have a guard accompany you, and you go along and make the sepulchre as sure as you possibly can!"

The priests went to the sepulchre at the foot of Golgotha with the Roman guard, and watched the sweating bodies toiling (which they knew was the deliberate breaking of this annual Sabbath day—but by this time they were willing to take any risk, and probably discounted it as "an ox in the ditch") to drive great wooden and stone wedges behind the huge round stone blocking the entry to the tomb. They then insisted that a full-time guard of several heavily armed soldiers be retained in the small stone court in front of the stone.

After the next day, when it was again Friday, and an ordinary working day, the women, Mary Magdalene, and Mary the mother of James the Less and Salome, continued their work throughout that day of the preparation of spices to return to the tomb prior to the fourth day.

They rested on the weekly Sabbath as they were commanded: Then, late at night after that Sabbath day, knowing they could go to the work of layering the body with yet another wrapping of graveclothes, bringing additional sweet-scented spices and ointments with them, and that their work would best be done under cover of dark when most were asleep, they started toward the tomb in the hopes they could ask the men there to roll back the stone long enough for them to give the body another complete dressing.

It was still quite dark, in the early hours prior to dawn, as the women made their way up the gradual slope toward the top of Golgotha.

Little did they know what had been occurring inside that tomb a few hours earlier!

CHAPTER 20

A Step Through Stone

Jesus had died late on the afternoon of Wednesday. True to His predictions, and the divine will and purpose of God, the Father in Heaven began His masterclock countdown at the precise instant of Jesus' death, the precise instant of the slaying of the Paschal lamb by the high priest in the high court.

That was about three o'clock on Wednesday afternoon.

One day and one night would pass before the late afternoon of the following "high day" (see John 19:31), and one more day to three o'clock in the afternoon on Friday, while the women were at home preparing the spices. All during that Sabbath day while the religious Jews were resting according to God's commandments, the body lay inside the cold, pitch blackness of the sealed tomb, with only the tiniest slivers of light seeping in from the minute cracks in the rough stone, which had been wedged tightly against the base of the tomb, and barely illuminated the pinkish white of the newly hewn stone.

As the minutes ticked away late that Sabbath afternoon, three full days and three full nights were about to elapse from the time Jesus had screamed out His last human utterance, said quietly to God He was commiting His spirit into His Father's hands, had died, and was buried.

At roughly three o'clock, some 72 hours after His death and burial, the tomb was suddenly filled with the brightest light! The mummified form stirred, then seemed to collapse completely, as, miraculously, Jesus materialized beside the bier, standing up!

He stooped, picked up the graveclothes, and began to unwrap and fold them neatly, taking the portion that had covered His face, and laying it in a separate place.

The tomb shone with a strange, bright light! Standing by were two powerful angels, dressed in shimmering white! Their faces were beaming with radiant smiles, as they waited to serve the risen Christ!

Finishing His simple task, Jesus looked at them, nodded, and stepped through solid rock into the Sabbath afternoon of Jerusalem.

Jesus had stepped back into eternity! He had dematerialized!

Probably, Michael and Gabriel themselves had come to His Resurrection—as the only known archangels besides the fallen Lucifer, now Satan.

Jesus would have instantly begun asking their help in seeing to it the events of the next 50 days took place according to divine plan! First, Jesus would wait until precisely the appropriate instant, and then ask His Father for another shocking earthquake, like an "aftershock" following that of His death, three days and three nights earlier, and roll back that huge stone to let the world look in!

But it had to be done at just the right moment—when there could be no question in anyone's mind about the miraculous nature of the event!

Now, Jesus was back in "that other dimension" again; the spirit world of spiritual essence! Jesus had once again become a *Spirit Being* with all the divine powers of the universe at His disposal, with a determined smile on His face, which still showed the livid bruises and tears of the terrible beating that He had taken, but now glowed with a translucent hue.

In an instant, from a battered, bruised, torn body, smelling heavily of the mixed spices and ointments that had been used to dress and to wrap His wounds, Jesus became, in the flickering of an eyelash, in an instant, *spirit!* He and the two angels whisked themselves outside the tomb in their dematerialized state and took a place in the garden nearby, talking animatedly.

Jesus prayed to His Father in Heaven, communicating directly with Him, as He waited for some of the most vitally important events in the fabulously exciting human drama that would be taking place within the next few hours. Instantly, possessing the mind of God Himself, Jesus could transport Himself

into the home where the woman labored over the spices, back to
Herod's palace, to the high priest's residence, up to Galilee, and
anywhere else He wished. Now, He was able once again to
overcome the physical laws of gravity, as well as overcome the
very elements themselves, not being constrained by any material
substance, not even solid stone!

About twelve or thirteen hours passed, during which time
Jesus carefully put certain thoughts into the appropriate minds so
that all the preparation would be made for collecting His disciples
once again in Galilee. All the while Jesus was waiting for those
moments in the predawn darkness before that Sunday morning
when He would miraculously allow the world to look inside His
empty tomb!

While the women were toiling their way up the gentle slope,
they once again heard a rumbling in the earth, and quickly
dropping to all fours, held on to the grasses until the rolling of the
earth had subsided. They wound their way along the path, dropping down into the garden, and saw the strangest sight in the
world!

Jesus had prayed to His Father, a great angel had come down
directly from the throne of God, and accompanied by a great
earthquake, the wooden and stone wedges seemed to split and
crumble; and with a roar, the great stone had rolled straight back
up the hill and toppled over!

The tremendous radiance of the angel was like flashing lightning, like a million strobe lights blindingly exploding all at once.
The Roman soldiers were so frightened that their spears fell with
a clatter to the stones, and with eyes glazed, they toppled forward
on their faces in a dead faint.

It was still very dark when the two women and the others
with them got to the garden and looked in amazement, mouths
open in shock, as they saw the stone rolled back! Frightened,
wondering what had happened, they looked into the tomb.

No one!

But looking to the right they saw in a niche in the stone what
appeared to be a young man sitting on the right side, dressed in a
white robe. "How did he get in here?" they wondered, "and who
is he?" When he said, "Don't be startled—I know you are looking
for Jesus of Nazareth who was crucified. He is not here! He has
risen, exactly as He said he would!

"Take a look. Here's the place where they laid Him! And now go and tell His disciples and especially Peter that Jesus will go before you into Galilee.

"Remember how when He was still in Galilee with you He told you that the Son of man must be delivered up into the hands of sinners and be crucified, and the third day rise again?

"Well, it is exactly as He said—and He will be in Galilee alive to see you there."

The women fled from the tomb, shaking terribly with astonishment. Not even stooping to check on the Roman soldiers, they hurried out of the garden, up the slight incline, turned to their left, and wound their way along the gentle slope back to the gate of the city of Jerusalem until they found where Peter and some of the other disciples had been hiding.

Mary got to Peter and John and said, "Someone has taken the Lord out of the tomb and we don't know where in the world they have laid the body!" Mary Magdalene was nodding assent. But most of the disciples, having been huddled in great fear, discussing what they were going to do from now on, and waiting for everything to quiet down so they could filter out of town—knowing they probably could not do so until the completion of the eight-day feast, and fervently hoping they would not be discovered in the interim—simply refused to believe the words.

Unable to contain his curiosity, Peter started out the door. No matter the risk, he simply had to know!

John, who had already taken a risk in remaining near the brutal scene of the crucifixion itself and having been there at a distance with the mother of Jesus to watch the murder, said, "Hold it, I'm coming, too!"

They hurried to the burial site, with both of them stopping just short of the tomb to look about in amazement at the gaping blackness of the hewn sepulchre, the big stone lying on the ground, and the guards still lying where they had fallen. Peter hesitated, and John ran the few steps, stooped and looked in, seeing the stained and ointment-soaked graveclothes lying on the rock sepulchre. He hesitated, afraid to enter.

Peter brushed by and stepped inside the tomb.

He looked around, seeing the linen clothes and the napkin that had been on Jesus' head rolled up in a place by itself—and, hearing the shuffling of John's feet, looked over his shoulder to see John also enter the tomb.

Suddenly, they believed the women had been right! Someone had come and taken the body away! Who in the world had done it?

Frightened thoughts raced through Peter's mind as he mumbled to John that they had better get out of here: it was bad enough venturing out in public, but surely now the Pharisees and chief priests were going to claim that Peter and the disciples had contrived to "steal the body away" and they themselves would end up crucified on that same hill within a few hours if they didn't hurry!

Peter and John had outdistanced Mary, who, after delivering the story to the frightened disciples, decided to go back to the tomb and see if any of the Romans or anyone else could give her a clue as to where Jesus had been taken.

By the time she got there, Peter and John were nowhere to be seen. A small crowd had gathered, including a man who appeared to be the keeper of the graves, for he was so disfigured.

Mary Magdalene looked into the tomb while she was by herself, and saw, shockingly, two angels in brilliant white, one sitting at the head of the sepulchre and the other at the feet right where Jesus' body had lain. Amazed, she saw the grave clothes between them and noticed the napkin that had been used to cover His face rolled up and laid on a nearby rock shelf. Tears streaking her face and her sobs quieted by the shocking sight she saw, she heard one of the men say, "Woman, why are you crying?" She answered, with a voice that was shaking with fear and grief, "Because they have taken away my Lord, and I don't have any idea where they have laid Him."

She backed out of the tomb, turned towards the pleasant garden place where a few other people seemed to be gathering, and found her way partially barred by a terribly disfigured man whom she supposed had to be the keeper of the garden. She knew it was commonplace that hunchbacks, wounded war veterans, those whose faces had been terribly disfigured in battle or through injury would oftentimes be employed as gravediggers, the keepers of tombs and their accompanying gardens, so she was not startled. Thinking he had to be the gardener, she didn't think it strange that he said, "Woman, why are you crying? Who are you looking for?" She looked at him and said, "Sir, if you are the one who has carried him away, please tell me where you have laid him, and I will take him away."

Jesus said to her, "Mary!"

What was that tone? That familiar timbre of voice? There was something about that one eye—the other seemed to be almost closed with terrible bruises and livid wounds, the lips torn and blue, and the skin pallid.

It was Jesus! Stunned almost to the point of fainting, she said, "Master!"; reaching out a hand, incredulously, thinking, "It can't be! But it is!" She tried to take His hand. Jesus withdrew His hand and said, "No, don't touch me! I have not yet ascended unto my Father—but I want you to go to my brethren and say to them, I ascend unto my Father and your Father, and to my God and to your God."

With that He disappeared. The words were still ringing in Mary's ears as she looked around in dumbfounded amazement and could not see anywhere the figure she had supposed had been the gardener. She noticed several additional Roman soldiers arriving, helping the guards to their feet, taking up positions to guard the entry to the tomb, and a runner being sent back to Pilate's residence.

She hurried up the pathway, went back into the city, and came to the disciples' hideout. She related every word that had been told her—but the disciples looked at her as if she were crazy.

Thomas, especially, shook his head, clicking his tongue, and muttered something about the stress of the last few days being entirely too much for the womenfolk to take. Expressions mixed with sympathy and pity, a "There, there, Mary" from Thaddeus and Bartholomew, an embrace and a pat on the head by Simon the Canaanite, but Mary continued to insist that what she had seen and heard was true, while the disciples continued to disbelieve.

About the same time Peter and John were running hurriedly back to where the rest of the disciples were hiding. Also about the same time, some of the Roman guards managed to finally fight their way through the throngs into the city, and arriving at the place where the chief priests could be reached, after a great deal of delay, much clamor, arguments, dust in the air, and explaining over and over again above the hubbub that there was an absolute essential message they had to deliver, a hasty convening of the Sanhedrin was called.

The soldiers were fretting worriedly outside, and after the noises had subsided, the timorous servants said, "The honorable Sanhedrin is seated, you may come in." The delegation of soldiers removed their metal helmets, held them under their arms, strode forward in cadence, stopped before the assembled group and looked upon them with a combination of fear and disdain.

The leader—the same brawny man who had so raucously gambled over Jesus' clothes, and then thought up the cute trick of grabbing a sponge from a passing housewife's shopping bag, dipping it in vinegar from her purchases, and sprinkling some hyssop from her cleansing materials into it and then pressing it against Jesus' lips; the same one who had jammed his spear into Jesus' lower side—began relating the entire series of events, heavily colored from his own prejudicial point of view.

He had already forgotten some of his earlier fright. After all, hadn't the sun come out again? Hadn't the world seemingly returned to normal? Wasn't he once again among his own companions, trotting along at double time with his sword clattering against his thigh, his spear at trail, and the familiar weight of his military uniform on his flesh?

It was absolutely essential, he knew, based upon the earlier sealed order he had been given, that he report to this hated, pretentious group of theological puppets, if he were to avoid incurring the immediate displeasure of his highest senior office, Pilate. Therefore, swallowing to keep the bile from rising in his mouth, fighting down a combination of fear over the events of the last several hours and his innate distrust and hostility toward these conniving religious leaders, he tried to relate from his own point of view, the events of the past few hours.

He told his tale of the enormous earthquake, the opening of the sealed order from Herod, suspiciously following Joseph of Arimathaea and Nicodemus and their house servants and the weeping women down to the tomb, seeing to it that the body was thoroughly wrapped and prepared for burial, and even to the sealing of the tomb, and his own standing by for a portion of the first watch after the giant stone was sledged into place with heavy mauls, stone and wooden wedges. When he had finished, his voice grew surprisingly contrite.

Had not he been called upon for extra duty? Had not he and his cohorts obeyed every order given them from Pilate, which was to say directly from the Caesar himself? Had they not gone without sleep, presiding over the changing of each guard, personally questioning the outgoing coterie of soldiers, and personally admonishing the incoming group to keep a specially watchful eye because of the huge mob of people in Jerusalem? Hadn't they been especially careful following the massive earthquake which had thrown such terror into the citizens all over the area?

Hadn't he, the officer, rebuked one of his own soldiers who had said that perhaps this was a "son of the gods"?

From that late Wednesday through all of Thursday, Friday and the following Jewish Sabbath these men had stood faithfully, until two or three of them had even fainted in the blazing sun. Requiring resuscitation, they had to be dragged unceremoniously away, their breastplates and helmets banging along the stones, to repose under one of the olive trees in the shade.

Hadn't they gone to every length to call out extra guardsmen?

And still, in spite of all of this—the brawny man now wondering how he would ever explain it rationally—it appeared that these clever followers of Jesus had pulled some strange trick.

The last guard of about the noon-to-four watch of the preceding few hours, in their unsound condition (probably resulting directly from their earlier fright over the grossly exaggerated tales of the extent of the earlier earthquake and the blackness across the land), upon hearing the faint tremor of the "after-shock" which seemed to rumble across the country on this late Sabbath afternoon, had simply fainted away!

"I cannot excuse them," he may have said, "but I hope you will all understand that these men are not accustomed to living in an earthquake area, and most assuredly have never seen anything so strange as the events of the last several days!"

Having made his speech, he came to the final moments, to the critical words he would have to relate.

Shifting his tassled Roman helmet from his right elbow to his left, he gulped, straightened his sword, thrust his left leg slightly forward as if in belligerent stance, and began.

"Nevertheless, we have done our duty. Exactly as the great governor Pilate has commanded, we stood watch as best we possibly could. Though I have already given orders to severely discipline the men who so frightfully failed in their task, I can only relate that it was beyond their power to stop the events of the past few hours, and it now appears that the large stone at the entrance of the sepulchre has been rolled away and the body of the one you call Jesus Christ of Nazareth, the 'King of the Jews,' is gone!"

"Oh, *no!*" the religious leaders thought. "This blithering, illiterate Roman jackal is telling us he and his armed men couldn't guard the tomb of a dead man!"

Their minds refused to believe it could have been a "miracle"! They were too committed now, too involved. The events of the past three days had so seared their minds they could only take each shocking setback with fierce, determined resolve to "see this thing through" to the bitter end, no matter what the consequences.

Some of them thought the Roman was lying, and accused him of it.

"No sir!" said the officer, "It's no lie! I can provide dozens of witnesses! No force of many, many men could have removed that stone!"

Minds working quickly, the leaders wondered how to turn this alarming bit of news into an advantage. No doubt, His bothersome disciples, especially that blustering swaggering fellow, Peter, who had hacked off big old Malchus's ear (they conveniently refused to admit into their minds that his ear was pinkly shining from beneath his thick, black hair at this very moment, right over there at the doorway behind the Roman delegation), would come out into the open, probably even claiming Jesus had risen again!

Smart! What a coup! They would have to counteract it right now!

Another hurried caucus.

Crowding together, one of their number came forward to the soldier, and calling him slightly aside, told him, "Look! You take these four bags, the larger one is for yourself; the other three are for the two soldiers who were standing the last watch, and the other for your companion here. As you will see, they are heavy with gold, and they represent a very large sum!

"Now we all know that very likely this was a silly trick by some of his own cohorts.

"No doubt the soldiers were unaware when these men snuck up behind them and probably used some magic trick that this strange person from Galilee had taught them in order to overcome them.

"Even though you may not have been there to see it, we all know that what truly has happened is that some of his disciples must have come in some secret manner, stole the body of the man away, and probably hid it somewhere, intending to claim that the man has been actually resurrected!

"Look, here's the money; let's be consistent with the story. You tell it as I'm telling you to tell it!"

"But, that's not what *really happened—*" the soldier began. "And besides, I have no authority—"

"Silence!"

"Look! Don't worry about getting in trouble with the centurion, or with Pilate himself! We'll take care of that, and get you off the hook.

"You see in the last three days, because of Herod's deference to your Roman governor, arraying this Jesus in robes in showing him that he was willing to patch up his difference, we honestly believe that there will be no difficulty whatsoever if we speak to Pilate ourselves! He is obviously nervous over his own involvement.

"Therefore, take the money. If any of this strange tale of the alleged escape, the way you tell it, reaches Pilate's ears, we will tell him the truth, and you might as well figure how many years you can stay alive aboard a galley!" (Compare with Matthew 28:11-15.)

The Romans bobbed their heads, tucked the money away in their inner garments, and went out and did precisely as they had been told. Their own lives now depended on it!

In the hours and days that followed, these soldiers continued in the bivouacs and the wine shops, along the streets, in the public bazaars, and the court of the temple itself, to repeat the tale as often and as loudly as they possibly could. It was true, they claimed, that a strange magical "trick" had been performed by the disciples of Jesus who had contrived to come and steal the body away—and Jesus had never been "resurrected."

Nevertheless, the Romans continued to affirm that not only had they seen him die, but the one brawny man, displaying the dried blood on the tip of his own spearhead, affirmed that this was "the very spear which took the life of the so-called Jesus of Nazareth who was called the King of the Jews!"

The tale spread quickly enough, and became the stuff of which mythology is born, traveling down through history so that it has survived to this day.

Jesus was busy all through that Sunday following His Resurrection on the preceding late afternoon. He was now setting about the business of arranging many eyewitness events which would establish incontrovertible proof that He, Jesus Christ of Nazareth, the same person who had been scourged almost to death, and who had died on His stake at Golgotha, was in fact *alive!*

At some moment after refusing to allow Mary to touch Him, Jesus actually appeared in heaven before His Father.

One can only guess at the extraordinary emotional power of the scene, the conversation that must have ensued, with millions of angels, the twenty-four elders round about the throne, the blazing blinding light that was God the Father Himself, and the bedraggled figure approaching that great throne on a translucent "sea of glass."

As a Spirit Being, with the very power of the universe once again about to be given Him, Jesus approached His Father and reported that the work He had been given to do was finished.

The details that may be gleaned from this heavenly coronation ceremony are scanty (and they rightfully belong as the setting for the beginning of another book).

Following the coronation ceremony in heaven, in the space of microseconds, Jesus could hurtle Himself through that other spiritual dimension, now endowed with *all power,* back to earth, and join two of the men who had been with Jesus a great deal through His ministry, Cleopas and probably Peter.

These two were strolling along that Sunday afternoon toward a village called Emmaus which was three-score furlongs from Jerusalem.

As the men were walking along the roadway, Jesus came up behind them, having stepped out of His spirit dimension and again assumed the flesh and bone of His disfigured state.

He looked so totally different they couldn't have recognized Him, and since He seemed to be walking their way, they continued to speak wonderingly of the shocking events of the past few days not suspecting the stranger who was strolling along beside them.

It was then that Jesus broke into the conversation. They were amazed that a stranger could have been in the environs of Jerusalem, yet seemingly not know of the events that had occurred (demonstrating again the fact that Jesus' life and death was the center of public interest).

After their hopeless tale about His death, burial, and the puzzling empty tomb, Jesus, seeing their doubts chided them, "Oh, you foolish men, and slow of heart to believe in everything the prophets have spoken! Wasn't it thoroughly planned that Christ should suffer all of these things and enter into His glory?"

There followed a quick synopsis, as they walked along, of every major prophecy from Genesis to the end of II Chronicles (the Hebrew order of the books of the Old Testament), with Jesus interpreting to them in every scripture the events concerning His own life and ministry.

They were amazed that this stranger could know all of these things, wondering at His words, as they drew close to Emmaus. When they made as if they would turn off the main road to go to the village, it appeared as if this stranger would go further.

Cleopas and the other disciple begged Him to stay with them, saying "It's almost evening, and the day is nearly gone."

They went in, and after a light supper was prepared, sat down to eat.

Just at the beginning of the meal, as was custom, they asked their guest to ask the blessing.

He picked a piece of the flat bread, asked God's blessing, broke off a piece, and gave one to each of them.

At this moment, Luke says, "their eyes were opened" and they knew who He was! With all of His words ringing in their ears, talking rapidly and earnestly all the way along the roadway to Emmaus about the things Christ would have to suffer, His life, His calling, the training of His disciples, the manner of His death, and especially the prophecy that He would be exactly "three days and three nights" in His grave, but be resurrected, they sat in absolute astonishment as, having reached out to take a piece of bread, and with a jolt realizing it was Jesus, even as they looked at Him smiling at them across the table, He vanished!

They cried out in a combination of ecstatic joy, fright, doubt and wonderment!

Shaking their heads, they looked at one another in absolute astonishment.

With their scalps prickling and every hair standing almost straight up, they sat in stunned silence.

Had this really happened? But the piece of bread was still in their hand, and *they* had not broken it! The place was set, the meal was steaming in its common bowl, and yet Jesus, who had just been sitting across from them, unrecognizable to them at first, had instantly disappeared!

They said, "No wonder our hearts seemed to burn within us while He was talking so earnestly to us on the way as we walked along, and gave us such understanding of the scriptures!"

Hastily, they took a few quick bites of the meal, got up, and began to trot along the road to return to Jerusalem as fast as they could, until they found the private place where the disciples had been huddling in fear.

When the eleven were all gathered together, they related "how the Lord is risen indeed and has appeared to Simon!" They were busily explaining all about the conversation, the stranger who had appeared to join them, relating all of the things He had said to them while the astonished disciples were listening with a mixture of doubt and wonderment, when, shockingly, Jesus flashed into human form right in their midst!

They were scared half out of their wits!

They thought it was some spiritual apparition and were terrified!

They knew they had locked the door, and that a maid was even standing careful guard nearby to give them warning in case the house was searched, because they were terribly afraid their hideout would be discovered by the religious leaders or Roman soldiers, and they themselves be made to suffer some terrible persecution for being His chief followers.

Jesus said, quietly, "Shalom!" Astonished, they stepped back, eyes wide in dumbfounded amazement.

With a smile on His lips, Jesus said, "What's bothering you? Why are you reasoning around in your minds? See, these are my hands and my feet! It is I, really!

"Come on, reach out and handle me, and see for yourselves! A spirit has not flesh and bones as you see that I have!" With that, He had displayed both sides of His hands, showing them His feet, with the large bluish-black wounds still visible, made doubly grotesque by the shocking whiteness and pallor of His skin.

As if to give emphasis to the fact that He was in their midst again with bodily form as a human being, in the very same body which had been quite literally resurrected, *changed into spirit* (although manifested as flesh), and that He now possessed the ability to instantly materialize once more in His fleshly form, asked, "Have you got anything here to eat?"

They were sitting down to a meal of broiled fish, and so, reaching into the pan at the center of the table where their evening meal was rapidly cooling, one of the disciples took out a small broiled fish and handed it to Him.

As their startled eyes widened, He sat down with them at the table, and began to eat the fish!

Following the meal an animated discussion ensued, and Jesus once again reiterated some of the words He had spoken to them at His last supper.

He said, "May peace descend over you! Even as the Father has sent me and commissioned me to fulfill His purpose on this earth, so I am commissioning you!"

As a symbol of His many earlier teachings about God's Holy Spirit, He breathed on them each, and said, "Receive you the Holy Spirit! Whatever persons' sins you forgive, they will be forgiven; and whatever persons' sins you retain, they will be retained!"

Following the brief encounter, Jesus dematerialized again! The disciples were left in bewildered, excited amazement about this stunning event.

The next days passed swiftly. The city throbbed with frenzied activity at the end of the Days of Unleavened Bread as the thousands of sojourners were gradually emptying hostels, inns, guest homes, and outlying camps in the environs of Jerusalem. It was eight days later, at a propitious moment, as the disciples were preparing to leave Jerusalem and go back up to Galilee that they were assembled in the same upper room behind locked doors.

This time, though, Thomas, who had earlier said, "Except I should see in His hands the very wounds those spikes made, and put my own finger into those wounds, and put my hand into that wound in His side, I will not believe!" was with the group.

During this evening meal, Jesus suddenly materialized in their midst again!

They were all awe-stricken.

Jesus looked at Thomas and said, "Thomas, come here!"

Thomas took several hesitant steps forward, eyes searching the disfigured face, studying intently to see if there were anything familiar about this person whose voice seemed identical, yet filled with an even greater note of authority.

"Come on," He said, "Go ahead, Thomas, I want you to put your finger right here into my hand."

Thomas reached out his finger and actually put it *inside* the large tear between Jesus' index and second fingers where the bones had been separated and the flesh grotesquely torn. Thomas' finger was tingling from its contact with the cold flesh and the bare bones of Jesus' hand. The figure took off His outer garment, and pulled up His shirt underneath to reveal a gaping, livid wound in His side. Jesus said, "Go ahead, put your hand into my side!" Trembling with nervousness and fear, Thomas reached out and actually put his hand completely *into* the gaping aperture that had been left by the Roman's spear.

How cold it was inside! Thomas's stomach was churning, his mind reeling, his eyes glazed with shock!

It was He! It really was! This was in fact the very same Jesus he had himself seen proved dead, standing here before him alive!

Thomas dropped to his knees and with tears filling his eyes in sick shame at his blustering statements of disbelief made before the other disciples said, "My Lord and my God!"

Jesus said kindly, "Because you have seen me, you have believed! I'll tell you, *blessed* are they that have *not* seen and yet have believed!"

From that time on, the disciples continued to be dumbfounded by the signs and the proofs Jesus presented to them. Only a few are recorded in the Bible (see John 20:30, 31) among the many other signs Jesus did right in the startled view of His disciples.

Their senses alive with expectancy, they made hurried plans, each still timorously wondering what would occur next. Would he now rally the people and set up His Kingdom? These miraculous events had so shocked their systems that it was all they could do to believe as they made plans to depart into Galilee.

Days passed. The doubts assailed them again from time to time. Though there had been several mysterious appearances there was room for them to wonder whether they were in fact seeing an apparition or whether it was just all a vivid dream; whether they were all collectively imagining it, or whether it was indeed a fact!

However, Thomas now became one of the chief proponents of the fact that Jesus Christ of Nazareth had been resurrected!

Over and over again he told of the actual *feeling* of putting his physical hand into that actual human wound and experiencing the coldness (for His blood had been drained completely out of His body; His life was now of spiritual essence, and whenever it would be miraculously transformed into human form, it would not require the circulation of human blood for the heating of bodily systems). Thomas's was the most insistent voice among them all that Christ had actually risen.

In the days that followed their return to Galilee, aged Nathaniel happened to be in the vicinity of Peter's home in Bethsaida when they all decided to go fishing. Aboard the boat in the Sea of Galilee were Peter, Thomas, Nathaniel who was living in Cana, and the two sons of Zebedee, James and John, along with two of the other disciples. Peter had said that he was going fishing. The family business had been allowed to almost disintegrate during the unnerving events of the past months, and Peter desperately needed a catch to meet expenses. His wife had no doubt told him of their dwindling family finances, and, knowing that his other employees had left, the men volunteered to go and help.

It was a large boat featuring weighted casting nets. They labored nearly all night long and succeeded in catching absolutely nothing!

As the faint hues of light began to paint the skies to the east, they were still heaving the nets in the hopes that this early morning hour would give them at least some success. Their backs were tired, their legs were aching, their arms leaden and heavy from the dozens upon dozens of casts they had made on all sides of the boat, with their cast nets, playing out the line, allowing the net to sink on or near the bottom, and then two or three of them hauling it in together, to discover with disgust nothing but an occasional bit of aquatic vegetation.

They rowed closer to shore, the sails limp and secured, and, grunting with their efforts, glanced over to their right, where the rays of the sun were gradually edging down the mountainside, and saw a lonely figure standing on the shore.

In that early morning hour the lake was as still as a pond, and the slightest sound carried remarkably.

It was commonplace that some folk would hail fishing boats and would ask to purchase a small part of their catch even before they could return to one of the towns and carry the fish to market, so they were not surprised when the figure lifted his hand, and said in clear tones, "Fellows, have you caught anything?"

Several of them chimed "No! No luck yet."

The boat had eased along until it was in the shallows and they had been casting out the left side, with the prow angling toward the south. They knew that any fish on the right side would surely be frightened away instantly by the shadow of the descending cast nets. Nevertheless, the figure on the shore said, "Cast the net on the right side of the boat—and you'll find fish!" How could he see that far? Had he noticed the shimmering of the water that meant a large school of fish that they had somehow missed?

They hustled to the other side, and spreading the net as far as they could, waited until Peter, with all his strength, heaved the weight like a bolo. As he let it loose, the other men dropped the thin strands of net they were holding. The big net sailed out over the lake, the weights splashed down and began to sink. Shockingly, brilliant iridescent hues of shimmering fish appeared trapped within it!

Quickly running fore and aft, crossing the lines so as to bring the mouth of the net closed, they began to heave together to trap as many of the fish as possible. It was so heavy they had to call for additional help, and could scarcely drag it in for the incredible weight of fish they had caught!

John, peering intently at the shore, having heard the timbre of that voice, and seeing the miraculous event that was taking place, said loudly to Peter, "Peter, it's the Lord!"

Peter and several of the others, in order to preserve their clothing from the slime and scales, as well as from the rivulets of sweat running down their bodies as they toiled, were laboring along the deck of the boat stark naked.

When Peter heard John's startled statement, he quickly picked up a lengthy shirtlike garment that reached to his knees, and, taking a run along the boat deck, flung himself headlong into the sea in a full racing dive. John gave quick orders and they got into the dinghy trailing along behind, quickly secured the net to the smaller boat, and began to toil along behind the receding splashing head and arms of Peter as he swam vigorously toward shore.

It was slow hard work, dragging the net filled nearly to bursting with dozens of fish, but they finally felt the prow of the boat bump bottom and dragged the boat to the beach.

Looking around, they saw a full fire going with utensils, bread baking, and a fish frying on a grill.

Jesus said, "Bring some of the fish you have just caught." Peter jumped back into the boat, and scrambling to the transom, began to heave on the line, tugging the net out of the water and onto the shore.

Excitedly, the disciples began to separate the fish by hand. Some of them were as large as any they had seen in the lake before, and when they had finished counting, throwing the fish into the boat as they disentangled each from the net, they discovered there were exactly one-hundred-and-fifty-three fish in the net! They selected several of the larger ones, cleaned them, and took them to the fire.

It was a remarkable occasion—the disciples all knew by now it was the Lord. They wanted to talk to Him directly, and even satisfy their curiosity by saying, "Is it really you, Lord?" but none dared to be so presumptuous.

Jesus said, "Come on, let's have breakfast!" As each had found opportunity to wash their hands and face, run their bedraggled fingers through their hair, and find stones and driftwood to sit on, Jesus had busied Himself about the campfire, and now the delicious smell of broiling fish and fresh baked bread filled their nostrils.

They all sat down and, after Jesus prayed briefly, began to eat.

As Peter was breaking open a steaming fish and relishing his breakfast, he began to realize this was the third time Jesus had shown Himself to the whole group of them since He had been risen from the dead.

As they were finishing that breakfast, Jesus looked at Peter and asked, "Simon, son of Jonah, is your affection toward me greater than it is toward these others?" (Jesus used two different

Greek words in His questioning of Peter—the first having more the force of our English word "like" and the second connoting a deep abiding love.)

Peter said, "Yes, Lord, you know very well that I like you very much!"

Jesus answered, "Then feed my lambs!"

The others watched, hands pausing in midair, as they waited to see what the outcome of this obvious pointed remark would be.

Jesus asked, "Simon, son of Jonah, do you love me?"

"Yes Lord, you know how much I love you!" answered Peter.

"Then *tend my sheep!*" Jesus said.

Peter began to groan within himself, suspecting what was about to happen—his tortured memory flashing back to that moment when Jesus' eyes had met his while Peter stood just outside the open room warming his hands and cursing vehemently that he didn't know Jesus.

Sure enough, Jesus repeated the question for the third time, using the same word Peter had been using, "Simon, son of Jonah, do you *love* me with all of your heart?"

Peter was deeply ashamed. He said, "Lord, you know everything, and you can see deeply inside of me. You surely must know that I love you!" Jesus nodded, smiled, and looking straight into Peter's eyes, said, "Feed my sheep!"

"I am telling you the truth, Peter, when you were a young man, you were your own man; you could put on your clothes, and go wherever you wished. But when you grow old, there will come a time when you will stretch forth your hands, and another will have to dress you, and they will finally carry you where you wish they wouldn't!"

(John said many years later that Jesus said this signifying the manner of death that would finally come to Peter which would glorify God. [Tradition says that he was crucified upside down.])

When He had made this remarkable statement Jesus finally said to Peter, "Follow me!"

Peter turned about, and seeing John just to his left, said, "Lord, what will happen to John here?"

Jesus said, "If I decide that he ought to remain alive even until he sees me return, what is that to you? Your job is to *follow me!*" Following this meeting, and the earnest conversations that they had, Jesus vanished out of their sight again!

It happened repeatedly—in many parts of the country, with different groups at different times. On one occasion, as attested to by the Apostle Paul years later, more than *five hundred* of those who had known Jesus were gathering together in a special meeting when He had appeared before them, and *they all saw Him!*

Later, He would tell them, "All power is given unto me in heaven and in earth. Go ye therefore into all the world, preaching the gospel unto every creature, and whoever really believes and is baptized shall be saved—he that does not believe shall be judged!"

He told them, "I will send the Holy Spirit of my Father upon you as I have promised—and I want you to go back to Jerusalem and remain there until you be empowered with His spirit from on high."

Luke later wrote that Jesus had showed Himself alive following His Resurrection by *many infallible proofs,* being seen by different groups of the disciples on different occasions over a *40-day period,* and continually explaining things to them concerning the Kingdom of God.

On one such appearance, the disciples had asked Jesus, "Lord, will you at *this time* restore the Kingdom to Israel?" Jesus said, "It is not for you to know the times of the seasons which the Father has under His own control—but you will receive *power,* after the Holy Spirit is come upon you, and you are all going to be personal eyewitnesses for me, both in Jerusalem, and in all the province of Judaea, up in Samaria, and even unto the uttermost parts of the earth."

It was while He spoke these words on the Mount of Olives in Jerusalem, that His garment seemed to shimmer with a brighter light, and with those words ringing in their ears, the disciples blinked in shocked amazement as they saw Him begin to rise off the ground! He seemed to be gradually lifted above their heads, up over the city of Jerusalem, until He became only a small dot in the sky and finally disappeared in the clouds.

Eyes blinking, necks aching from the strain of trying to see where He had gone, they heard a loud voice, and with amazement looked to see two men standing beside them in white apparel. A booming voice said, "You men of Galilee, why are you standing there staring off up into the heavens? This *same Jesus,* which is now taken up from you into heaven, shall *so come* in like manner as you have seen Him go into heaven." Finally, according to Jesus' instructions, they went down from the top of the Mount of Olives and back into the city of Jerusalem, into the familiar upper room where they began to eagerly discuss their preparation for the soon coming day of Pentecost.

For 40 days now they had never ceased to be amazed at the sudden appearances and disappearances of Jesus. They had touched Him, handled Him, thrown their arms about Him, embraced Him, walked with Him, talked with Him, sat down to eat several meals with Him, seen Him in Galilee by the lake, in the streets and towns up and down the length and breadth of the country, on the Mount of Olives, in Jerusalem, where they had been assembled behind huge locked doors, in the garden of Gethsemane, on the road to Emmaus, and many other places. Years later John was to write that the many amazing signs and miracles Jesus performed to convince these doubting men of the fabulous miracle of the Resurrection were so elaborate and so strange that if every one of them should be put to writing they would be so shocking the world could neither tolerate nor understand them.

In the years that followed, the brothers and sisters of Jesus disappeared from history. That period from about A.D. 70 until well into the second century has almost been obliterated from history.

Whatever became of James, Joses, Simon and Jude? What of the girls? Did they ever marry? It is very likely most or all of them did—and that they had children. Was there a wizened old grandfather who could pray to God on his deathbed that he was thankful he had kept his great secret until the end? Had he determinedly refused to reveal his family origins to the bride of his youth, when, as a fugitive, he had found his way into a tiny fertile valley in one of the Ionian islands? Had he been content to see his strong young sons and daughters growing up in his household, their whole lives before them, hoping desperately they would not be discovered and linked by family kinship to the One the Romans' were calling *Crestus* who was called the leader of a vast and growing insurrection which was threatening the very foundations of the empire itself?

Perhaps so. Perhaps not.

Whatever became of the dozens of "schoolnotes," personal

letters and memoranda, classwork, bills of lading, Bible study notes, requisitions, sketches and drawings of household plans, itemized lists of building materials, and signatures on agreements between providers and suppliers of all the essential ingredients in the building trade which had been written in Jesus' own hand? Perhaps the preservation of even one of them could have resulted in vast religious wars—and as surely as any could have been preserved, there would probably be so many reams of alleged "writings of Jesus" on the earth today that their composition would have required a thousand men a lifetime of a thousand years apiece at an electric typewriter.

In God's wisdom, none of the family members were ever revealed—though surely, somewhere, on the earth at this precise time, are the living descendants of those children of Joseph and Mary, the half brothers and sisters of Jesus Christ of Nazareth.

Jesus did not walk away into lost history when He disappeared into the clouds—but took His seat at the right hand of the blazing omnipotent power of God the Father in heaven, and has been actively busy every instant of the time ever since!

Jesus Christ is sitting *at the right hand of God the Father in heaven right now!*

He sees through the top of your roof, into the room where you are living, down into the top of your own mind. That great God who made the universe, who brooded over the tumultuous waves so many billions of years ago after Satan's rebellion, who raised the continents and who stooped in the muddy clay by a creek bed near what is called the city of Jerusalem today to form Himself a man; that great Being who appeared to Moses, divided the Red Sea, wrote the Ten Commandments with His own finger, wrestled with Jacob, spoke to the prophets, "emptied Himself" and came down to His own creation to be born in the figure of a man, and who redeemed the entirety of this physical creation— mankind—by perfecting a plan that is dizzying in its vast spiritual, superhuman, supernatural potential, that One is the real Jesus!

The most carefully concealed secret in all of history was kept until the last instant when Jesus suddenly realized He was left *alone*—that God the Father had totally forsaken Him! Can we really understand the awesome depths of Jesus' own final sufferings. When we read the words of Paul are we able to comprehend its overwhelming significance? "... when he had, *by himself* purged our sins he sat down at the right hand of the Majesty on high " (Heb. 1:3).

By taking upon Himself the sins of all humankind—as the Lamb sacrificed for a sin offering; by dying from the merciless beating and crucifixion He suffered—He "became sin for us," and in this one fell swoop, gave that *one life* which was worth more than the sum total of all of the rest of our lives put together!

Today, "we see Jesus, who was made a little lower than the angels for the suffering of death, crowned with glory and honour; that he by the grace of God should taste death for every man.

"For it became him, for whom are all things, and by and through whom are all things, to bring *many sons* unto glory, to make the Captain and Author of their salvation perfect through sufferings" (Hebrews 2:9-10, paraphrased).

This is the real Jesus: God the Creator changed into human life, reared of Joseph and Mary, who grew up in the streets of Nazareth; was educated to the full; had the Holy Spirit without measure; and who fulfilled His purpose and destiny in His three-and-one-half-year ministry.

The real Jesus overcame Satan the Devil, the world, and the pulls of His own flesh; He called, trained and commissioned His disciples to become the foundation of His New Testament church.

The real Jesus qualified to become the future World Ruler by *dis*qualifying the present world ruler, the "god of this world," "prince of the power of the air," who is Satan the Devil, the deceiver of all nations.

That personality, the real Jesus, is *vastly* different from the "Jesus" of this present world!

He was crucified, as He said; He was placed in a tomb where He remained for exactly three days and three nights, and was resurrected precisely 72 hours later. He appeared to doubting disciples and relatives alike, until those men were absolutely convinced beyond the remotest shadow of a doubt that He was alive. They were so convinced that most were later *martyred* for preaching the message of the Resurrection.

The apostles preached that fact, and vast miracles began to occur. The apostles were believed, *because* they believed.

Maybe it's time that you too recognized what Paul recognized: that there isn't anybody on the face of this earth whose thoughts and acts are not obvious in God's sight. All things are absolutely naked and opened before the eyes of Him who created us.

"So understanding, then, that we have a Great High Priest who has passed into the heavens, Jesus the Son of God, let us hang on to our Christian calling—because we don't have a High Priest who can't be touched with the feeling of our own infirmities; He was in every point tempted just as we are, yet He never sinned!

"Therefore, let's all come boldly unto that throne of grace—so we can obtain mercy, and find grace to help in the time of need" (Heb. 4:14-16, paraphrased).

Jesus of Nazareth. The Christ. The Creator of the universe.

A tiny baby. A young lad learning to say "Mama" in the Hebrew tongue while hiding in Egypt. An obedient, bright Jewish boy learning His father's trade in Nazareth. A strong, stocky young journeyman carpenter who amazed the doctors of the law in Jerusalem when He was only 12. A mature, hard-working provider for the family for the next 18 years until He was 30. A strong, average-looking, average-sized, perhaps reddish-haired Jewish man who wore everyday clothing, and who grew in depth of understanding through each human trial. All this was the real Jesus.

Jesus the Man. The Man who could grow irritated, and control it; who could grow hungry, and not resent it; who could be angry, and never sin; who could appreciate the supple beauty of Israelitish girls, and never lust; who could laugh with gusto, yet weep with grief when others lacked faith. All this was the real Jesus too.

The Jesus whose face has never been painted; whose personality has never been understood; whose life and teaching has been so sadly ignored; whose purpose has not yet been fully proclaimed.

This Jesus was loved by the little people; the harlots, lepers, the Roman officers, the poor and the sick, the elderly and the lonely.

The common folk flocked to His side, not because of how He looked, but because of what He did, and what He said. The deaf could never recognize Him, because He looked so common; the blind could find Him easily, because of the authority with which He spoke!

This Jesus, the real Jesus of your own Bible, is the kind of a guy you can love! Jesus of Nazareth. Son of Mary and Joseph; Son of Man; Son of God! About 33½, probably rusty-complexioned, about 5'6" or so, broad-shouldered and well proportioned; rough hands, neatly groomed hair; trimmed beard, ready smile, deeply contemplative now and then, with a full, authoritative voice and a direct, masculine manner. Still, you would never have worshiped Him because of the way He looked—only because of Who He Was, and Is!

Mary of Bethany knew the best possible position a person could assume, just prior to His death, when even His closest friends and disciples couldn't know. She knelt down, put out her hand, and took hold of Jesus' foot. It was a good place to start.

It still is.